The Necessity of Politics

MORALITY AND SOCIETY

A SERIES EDITED BY ALAN WOLFE

The Necessity of Politics

Reclaiming American Public Life

Christopher Beem

WITH A FOREWORD BY
Jean Bethke Elshtain

THE UNIVERSITY OF CHICAGO PRESS
CHICAGO AND LONDON

Christopher Beem directs the Civic and Civil Community Program at the Johnson Foundation and is the author of *Pluralism and Consensus: Conceptions of the Good in the American Polity.*

The University of Chicago Press, Chicago 60637
The University of Chicago Press, Ltd., London
© 1999 by The University of Chicago
All rights reserved. Published 1999

08 07 06 05 04 03 02 01 99   1 2 3 4 5
ISBN: 0-226-04144-1 (cloth)

Library of Congress Cataloging-in-Publication Data

Beem, Christopher.
    The necessity of politics : reclaiming American public life /
Christopher Beem.
        p.   cm. — (Morality and society)
    Includes bibliographical references (p. 261) and index.
    ISBN 0-226-04144-1 (cloth : alk. paper)
    1. Civil society—History.   2. Civil society—United
States—History.   3. United States—Politics and government.   I.
Title.   II. Series.
    JC336 .B44 1999
    320.973—dc21

                                                98-49098
                                                CIP

To Rachel, Connor, and Sam

Contents

Foreword

Jean Bethke Elshtain

As Christopher Beem argues in this timely, cogent, and provocative book, civil society is on the tip of our tongues nowadays whenever the question of how well democratic societies, whether old or new, are faring is put. That this is so is perhaps unsurprising. For we seem to have arrived at a point of recognition, namely, that neither markets nor states suffice to order a decent way of life in common. As Beem points out, that's the easy part. More difficult by far is sorting out precisely what political configurations—governments and states—have to do with sustaining or depleting those plural associations that, taken together, constitute a *civil* society. Too often, in Beem's view, civil society advocates eliminate politics, whether formal governmental structures or such institutions as political parties, from their purview. This will not suffice, as politics is an essential and constitutive feature of civil society in modernity. This, of course, leaves open numerous and vexing questions concerning the precise role and nature of official political structures.

The civil society framework is one grounded in a recognition that our social and political worlds are enormously complex and that they emerge and take shape concretely over time. No social engineer could design a civil society. No linear model can explain one. A civil society is a system, but it is an open system. If environmental thinkers have shown us how the cumulative effect of misuse of an environment can, at one point, be more than a natural ecology can bear, so civil society analysts argue much along the same lines. They call upon us to evaluate the ways in which depletion and misuse of civic and moral resources can have debilitating, perhaps at one point even catastrophic, effects.

Beem is not favorably disposed toward theses of decline. At the same time, he is no cockeyed optimist determined to envelop every "new" thing that comes down the pike in the roseate hue of benign progressivism. That which is new is not necessarily good. For example: If I live in a culture that encourages unlimited consumption, no single act of mine will be seen as harmful in a direct way to others. But hundreds of thousands of persons consuming voraciously in a way that encourages or even comes to require what Pope John Paul II, in various of his encyclicals, including Sollicitudo Rei Socialis and Centesimus Annus, calls "super-development" may produce corrosive results. We come to understand this by assessing the effects of certain tendencies and trends over time rather than by trying to force all the particulars of a complex situation into a single, predetermined framework. That is to say, civil society argument relies on a form of *social learning* rather than on the creation of entirely abstract systems of thought, blueprints for beautiful hotels that have this overriding flaw: no single living and breathing guest has ever stayed overnight.

What is the tone and texture of *lived* life on the ground for women, men, and children, for the young and the old, for the healthy and the infirm, for white, black, brown, and yellow? Civil society begins by recognizing our complex interdependencies. Rather than a world of "zero-sum games" in which my winning comes at your expense, civil society views us as rising or falling together and urges us to recognize and to foster decent and life-affirming interdependency. We are called to various forms of "love of neighbor." But it is hard to put this into practice unless one has a neighborhood; unless there are institutions that are present and strong; unless there are processes of moral formation through institutions, beginning with families, that call us to responsibilities as well as to rights; to recognition of human finitude as well as to action in freedom.

Thinking about what civil society is reminds us that human beings are complex creatures who, in wanting to do good, turned at various points to government to take over when charity did not suffice. (And, needless to say, in the interest of maintaining the rule of law and the fundaments of order.) Wanting to reap the rewards of self-discipline and hard work, persons turned to economic structures to generate jobs and prosperity. In the minds of some, unfortunately, government became not only a line of defense against social distress and unacceptable levels of injustice, but also the only font of ethical decency and concern. Strong statists often despaired of, or even disdained, civil society because it didn't seem up to the tasks they believed needed doing and, as well, because the plural complexities of civil society challenge all top-down models. Similarly, the market, many optimistically believed, should be the source of social well-being as individual opportunities and rewards ushered into an overall social benefit. The economy alone, some market enthusiasts insisted, was powerful enough to fend off efforts to locate too much power in governments. And there matters often got stalled. But what we have learned in the past half-century is that, even as families and churches and other associations of civil society have been buffeted about and even undermined by external powers of many kinds, there is no substitute for them. Without civil society, a political culture cannot sustain a decent moral and social ecology.

But—and this is where Beem's analysis grows pointed and incisive—it is a huge mistake to assume, therefore, that government and politics are always problematic and even suspect from the civil society perspective. Rather, in his view, politics is *essential* to any defensible vision of a civil society. And if you put politics in, civil society is bound to take on and to take up certain aspects that are missing from a civil society vision in which government is either a shadowy menace or something like a ghost in the machine. This is a book that is bound to incite controversy and to contribute to our ongoing grappling with where our own democratic political culture is going or, more important, where precisely we are at present. Beem understands that getting the description right lies at the heart of compelling social commentary. Indeed, if I may be so bold, I would argue that most of our deep moral and political disagreements are, in the final analysis, disagreements about the facts of the matter: are things better or worse and how do we know? Beem helps us to get things right by offering a corrective to any and all visions of civil society sanitized from politics.

Acknowledgments

This book began during my tenure as director of the Council on Civil Society, a project co-sponsored by the University of Chicago Divinity School and the Institute for American Values. Working for and with the Council was a unique privilege, and I am grateful to David Blankenhorn, President of the Institute, for the opportunity, and to the Earhart Foundation for their financial support. I must extend a special thanks to Council member Don Eberly; our extensive conversations on these matters were enormously helpful to me.

The work was completed while directing the Project on Religion and American Civic Life at the University of Chicago Divinity School. The project was overseen by the Council's Chair, Jean Bethke Elshtain. She bears no responsibility for anything I say here, but her support—evinced most ably by her foreword—is something for which I am very grateful. I am also grateful to the Divinity School's dean, Clark Gilpin. Indeed, were it not for these two advocates, it is likely that the book would not have been written at all. My thanks, as well, to Luis Lugo and the Pew Foundation for financial support.

There are many others I would like to thank for their help on the manuscript. David Ost helped me work through the section on Solidarity. Mary Stimming offered important feedback at a very critical time. Jim Sleeper read the manuscript and helped me think through the last section of the book. Two readers for the University of Chicago Press offered extremely helpful suggestions. John Tryneski, Michael Koplow and many others at the Press shepherded this work through the publication process. Everyone has my sincere thanks.

As usual, my greatest debt is to my wife, Pattie, for her support and good sense, and for her accompaniment through the hinterlands. This book is dedicated to our children—the delight of our lives and three very concrete reasons for me to focus on the future of this polity.

Chapter 1 was originally given at the inaugural meeting of the Council on Civil Society. Part of chapter 8 was originally published in *The Responsive Community 6, 3.* A version of chapter 6 was given at the Midwest Political Science Association meeting in Chicago, April 25, 1998.

Introduction

Throughout much of the world, and particularly in America, "civil society" has moved into the public square and become the subject of an important and formidable political debate. Suddenly, the prosaic world of family dinners, PTA meetings, and youth soccer has taken on profound social significance. "Bowling alone" has entered the cultural parlance. Despite a hotly partisan, even rancorous climate, Democrats and Republicans alike extol civil society as the newfound wonder drug for tackling a host of intransigent social problems—from fragmenting families to the underclass to a decline in civic engagement.

This sudden explosion of interest within and among the American public is born of the belief (or at least the hope) that civil society offers us a strategy for addressing our nation's social ills. In poll after poll, overwhelming majorities of Americans express their belief that our nation has abandoned its civic commitments; that our most important social institutions no longer hold nor merit the respect they once did; that civility, responsibility, and accountability have become rare and sullied commodities. Citizens likewise believe that our society is losing its moral center, that we citizens are growing ever more disconnected and isolated, cynical and unconcerned. When we do face each other, it seems that our encounters are ever more tenuous and fragile, often degenerating into acrimony.

I will argue that these contemporary circumstances are not as unusual as most Americans believe. The problems of anomie and atomism are as old as modernity, and just as old is the effort to address these problems through a distinctive, and imminently modern, understanding of what civil society is, and what it does. Nevertheless, while the contemporary debate may not be different in kind from those of generations past, that does not obviate widespread and very timely feelings of cultural disquiet. Continued good economic news may reverse, or at least mitigate, Americans' gloomy attitudes about their government and their society, but an abiding and pervasive sense remains:

Our nation's civic and moral condition has deteriorated in dramatic and disturbing ways.

Again, the civil society movement has risen in response to this perceived breakdown. Whatever else accounts for and drives the public dimension of this revival, it is properly understood as an effort to rebuild a more moral, more civic-minded American society. The movement is thus premised on the claim that our contemporary condition results primarily from the decline of the institutions that make up American civil society. Those mediating institutions that stand between the individual and the state—especially families, neighborhoods, and churches—traditionally helped to inculcate a shared sense of citizenship and concern for others. Because these institutions are in serious disarray, we are losing that shared sense, and, as a result, our social fabric continues to unravel. If we are to renew American culture, the argument goes, we must begin by restoring the local, mediating institutions that make up American civil society.

Of course, despite all the newfound interest, not everyone sees it this way. Some are inclined to write off this phenomenon as either the misplaced angst of a privileged, dual-career class or the latest cultural impact of the baby boomers. Like the pig moving through the python, baby boomers are advancing into middle age, and from that perspective now view with predictable concern the very same cultural trends they helped to foment. Others see the movement as yet another handy justification for abandoning the underclass: by prescribing civil society for the intransigent problems of the inner city, the ostensibly moral thing to do conveniently coincides with budget- and tax-cutting priorities. These critics thus contend that the whole thing is, at worst, a mean-spirited dodge; at best, they contend it is little more than the latest intellectual fad.

Whether or not there is any truth to criticisms like these, it is certainly true that waves of enthusiasm are usually as big as they are brief in contemporary American society. It is therefore surely possible that this movement, like so many before it, will be quickly relegated to political oblivion. But Americans' widespread dissatisfaction should not be so readily dismissed. Moreover, the effort to connect these concerns with the concept of civil society betokens a larger interest in some very fundamental social questions about politics, culture, citizenship, and morality.

I contend that the wave of interest in civil society is driven by a legitimate, indeed welcome, urgency, and I affirm the claim that revitalizing American civil society is a viable strategy for effecting cultural renewal. However, I also believe that the dominant view of civil society is, in many respects, both superficial and romantic. The very urgency that has caused this amazing revival also accounts for a series of disquieting, yet lingering questions: What is civil society, anyway? Is it really in decline, and if so, why? How exactly does civil society do what advocates claim it does? Why is it that some forms of civil society foster these goals, while other forms are largely antithetical thereto? And what, if anything, can society do to encourage the former and discourage the latter? The goals associated with the civil society movement depend upon the answers to these and similar questions. In this work, therefore, I step back and try to sort out the whys and wherefores of the movement, teasing out the complex conceptual legacies and reattaching the discussion to some long-standing debates.

Again, the ostensible goal of the civil society movement is to help to fashion a more moral, more civic-minded society. And that goal requires a shared commitment to a set of moral values and virtues and to a set of civic ideals; indeed, for our American democracy, that commitment constitutes our very identity as a nation. Thus, the very goal of the civil society movement is premised on a restored sense of civic, cultural, and social unity. Yet the institutions of civil society are, by definition, pluralistic. For all the value these institutions have in inculcating a thick moral frame of reference, they are insufficient to this fundamental task. Indeed, I will argue that the omnipresent and utterly American problem of race shows that the institutions of civil society are inherently ill suited to address some of the movement's core objectives.

If it is to operate as its advocates intend, the free and raucous world of American civil society must be directed, contained, and sustained by a minimal yet overarching set of moral principles. And that means that our society requires institutions with universal reach and import. I contend that the enterprise of politics is indispensable to the task of building or rebuilding a moral society. For good or ill, political associations and political institutions—including, most relevantly, the state—outline a minimal set of moral constraints within which all Americans are obliged to operate. Therefore, our polity is best able to achieve the goals of the civil society movement when both the state and civil society are operative and vibrant. For it is through the ongoing, and often quite contentious, dialogue between these two social institutions that we most adequately advance the task of half-building and half-discovering our shared American identity.

The Argument

In part 1, I describe the concept of civil society operative in the public debate. Civil society is an inherently lax and expansive concept, incorporating every social phenomenon that is not the state. I argue that throughout history, one's understanding of civil society has been narrowed analytically by one's normative objectives: in a phrase, civil society is what you want it to do. Because civil society advocates are united in their desire to refashion a former (and perhaps idealized) version of the American nation, a common and distinctive understanding of civil society has emerged as well. The civil society debate is distinguished by its affirmation of what I call "social capital institutions": namely, families, neighborhoods, and churches. The civil society movement in America centers on the claim that a revival of these institutions is the single most important means by which American society can achieve civic and moral renewal. The movement is just as united in its opposition to the market, political partisanship, and especially the state. These institutions, it is argued, have overstepped their legitimate social roles; their conduct is therefore inimical both to the vitality of these social capital institutions and to the goals associated with the movement.

In order to evaluate the movement's orienting objectives, it is necessary to attend more carefully to the analytical and normative dimensions of this concept. And to do that, it is necessary to place it in historical context: to know where we are and where we are tending, it is necessary to know where we have been. To that end, I go on to examine the theoretical wellsprings for the concept of civil society in America. In part 2, I outline the relevant thought of two major intellectual figures, Alexis de Tocqueville and G. W. F. Hegel. I show that their concerns regarding modern society were dramatically similar to our own, as was their use of the concept of civil society to control and ameliorate those concerns. An examination of Tocqueville and Hegel illustrates that the civil society movement in contemporary America is yet another manifestation of the perennial need to attend to what I call the modern problematic.

Tocqueville and Hegel left an intellectual legacy that scholars continue to mine, and thus each thinker gave birth to a tradition of thought about civil society that continues to this day. I discuss a series of twentieth-century American social critics who continue to apply Tocqueville's categories to an ever-evolving set of historical circumstances. These thinkers, I argue, are the most important trailblazers for the contemporary movement. More controversially, I argue that the Polish Solidarity movement bears a strong conceptual connection to the Hegelian tradition and its dynamic understanding of civil society. I then try to show that this movement, and its specifically Hegelian dimension, also informs the contemporary public concept. This dual legacy explains why the civil society movement understands a group of pluralistic, disconnected social institutions to be the central and consummate means by which American society can assuage and reverse America's pervasive sense of moral and civic breakdown.

Yet an analysis of the two figures also shows why civil society is wholly inadequate to that task. In part 3, I show that neither Hegel nor Tocqueville saw the institutions of civil society as sufficient means for achieving or sustaining (let alone reestablishing) ethical cohesion. In order to achieve that end, society does indeed require a vibrant, even cacophonous collection of social organizations and institutions. But it also needs an authoritative yet minimalistic, universal yet capacious, set of moral norms and values. An analysis of the contemporary purveyors of these two traditions—Solidarity and the neo-Tocquevillians—confirms the point: the antecedents to the public debate in America reveal the contemporary deficiencies of the civil society concept. If civil society advocates are to achieve their goals, they must recognize and acknowledge the inescapable moral aspect of politics.

In the final section, part 4, I show how a return to Tocqueville and Hegel can help restore this dimension, and thereby correct the movement's inadequacies. Because political associations are inevitably and sometimes virulently partisan, civil society advocates are inclined to believe that their behavior undermines the quest for a renewed civic commitment. I argue, to the contrary, that national political associations are particularly well suited to operate according to the terms of what I call "medium party politics." Following Tocqueville, I show that these associations make claims to their fellow citizens in terms of our shared moral and civic values. We citizens are constrained to evaluate their claims, and in the process, the American public moral consensus is made more concrete and more responsive to the exigencies of our present circumstances.

The civil society movement rejects political institutions, not only because of the presence of partisanship, but because laws and governmental institutions have subverted civil society and the civic dimension. The seeds of civil society, the common refrain goes, lie fallow in soil made poor by the incessantly avaricious state. Limit the state to its proper and circumscribed role, and civil society will reemerge, as will a rejuvenated moral fabric. This conception of civil society is, I argue, both romantic and myopic. What is more, in terms of the role of the state, I want to argue almost precisely the reverse. Employing Hegel's treatment of the state, I return to the issue of race and reexamine the role of the government in the Voting Rights Act of 1965. I argue that the government's actions conform quite well to Hegelian categories, thereby exemplifying the state's inescapable status as a moral pedagogue. The state is the central mechanism by which Americans express their thin but universal moral judgments back to themselves.

The civil society movement is responding to social problems that are at once contemporary and perennial. I do not maintain that our generation can address those problems any better than our predecessors. But I do want to claim that, at least in the case of Hegel and Tocqueville, our predecessors had a better sense of how this generation might go about addressing them. Combined, their insights offer an image of the democratic polity that is more adequate to the daunting task at hand.

Part One

The Concept of Civil Society

Chapter One

The Concept of Civil Society and the Contemporary Predicament

The vigorous public interest in the concept of civil society, particularly in America, is born of a desire to address some grave concerns about contemporary society. The public discussion is driven by the belief that there is something seriously wrong with the American body politic, and that this condition has resulted from the decline in the institutions of American civil society. Revitalization of those institutions, in turn, is understood to be an indispensable mechanism for combating the sorry condition of our moral and civic culture. In this chapter, I give an account of this position. I outline the concerns that drive the debate and then show how this understanding of what we need civil society to do has led to a distinctive conception of what civil society is.

The Contemporary Concern

The primary impetus to this discussion is the intuitive and widespread belief that our society is experiencing a breakdown. Americans are increasingly convinced that our society has lost much of the feeling of community that pervaded life in past generations. People seem less connected, less invested in each other. Bill Bradley quotes from a recent "Mood of America" poll that found that "76 percent of those surveyed agreed that 'there is less concern for others than there once was.' "[1] Relatedly, Robert Putnam cites polling data that show that "the proportion of Americans who socialize with their neighbors has slowly but steadily declined over the last two decades, from 61 percent in 1974 to 47 percent in 1994."[2] This ebbing of concern manifests itself in a decline in basic civility. A 1996 national survey in *U.S. News and World Report* showed that 89 percent of Americans consider our nation's incivility to be a serious problem.[3]

The decline in our civic culture is also associated with, and manifested in, more public outlets as well. At the bottom of this sorry pile is the proliferation of TV and radio talk shows. The former casually celebrate the prurient and the pathological; the latter routinely turn complex issues into simplistic bombasts, and sincere political disagreement into antipathy and mean-spiritedness. Both whip up the abusive rantings of their audience and then tout the result as a public exchange of views. One must wonder what it is within the contemporary American psyche that accounts for the proliferation and enormous cultural power of these shows, but regardless, their standing within American society confirms for many a serious decline in civility and citizenship.

Even at the top of our political culture, people perceive on all sides a crass political agenda that overrides any concern for the truth or the common good. Negative campaigning, the cynical manipulation of sound and image bites, partisan representatives offering their "spin" on recent events—none of these is strictly a new phenomenon, but the exponential growth and systematic exploitation of these tactics are universally acknowledged and, except by those who profit from this state of affairs, universally lamented. Mainstream national political groups like the Christian Coalition, the NRA, the AARP, and the NOW also present their debates on television, but their exchanges likewise routinely reflect a combative belligerence and often an astonishing disregard for the truth. The grand ideals that ostensibly undergird their positions are lost in a battle for debating points and, one suspects, good television.

This nearly ubiquitous public burlesque is significant in its own right, but it is perhaps more important for the tone it sets for American public life. Widespread distaste for partisan bickering has led many to reject participating in, and to deny the legitimacy of, the political process. Michael Sandel notes that "three-fourths [of all Americans] say they are dissatisfied with the way the political process is working . . . a similar percentage believe that government is run by a few big interests rather than for the benefit of all."[4] More generally, it is fair to claim that the shrill and rancorous exchanges that are now routine to television and radio set the standard for public debate, and indeed all forms of public behavior in this country. In large measure, people who act in an uncivil manner in their daily public actions are simply modeling the behavior that is daily paraded before them.

The various surveys and anecdotes noted above illustrate that the change in people's perception can be documented, and that fact is itself significant. As any Wall Street investor can tell you, if enough people believe something will happen, it usually does. But there is a more basic level to the argument. A well-ordered democratic society cannot maintain itself without some minimal level of social trust. And, in fact, the decline in civility, connectedness, and accountability noted above has resulted in a rather inevitable decline in this social sine qua non. In 1960, before the social tumult of the sixties, and before Watergate, 58 percent of Americans agreed with the statement that "most people can be trusted most of the time." In 1994, that number decreased to 37 percent.[5]

What's more, these fears are not merely intuitive, they are underscored by significant empirical evidence. Beliefs about a declining social fabric are tied to a verifiable increase in a variety of social pathologies. Very concrete and ascendant social problems, including the intransigence of the underclass, inadequate school performance, and the souring of relations between ethnic groups, races, and generations, are behind much of the contemporary feelings of anxiety, despair, and dread. William Bennett argues that "America now finds itself at or near the top of the industrialized world in rates of murder, rape, drug use, divorce, abortion, child abuse, and births to unwed mothers. Our elementary- and secondary-education system often places us at the bottom of the industrialized world."[6] Fordham University's 1996 "Index of Social Well-Being" looked at 1994 federal government statistics concerning sixteen social problems—including rates of unemployment, homicides, poverty, and infant mortality. It concluded that the nation's aggregate social well-being is at its lowest level in twenty-five years. The report also noted that "of the six problems concerning Americans younger than 18, four of them—child abuse, teen-age suicide, drug abuse, and high school drop out rates—worsened in 1994." Even more disconcerting, this aggregate rating has been falling more or less precipitously and more or less continuously since the survey began. The index level in 1973 was 77.5. By 1994, it had shrunk to 37.5.[7]

It is, of course, by no means assured that these trends will continue. Indeed, as the economic boom of the nineties rolls on, some of these numbers have declined marginally. Unemployment is down, consumer confidence is up, and both facts are reflected in people's outlook. Yet even in the midst of widespread optimism about the economy and about one's personal economic prospects, an August 1997 poll in the *Washington Post* showed that only 39 percent of Americans believed that our nation was on the "right track."[8] Results from the long-standing "right-track/wrong-track poll" have traditionally been tied rather directly to economic conditions. This apparent disconnect is, if nothing else, unusual, and thus speaks to the persistence of Americans' disquiet.

Civil society advocates routinely recount data like these as a prelude to their prescriptive account. For they believe these figures are more than simply lamentable; they reveal nothing less than the rending of the social fabric, the breakdown of civic culture. For civil society advocates, the Fordham report and polling data are thus of a piece. Without a common commitment to elemental standards of civility and to a shared set of basic moral propositions, the common enterprise of democratic government becomes untenable. These advocates thus frankly question whether our society will be able to maintain the most basic prerequisites of a free and democratic society. Robert Wuthnow summarizes the movement in just these moral and civic terms:

> The civil-society debate is . . . about the quality of social life itself, especially in those voluntary realms governed by freedom of association rather than by the coercive powers of law and politics, and in those spheres of life motivated by commitments other than profit and self-interest. The civil-society debate is vitally concerned with the extent and quality of social interaction, with relationships that build and sustain moral commitment and character, and with the collective values that implicitly or explicitly define us as a people.[9]

Wuthnow's summary also shows why this grave assessment of contemporary American culture is tied to the surging public interest in civil society. For these advocates also believe both that our nation's condition stems from the decline of the institutions of civil society, and that their revitalization is an indispensable mechanism for combating it. I argue that this understanding of the normative function of civil society has led to a distinctive conception of what civil society is, specifically what institutions are understood to be most important and most representative. To do so, it is necessary to outline briefly the analytical dimensions of the concept.

The Concept of Civil Society

In its modern formulation, civil society is understood as a subset of the broader social order; it is that part of society not under the direct control of the state. The *Blackwell Encyclopaedia of Political Thought* notes that while the term was originally "a generic term for society and state, synonymous with 'political society,' " it has "more recently" come to mean those "social and economic arrangements, codes, institutions apart from the state. . . . In general usage today civil society . . . refers to the non-political aspects of the contemporary social order." This modern definition sets some minimal parameters for the discussion and ostensibly allows for broad comparative studies. Nevertheless, agreement apparently only comes with vacuity; this "general usage" of the term is so broad as to make it almost useless. In order to say anything substantive, discussants must inevitably invoke their own, more specific definition.[10]

Where does this added specificity come from? Again, in its modern formulation, civil society is understood as a subset of the broader social order. Almost by definition, political theorists are motivated by their belief that the social order is to some degree deficient. They write books in order to improve or remedy that condition. Interest among political theorists in the concept of civil society therefore stems from the fact that they see it as a means for outlining and advancing their objectives for society itself. Thus, no matter how it is formulated, the modern understanding of civil society is a fundamentally normative concept. Whatever else it is, civil society is a mechanism that at once produces, maintains, and manifests some basic and essential social goods. Therefore, the way in which one adds further analytical specificity to the concept is of a piece with one's understanding of the normative function of civil society. What you think civil society is—your understanding of what the term means analytically; which institutions, groups, associations are included, and which are not, which epitomize the concept, and which are effectively ignored—is all largely determined by what you want civil society to do.

Civil Society in the Liberal-Democratic Tradition

In the broadest terms, the goal of the liberal-democratic tradition has always been to achieve a high degree of individual freedom and autonomy while maintaining a viable, sustainable social order. Therefore, within this tradition, the understanding of what civil society is and what it does is focused around this fundamental objective. Among liberal-democratic theorists, civil society commonly refers to a vast array of independent groups, associations, and institutions. These groups are voluntary—some are more structured than others, some are more effectively permanent than others—but they are all made up of unrelated individuals who come together to pursue a specific common interest or concern. Examples of such groups can include neighborhood groups, churches, civic associations, labor unions, political parties, and the like. A vibrant liberal-democratic society is inherently pluralistic and continually generates opportunities for local or group interaction. Civil society is thus a collective noun, referring to the sum of these groups.

These associations are understood to be free and independent because they are not under the direct control or oversight of the state. As a result, they create independent loci of political power (and often, competing political narratives) that temper the power and reach of the state. The everyday operation of the institutions of civil society is thus understood to preserve individual freedom. Yet civil society also helps produce and maintain the order and consensus that any society demands. For while these groups have their own identities and aims, their normal, everyday operation reflects and reinforces the norms of democratic society. Through group interaction, citizens come to recognize their commonalities and differences. They learn to exploit the former through concerted political action and to resolve the latter through reasoned argument and compromise. So civil society is also where one learns the skills and habits of civility and good citizenship.

The modern conception of civil society fosters the common and rather deep-seated belief that these two goals are ultimately one and the same: a robust democratic society will possess a civil society that both secures pluralism and instills civic virtue. Democratic civic virtue centers on traits like independence and self-reliance—virtues that certainly check the usurping power of the state. Likewise, the abundance of associations and groups serves concretely to reinforce the prevailing democratic ethos. Exposure through civil society to the very fact of pluralism instills within all citizens the necessity and legitimacy of virtues like tolerance and open-mindedness, moderation and compromise.

Yet while there is a natural affinity between these two goals, it is too much to conflate them completely. For at least when taken to extremes, the two objectives associated with the concept of civil society are not only distinct, they are contradictory. In the first instance, when civil society is operating as it should, it stands in healthy opposition to the state. To this end, pluralism—even sectarianism—is a good thing. In

Madisonian terms, the more independent organizations there are, the freer the society and the more stable the democracy. The second objective, however, requires a fairly strong sense of moral cohesion. Despite our inevitable and fundamental differences, civil society serves to inculcate a shared set of values, norms, and beliefs. As a result, pluralism is legitimate only insofar as it operates within the parameters established by our common understanding of civic virtue: thus far, and no farther. Civil society, in this instance, is a force for building social cohesion. This tension, of course, reflects the fundamental liberal objective: a society that is free yet ordered. To anticipate, it is a tension that I believe the contemporary debate is unable to resolve. But at this point, I merely want to show that this tension explains the significant differences that remain within the liberal-democratic understanding of this concept.

Many liberal theorists stress the preservation of political freedom—the institutions of civil society stand against the innate acquisitiveness of the state. Ernest Gellner, for example, argues that civil society both manifests and preserves the political, cultural, and economic freedom that is the unique achievement of liberal-democratic society. But others, like Michael Sandel, see the problem precisely as too much freedom, or at least, too much of a certain type of freedom. The rise of this unfortunate conception, which celebrates individual choice, has compromised the health of the polity. Sandel therefore argues that civil society is the mechanism whereby a more substantive conception of freedom is developed and maintained. Alternatively, far from perceiving a necessary connection between civil society and capitalism, leftist thinkers like John Keane want to use civil society as Antonio Gramsci did—as a means for jump-starting a socialist agenda, for extending democracy to the economic realm. Similarly, social democrats Jean Cohen and Andrew Arato highlight civil society in their call for a more inclusive, vibrant, and thus inherently more progressive democratic dialogue: the creation of a Habermasian public square. Finally, Robert Putnam and other neo-Tocquevillians see civil society as a necessary device for reinstilling the demands of democratic citizenship.[11]

These normative differences have also led to different analytical conceptions. Those theorists who focus on the task of preserving freedom believe that civil society refers to structured, formal, and effectively permanent institutions, where people without any affective ties come together to pursue a common and frankly political aim. Organizations that are similarly structured and permanent but profess a shared inter-est that is not directly political (the soccer clubs and choral groups that Robert Putnam saw in Italy, for example) are not the subject of much attention.[12] Similarly, those on the left are more likely to stress struc-tural institutions, like unions, that can stand up to the monolithic (and ostensibly oppressive) power of the state, while those on the right may be more inclined to highlight those organizations that foster a common conception of civic virtue. These examples can be readily extended; the point is simply to show that the contemporary theoretical discussion within the liberal-democratic tradition shows significant disagreement about which institutions exemplify civil society and what civil society ought to do.

Academic discussions are surely known for conceptual debates like these. In light of the long and variegated history associated with this concept, this lack of agreement is therefore perhaps to be expected, if not necessarily welcomed. But civil society has broken out of the con-fines of academics. For the first time, the term has also taken on a dy-namic and significant role in public political discourse.

The line of demarcation is, of course, fuzzy, but one of the first things that distinguishes the public political dimension of the civil society re-vival is precisely the lack of this theoretical contention. The social critics (coming from think tanks, periodicals, foundations, and politics) who take part in this public discussion start with the assumption that the theoretical issues outlined above are effectively settled, or at least they believe that settling such questions is not prerequisite for the meaning-ful application of the concept. Even among the many academicians who have joined the public debate, the writing is comparatively devoid of arcane language and conceptual argument. Rather, they, too, accept the broad outlines of the public conception, and quickly move on to the more substantive question of application.[13] The public debate is not centered on questions about the amorphous nature, content, and normative function of civil society; advocates are often content to de-fine the term in a couple of sentences. Instead, the operative question is this: How do we get it back so that it can once again do what it used to do?[14] This specific question is behind the dynamism and the distinctiveness of the public debate. For it reveals the depth of concern that drives it.

From the time of its founding, the success of the United States has been tied to the vibrant and prolific character of our civil society. Joining associations was understood to be a uniquely American passion. In Tocqueville's famous words,

> Americans of all ages, all stations in life, and all types of dispositions are forever forming associations. There are not only commercial and industrial associations in which all take part, but others of a thousand different types—religious, moral, serious, futile, very general and very limited, immensely large and very minute. Americans combine to give fetes, found seminaries, build churches, distribute books, and send missionaries to the antipodes. Hospitals, prisons, and schools take shape in that way. Finally, if they want to proclaim a truth or propagate some feeling by the encouragement of a great example, they form an association. In every case, at the head of any new undertaking, where in France you would find the government or in England some territorial magnate, in the United States you are sure to find an association.[15]

There is much more to say about Tocqueville in what follows, but the first point is simply historical: the American proclivity to join associations was part of our culture, our identity as a nation. What's more, compared to other nations, Americans' level of voluntary activity, especially in church groups and the like, remains extremely high. But Tocqueville also believed this proclivity was largely responsible for the success of American democracy.

Contemporary civil society advocates are profoundly indebted to Tocqueville's analysis. They fully accept his claim that the institutions of civil society develop and preserve a shared set of essential virtues and mores. Their assessment that American society is experiencing a cultural breakdown centers on the belief that these virtues are no longer sufficiently manifested in American society. And that means that they have therefore also come to doubt the vibrancy of those institutions. In short, these critics are convinced of a serious decline in American society and culture, and, following Tocqueville, they contend that this condition results primarily from a decline in the institutions of civil society.[16] Because these institutions have declined or changed in a significant way, civil society has ceased to fulfill adequately its normative function, and a pathological social order is the result.

Given this diagnosis, the proposed treatment plan is self-evident. If the sorry condition of civil society is the preeminent reason for our problems, then American renewal requires that we reinvigorate these institutions. We must therefore determine what has happened to cause or precipitate their decline, and figure out what we as a nation need to do to stop that decline and facilitate their recovery.

All of this means that while the contemporary debate manifests the lineage of the liberal-democratic tradition, it is nevertheless distinctive. In other words, the two-sided desideratum that has characterized the liberal-democratic understanding of civil society—namely, that civil society both culls the power of the state and cultivates democratic virtues—has, in the public debate, come to center on the latter objective. In Nancy Rosenblum's words,

> The orthodox preoccupation with associations as buffers against government and avenues to political participation, and with freedom of association as an aspect of personal liberty, has been eclipsed. Today, the dominant perspective is moral: civil society is seen as a school of virtue where men and women develop the dispositions essential to liberal democracy.[17]

Of course, the public debate is properly characterized; it is, after all, a debate. Any public movement that extends to the farthest reaches of the American political spectrum is surely not going to manifest univocal affirmation. Nevertheless, this debate has a hegemonic center. While unanimity does not obtain, there is a significant amount of agreement regarding the assessment of the contemporary social order—how and why it is deficient—and of what we should do about it. This goal, in turn, produces a distinct and unusually united understanding of what civil society is. There are surely counterexamples. Nevertheless, the themes I outline below are prevailing and pervasive. They fairly describe the dominant conception of civil society within the public debate. These distinctive features are in line with, and reflective of, the conservative turn in American politics, and I suspect that fact goes a long way toward accounting for its dominance within the contemporary public discussion.

The Triumvirate: Family, Neighborhood, and Church

I have argued that the concept of civil society has both an analytical and a normative dimension: civil society is what civil society ought to do. The public debate reinforces this argument, for just as this debate manifests a startling consensus about the goals of a revival of civil society, so, too, does it present a dramatic similarity regarding the institutions that are understood to exemplify that concept. Senator Dan Coats presents "families, churches, neighborhoods, voluntary associations" as representative institutions of civil society. When these institutions are resilient, when civil society is strong, he argues, "it infuses a community with its warmth, trains its people to be good citizens, and transmits values between generation."[18] Senator Bill Bradley offers a strikingly similar list, and a strikingly similar objective:

> Civil Society is the place where Americans make their homes, sustain their marriages, raise their families, visit with their friends, meet their neighbors, educate their children, worship their God. . . . It is where opinions are expressed and refined, where views are exchanged and agreements made, where a sense of common purpose and consensus is forged.[19]

These assessments are representative. The institutions of families, neighborhoods, churches, and voluntary associations are routinely touted by civil society advocates. This is what the public discussion means when it invokes the term *civil society.* These are the institutions that they believe require reinvigoration. At this point, I do not want to take issue with this idea, but I do want to point out that while political and civic associations are central to the liberal-democratic discussion, the institutions of family, neighborhood, and church are not at all common to the broad history of the concept, nor even to the liberal-democratic conception. I propose, therefore, to look more closely at these three features, in order to help explain the distinctive understanding of the concept as it is presented in the contemporary public debate.

Social Capital and "The Density of Associational Life"

The objectives of the civil society movement center on the idea of civic and moral renewal. That problem, in turn, is tied to the perceived decline of the institutions of American civil society. The concept that ties these two premises together, and the term that grounds and permeates the civil society debate, is *social capital.*

The term has a number of derivations and uses, but the most relevant was developed by the late James Coleman, a sociologist at the University of Chicago. It describes a sort of by-product of economic interaction. When people interact, either in the production or distribution of their product, they inevitably develop certain expectations about the

other's behavior. And if those expectations include feelings of trust—
i.e., the idea that the person or persons you are dealing with can be
relied on to do what they say and to do their jobs well—then that
interaction aids in the production of certain shared ends. Thus, social
capital, like human capital and physical capital, enhances productivity,
for it increases a group's ability to achieve a given set of objectives.
People who trust each other cooperate more easily and more frequently
and can more readily achieve their objectives. For example, transac-
tions can be handled with a handshake rather than a lengthy contract.
If, on the other hand, social capital is depleted, productivity declines,
and exchanges, including the most basic features of ordinary social
intercourse, become more difficult. Coleman's concept is multidimen-
sional and complex, but this description fairly establishes its use within
the public discussion.[20]

The reason civil society advocates are interested in this concept is
clear. They employ the notion of social capital because it directly reflects their goals: the idea is that healthy interaction between individuals is an important and even an essential asset for any society. This
interaction is what enables us Americans to build community, to re-
commit ourselves to each other, to reknit the social fabric. Trust between individuals thus becomes trust between strangers and trust of
a broad fabric of social institutions; ultimately, it becomes a shared set
of values, virtues, and expectations within society as a whole. Without
this interaction, on the other hand, trust decays; at a certain point, this
decay starts to manifest itself in serious social problems. Thus, the concept buttresses their analysis of contemporary American culture. Social
capital has, in Don Eberly's words, been "drawn down." An absence
of trust, community, and concern for others is behind both the plethora
of social pathologies and, more broadly, a widespread anomie. What is
more, the concept of social capital contends that building or rebuilding
community and trust requires face-to-face encounters. Robert Putnam,
who is the most important exponent of Coleman's writings, thus distinguishes between social capital, which involves "our relations with one
another" and political participation, which "refers to our relations with
political institutions."[21] The concept of social capital confirms that the
institutions of civil society are indispensable to our society's health and
vibrancy. Finally, the idea of social capital is important because it gives
informal, nonstructural instances of civil society essentially the same
standing as more permanent institutions. Most theoretical discussions
are apt to ignore informal interactions, because they do not advance the

ends in mind. But while social capital may be advanced in permanent institutions also, these are not the heart of the matter. Putnam notes that "bowling in a league or having coffee with a friend embodies and creates social capital."[22] These interactions, more than those commensurate with more formal institutions like politics and economics, are where we develop feelings of trust and solidarity.

Again, the concept of social capital has become central to the civil society movement. Indeed, the reason for the distinctive analytical dimension of civil society hinges on the fact that social capital is understood as the means by which civic and moral renewal can be effected. The family, neighborhoods, and churches are important because all three of them reflect what Putnam calls "the density of associational life,"[23] and hence they are seen by civil society advocates as especially effective institutions for inculcating social capital. I will therefore refer to them as *social capital institutions.* In what follows, I will take up each dimension, outlining its importance to the movement.

The Family

In the academic arena, most theorists ignore the family as an institution of civil society.[24] Explanations for this absence are not forthcoming, of course, but they are not hard to postulate. While it is surely a social institution, the family is also understood to be primarily private. Indeed, it is often seen as a haven from the public world. While the family is an institution of structure and some permanence, the bonds that unite the participants are grounded (at least according to all but the most virulent economic rationalists) not in interest but affection. And while the family is in some sense a locus of independent power—political thinkers as far back as Plato have recognized that the family can be the enemy of the state—on its own, that power is judged insufficient to challenge the state's centralizing tendencies.[25] Whatever the merits of this speculative assessment, the contrast between the academic literature and the public discussion is striking. Among the former, there is almost a universal lack of interest;[26] among public civil society advocates, the family is the first and most important institution of civil society. It is almost universally understood to be the primary (in both senses) mechanism for the inculcation of social virtues and civic norms.

Participants in the public debate routinely note the grave condition of the American family, recounting a litany of disturbing facts about absent fathers and the prevalence of divorce and births outside of marriage and the proliferation of substandard child care. These critics argue that the family is where Americans start to learn the basic social virtues. Therefore, these phenomena amount to a cultural failure in child rearing, the results of which can be seen in a host of social problems. Ultimately, this failure jeopardizes democratic society itself. As Mary Ann Glendon writes, "[I]mpairment of the family's capacity to develop in its members the qualities of self-restraint, respect for others, and sturdy independence of mind cannot help but impair the prospects for a regime of ordered liberty."[27] Civil society advocates want to reinvigorate a more virtuous, more civically engaged American culture. Most relevantly, they want to reinvigorate the institutions that inculcate social capital. Putnam notes that "the most fundamental form of social capital is the family."[28] And for this reason, the family emerges as a vital, indeed, a primary area of inquiry and concern.

There is, in fact, a dramatic overlap between public intellectuals associated with the civil society movement and those who are involved in the public debate concerning marriage, fatherhood, and the family. Don Eberly, David Blankenhorn, Mary Ann Glendon, David Popenoe, Jean Bethke Elshtain, and William Galston are all significant figures in both movements. In political circles, Dan Coats, William Bennett, Bill Bradley, and Bill Clinton have all outlined public policy initiatives that focus directly on the family in their effort to revive civil society. None of these would claim that the family is the only relevant institution, or that the decline in the family sufficiently accounts for our nation's social problems. Nevertheless, I am hard-pressed to name one public advocate who does not argue that the family is singularly representative of the social role of civil society, and thus singularly important to the revival of American culture.

Neighborhoods and Communities

The question of neighbors and neighborhoods also reflects a distinction between the academic and the public debates. But here the difference is more subtle. Liberal theoreticians typically list relations between neighbors in their accounts of civil society, but those relations are normally relevant only insofar as they take place between unrelated individuals within a structured organization—a PTA meeting, a neighborhood watch group, a community organization, and the like. The public discussion includes these more structured groups as well, but it also extends the idea of the relevant interaction to include, and often even highlight, adamantly informal meetings—gossiping with a neighbor over a fence, exchanging pleasantries about sports or the weather with the lady at the dry cleaners, inviting the neighbors over for coffee, cards, or a barbecue. Bill Bradley asks, "How many of us know the names, much less the life stories, of all the neighbors in our section of town or even on several floors of our apartment building?" Bradley acknowledges that "it may sound painfully small time, even corny, to focus on these things," but he adamantly avers that "upon these things lie[s] the whole edifice of our national well-being."[29] The public debate sees civil society as a means for reinstituting social trust and a shared sense of civic virtue, and to this end, informal interactions and informal ties are very significant, and perhaps even determinative.

This understanding obviously highlights the use of the term *social capital* among the public civil society advocates. Yet there is another essential point about neighbors that should be addressed here. The public discussion about civil society draws a connection between neighbors and neighborhoods on the one hand, and civic virtue on the other, primarily because of the essential support function neighborhoods provide for the family. Parents need to hear that their efforts are valued, and they need the concrete support of advice, experience, and time from those around them. Most importantly, parents need others to reinforce the moral values they seek to implant in their children; in this regard, the neighborhood serves an almost indispensable function. The idea that families and neighborhoods are mutually supportive, that they are, so to speak, morally on the same page, is fundamental to the public discussion of civil society. David Popenoe, who has written most directly to this issue, puts the matter this way:

> For the moral development of children, no aspect of community support is more important than the community's ability to reinforce the social expectations of parents; that is, to express a consensus of shared values. Young people need to hear a consistent message about what is right and wrong from all the important adults in their lives; they need not only a social community but a moral community.[30]

A recent report on Chicago neighborhoods confirms Popenoe's finding. A ten-year study led by Felton Earls and Robert Sampson found that neighborhoods with "a shared responsibility for public order" had crime rates dramatically lower than those found in similar but less cohesive neighborhoods.[31]

For a variety of reasons, contemporary America possesses few (or at least, comparatively fewer) neighborhoods that can fulfill this function. For civil society advocates, that fact helps to explain the sorry condition of America's families, and, in turn, America's youth. Jean Bethke Elshtain argues that "where neighborhoods are strong and families are intact, drug and alcohol abuse, crime and truancy diminish. But of course, families and neighborhoods in 1996 are far less likely to be strong and intact. As a result, all forms of socially destructive behavior are on the rise."[32]

Finally, it is important to consider the impact of this set of concerns for the American social order. At the end of his article, Popenoe argues for a new public policy initiative—a "new localism"—that would seek to reinvigorate neighborhood life. Along with fostering residential stability and increasing public space and facilities, Popenoe recommends the enforcement of "community moral standards," and the protection of "homogeneous neighborhoods." He maintains that without these policies, communities can never again become "moral communities," and without moral communities, there can be no social virtue.

Concepts like "community moral standards" and "homogeneous neighborhoods" are certainly not morally straightforward. Among many citizens, they invoke painful memories, and indeed, reminders, of prejudice and discrimination. Popenoe notes, "I am not thinking here necessarily of racial and ethnic enclaves but of family-focused enclaves of people who share similar values and have a similar lifestyle." But he also acknowledges that "[t]here are obvious concerns about racial and ethnic discrimination and about constitutionally guaranteed human rights." This acknowledgment alone is not likely to assuage the misgivings of many marginalized persons. Popenoe's final response is not to deny the truth of these misgivings, but to argue that Americans must address the need for moral communities despite these fears: "There is no evidence that realistic social alternatives exist for the traditional 'tribal' structure of family and community."[33]

The concerns associated with Popenoe's argument recall a book that has received a great deal of attention among civil society advocates, Alan Ehrenhalt's *The Lost City*.[34] Ehrenhalt looks at three Chicago area neighborhoods, comparing life in the 1950s with that of today. His study begins with the feeling of longing and loss that many Americans have for the social world in which they grew up. But while Ehrenhalt celebrates the decency, the strong sense of community, even the quiet nobility that characterized the 1950s, he also conveys the serious (and in the current wave of nostalgia, often overlooked) moral issues associated with that era. Ehrenhalt is out to show that the feeling of community and solidarity that characterized the 1950s did not come without a cost. Real community cannot take place without a common moral authority, which, in turn, cannot happen without limiting individual freedom and choice.

The connection is interesting because while both writers affirm a kind of new localism, they highlight different dangers. Popenoe argues that social capital is indispensable to any healthy democratic society, and social capital is built through local institutions and interactions: if you want a moral society, you have to start with autonomous and morally homogeneous neighborhoods. But Popenoe's analysis suggests that the viability of these neighborhoods is to some degree dependent on the tribalistic instincts that are innate to human beings. And that leaves open the possibility that a community's moral order might foster discrimination against an outsider. As Michael Sandel has acknowledged, "to accord the political community a stake in the character of its citizens is to concede the possibility that bad communities may form bad characters."[35] Ehrenhalt, on the other hand, is concerned with the effect of localism on the insiders—those who live within the community. While the 1950s surely exemplified a moral consensus, the authority that undergirded that consensus was necessarily stifling to some. Strong community limited the possibilities, the parameters, for acceptable individual expression.[36] Indeed, Ehrenhalt suggests, as many have, that the authoritarianism and conformist ethos of the 1950s is the root cause for the strong counterculture movement of the 1960s. In short, then, morally cohesive communities can also either stifle freedom or lead to its abuse.

The idea of neighborhoods as moral communities, the belief that these have declined, and the question of how society might get them back, all of this is central to the civil society debate. I will have much to say about this in what follows. For now, though, I am concerned simply to show that even on its own terms, a moral community does not come without a price.

Religion and Religious Communities

Religious organizations—churches, mosques, synagogues, and the like—offer a third analytical contrast between the academic and public debates. To be sure, while the theoretical debate often downplays the relevance of religion, it rarely discounts that relevance completely. Whatever one wants civil society to do, it is hard to deny that religious institutions exemplify the concept of an effectively permanent institution formed by the voluntary action of independent yet like-minded individuals.[37] What's more, it is equally hard to dispute that churches both inculcate and reinforce a set of social virtues and act as independent loci of political power.[38] Indeed, theorists often even acknowledge a long historical legacy of religious institutions standing up (often alone) against the state's centralizing tendencies. But despite this affinity, there is still ample difference between the academic and the public discussion. The latter goes further than simply to affirm the idea that religious institutions are part of civil society, or even to claim that religion is a bulwark of social morality. Rather, that discussion often maintains that religion's ability to foster a commitment to virtue is both unique and indispensable. The public debate about civil society therefore has a far more affirmative assessment of religion, and is far more open to raising questions about the standing of religious belief and religious institutions in American culture. In short, the civil society movement is concerned not just with religious institutions, but with the concept of civil religion.

Public advocates of the civil society movement note that, for whatever reason, church attendance and the public standing of religious belief have declined in America over the past generation. More importantly, they contend that this trend is in some sense behind America's cultural crisis. Adam Meyerson, editor of *Policy Review: The Journal of American Citizenship,* writes that "the root cause of crime is spiritual."[39] William Schambra approvingly quotes an op-ed piece by the economist Glenn Loury that echoes the belief that religious institutions are indispensable. Loury denounces the moral breakdown of the inner city and calls for new "agencies of moral and cultural development":

> The family and the church are primary among these. These institutions have too often broken down in the inner city. . . . Yet these are the natural sources of legitimate moral teaching—indeed, the only sources. If those institutions are not restored, the behavioral problems of the ghetto will not be overcome.[40]

To be sure, not all civil society advocates would make this point so strongly, nor would they all agree that religion and the family are the only salient sources of moral instruction. But there is practically universal agreement about the claim that cultural and moral decay—in the inner city and throughout American society—is associated with the decline of religion in American culture, as there is about the related claim that religion must play an essential role in any cultural recovery.

The specific relationship between religion and the social problems of the inner city Loury outlines is not unique. Indeed, the prevailing attitude about religion and religious organizations is most clearly apparent when civil society advocates talk about the failures of the welfare state. In large part, their argument is that welfare has failed because the federal government is too big and too distant to address the specific problems of poor individuals. But there is more to it than that. President Clinton, who has repeatedly appealed to communitarian and civil society themes, made reference to this belief in a speech to high school students in suburban Virginia:

> Don't you believe that if every kid in every difficult neighborhood in America were in a religious institution on weekends—a synagogue on Saturday, a church on Sunday, a mosque on Friday—don't you really believe that the drug rate, the crime rate, the violence rate, the sense of self-destruction would go way down and the quality and character of the country would go way up?[41]

Clinton reflects a commonly expressed belief among civil society advocates that there is at least a significant connection between religious belief and individual virtue, and that vibrant and widespread religious activity is part of a well-ordered, civil society. These words likewise reiterate the civil religion theme. Whatever differences there are between religions, these are not as significant as their overarching similarities. The civil society advocate presumes that all or almost all religions are able to foster a common commitment to the social order.

There are, of course, substantive points of contention here. I go on to show that specific proposals about what role religion ought to play in a democratic society raise a host of potentially polarizing questions. But it is enough in this context simply to note that the public discussion advances a more positive cultural role for religious belief and religious institutions. That means civil society advocates wish to reexplore and revalidate the explicitly religious roots that have traditionally defined our nation's moral consensus. It also means they are generally less

concerned about the oppressive tendencies sometimes associated with
civil religion. The fear of religion—the fear that gave birth to liberal-
democratic society—is not the whole story. The point is not to deny
the concern; rather, civil society advocates appeal to the metaphor of
balance. The idea that religion is so dangerous that it must be walled
off from the public realm, that any accommodation to religion is open-
ing the door to either religious tyranny or religious wars, greatly over-
states the danger. More importantly, it ignores and jeopardizes the indispensable benefits that religion brings to a society. These advocates
therefore conclude that our nation's cultural and moral crisis requires
that we reassess the dangers, and reconsider the role, of religion in
American society.

The public conception of civil society is by no means exhausted by
these three institutions. Advocates routinely cite voluntary associations, political parties, unions—indeed, all the more organized, effectively permanent, interest-oriented groups that are common in the academic discussion. Yet while these other institutions are not ignored,
they receive comparatively little attention; the triumvirate of family,
neighborhood, and church clearly constitutes the focus of the public
discussion of civil society. The participants in the civil society debate
are well nigh united in their judgment that these institutions are most
effective at redeveloping our nation's supply of social capital and that
these same institutions are currently most in jeopardy. Within the public debate, Dan Coats's words are emblematic:

> The decline of these institutions which instill values without
> public coercion has resulted in terrible human carnage, af-
> flicting every strata of society, but especially the inner cities.
> Without the restraining influence of healthy families, churches
> and neighborhoods—an influence which is literally "civiliz-
> ing"—a society, at worst, falls into chaos.[42]

This quotation from Coats highlights the movement's affinity with
the right wing of American politics. I have shown that the concept
of social capital highlights informal interactions like church picnics,
chats with neighbors, and family dinners. These interactions resonate
strongly with right-wing talk of family values, the desire to free ourselves from governmental intrusion, and the need to reestablish God's
sovereignty in our society. Moreover, common to both is a nostalgic
attitude toward ways of life associated with a generation ago.[43] While

there is enough latitude in the discussion to allow centrist and even left-leaning interpretations, there is an easy resonance between central elements from the conservative agenda and the civil society debate. Given this, and given the conservative turn in American politics generally, it is not surprising that the civil society movement is dominated by a conservative or neoconservative political perspective. The movement's understanding of what is wrong with American culture further refines and solidifies the connection.

The Antitriumvirate: The Enemies of Civil Society

To elucidate further the public concept, it is helpful to note that the movement is equally united in its belief that three social institutions— the state, the market, and partisan politics—are inimical to their goals. These institutions—what I call the antitriumvirate—are distrusted and disparaged because they both undermine the free flourishing of social capital institutions and further our nation's declining civility, trust, and solidarity. To be sure, these issues are equally partisan. There is nothing like universal agreement on any of these issues, either. However, there is a common dimension to these positions, a broad parameter to the debate that is common to civil society advocates. I will seek to identify both this broad agreement, as well as outline the various partisan positions.

The State

Recall the discussion about religious groups and the commonly acknowledged failure of the welfare state. At best, the prevailing notion is that regardless of intentions, the welfare programs of the federal government have contributed to the intransigent problems associated with the underclass. At worst, the state is seen as the fundamental cause of the decline of American civil society, and thus the ultimate cause of our current cultural crisis. Radical devolution of federal power is therefore understood to be prerequisite to any effort to effect American renewal. It is worth laying out this position in some detail.

This underlying animosity toward "big government" is a perennial idea in American conservatism, and was obviously reflected by the Republican majority elected to Congress in 1994. William Schambra presents the argument for devolution in a way that directly ties it to the civil society debate. Schambra argues that the birth of big government, and the subsequent decline of American civil society, began with the Progressive movement. Herbert Croly, Walter Lippmann, John Dewey, and others sought to solve the problems of growing pluralism and a growing economy by developing a stronger national government. But they sought to allay the inevitable loss to local communities by making community national as well. They therefore encouraged the development of a paternalistic, benevolent government that would ostensibly develop and ostensibly replicate the best elements of localism on a national scale. "It is progressive liberalism's grand intellectual attempt to reconcile the centralized, bureaucratic, therapeutic state with the idea of public-spirited citizenship and community."[44] To achieve this end, the government took on ever more power. Unfortunately, the objectives outlined by Croly and others were inherently misguided. While a large nation may be a political possibility, a national community is not. Again, meaning is a local phenomenon.

The story of the twentieth century can thus be understood as a protracted struggle—a struggle, Schambra acknowledges, that was overseen by Democrats and Republicans alike—to achieve the unachievable. But while this enterprise failed to produce real community, it was all too successful at taking over and thereby disabling the traditional, local institutions of American civil society and local government. As George Will argues, "There is . . . a zero-sum transaction in society: As the state waxes, other institutions wane."[45] The government thereby eviscerated the local institutions that actually did build community. Worse, this condition engendered within the citizenry a weak-willed spirit. In its effort to achieve national community, the government became the problem-solving institution. The drive, self-sufficiency, and resilience that characterized the American ethos were severely undermined. This misguided political policy thus weakened, if it did not outright destroy, the only means available for future restoration. For Schambra and like-minded civil society advocates, the 1994 elections offered new hope for American society (hopes that were, of course, either derailed or at least postponed by the elections of 1996 and 1998). In any event, the Republicans continue at least to promise the end of big government and devolution of federal power. By these measures, they contend, Americans might begin to undo the damage of the past and allow for the rejuvenation of civil society.[46]

Now as with the discussion of religion, there is substantial disagreement on this point. Despite some conservative statements to the contrary, there are very few on the left side of this debate who are willing to accept fully the devolution agenda. Robert Putnam, for one, refuses to be aligned with this position. "For good historical reasons," he argues, "progressives should resist the view, now being articulated by some simple-minded reactionaries, that government can be replaced by 'civil society.' "[47] But even on this fundamental point, the difference is one of degree and not of kind. Recall President Clinton's well-known comment that "the era of big government is over." Advocacy of the concept of civil society appears to include a rejection, or at least suspicion, about the idea that moral or civic renewal can be born of the actions of the federal government. There is likewise fairly universal agreement that community is a local phenomenon, and that big government is not conducive to this local dimension of American public life.

This is not to say that the state can play no role. Even the most ardent libertarian argues that a dismantling of the state is essential to the cause, but of course that dismantling is itself an act that can be undertaken only by the state. The state's role is thus indirect. Its minimal task is to stop killing civil society. At most, it should provide mechanisms that foster the reemergent growth of those institutions.[48] Here too, there are differences. Not surprisingly, politicians like Bill Bradley and Dan Coats are much more interested in addressing the renewal of civil society through public policy than is a libertarian like Daniel Boaz, but even the most liberal advocate downplays the ability of government to address cultural problems. Bill Bradley, for example, offers several policy suggestions that he says illustrate that public policy "can help facilitate the revitalization of democracy and civil society." But he, too, accepts the movement's prevailing ethos that the state "cannot by itself *create* civil society."[49]

At its most ardent, the civil society movement maintains that a diminished state is necessary to reinvigorate the unifying forces of American society.[50] The federal government has taken on many of the tasks of civil society without being able to achieve their normative ends. But liberals and conservatives are united in the belief that the state is only indirectly relevant to the orienting goals of the movement. Whether the state merely undoes what it has done or whether it moves proactively to restore civil society advocates agree that our nation is experiencing a moral and civic breakdown, and that the state is inherently ill equipped to address this problem. Glenn Loury has argued that

> the core social problems of our time require for their solution a language of values—we should do this; they ought to do that; decent people must strive to live in a certain way. This

is the language of the pulpit, not the conference room. In
the discourse of the "policy wonk," who speaks fluent "con-
ference-ese," there is no place for language like this.[51]

These normative ends are the whole of the matter. Government is
judged unable to achieve them, and therefore government is, at best,
beside the point. There is no other proposition that is so characteristic
of the public civil society debate.

The Market

When public advocates of civil society define the term, they most often
say that civil society means those social institutions that exist and operate between the state on the one hand and the market on the other and
thereby mediate the negative tendencies of each.[52] It is, in Bill Bradley's
metaphor, "the third leg of the stool." This is, of course, an analytical
description. It merely separates out a subset of social interaction for
study and examination. But my argument has been that these analytical
distinctions do not fall out of the sky; they are born of normative goals.
There is nothing within the broad history of the concept of civil society
that suggests that the market is disconnected from, and thus completely irrelevant to, the institutions of civil society. On the contrary,
civil society theorists have, historically speaking, been almost universal
in maintaining an intimate connection between the economy and civil
society. Sometimes, this connection was seen as negative; the emergence of capitalism, it was argued, undermined a more adequate and
decent set of social virtues. Other equally important figures argued that
civil society developed out of the drives of self-interest and the workings of the marketplace. The inclination within the public American
debate to leave aside the economy is not a historical given, but rather
is premised on the belief that the goals of moral renewal are, at best,
not advanced and are, at worst, compromised by the mechanisms of
the market. Like the traditional theoretical discussion, this analytical
distinction is thus born of an important, if not always articulate, animus.

So far as I know, there are no thinkers in the public debate who
would advocate an alternative economic system. Most accept the idea
that capitalism is not only a given, but a powerful social force that is
(on balance) benign. But they would claim that this condition is not
inevitable. Historically, the argument goes, American capitalism has

served the nation well because it operated within a well-defined subset of social interaction and a constraining set of social mores. These mores checked the worst proclivities of the marketplace, and inculcated a rather strong sense of corporate and personal responsibility. They would go on to argue that the cultural forces that have led to a decrease in social trust, civility, and accountability have also unleashed these proclivities, and a bad situation has thereby been made worse.

From its inception, capitalism's operative principles of self-interest and acquisitiveness have been frequently seen as inimical to the burdens of community.[53] These concerns are surely part of what is being expressed in the public debate, too. But legacies from the past do not get at the heart of this concern. For this contemporary debate, one must instead focus on the contemporary corporate climate. That is, how does the operation of the free market impact on American society today?

Consider the fairly radical changes in the corporate climate over the last five to ten years: plant closings, corporate restructuring, layoffs, changes from full-time employment to part-time and contracted worker status, a rising disparity between worker and upper-management incomes—all of these recent phenomena—are representative of a decline in the social contract between worker and employer that was fairly ubiquitous only a generation ago. Here again, some of these phenomena have declined in recent years. High growth and low unemployment figures have forced some companies to become more employee-friendly. But beyond the vicissitudes of current economic forecasts, it remains the case that compared to the world of the 1950s, say, corporations today operate under a significantly different social contract, that is, a different understanding of their obligations to employees and vice versa. In the summer of 1996, the *Washington Post* recounted the story of this change within the corporate culture of AT&T. The authors conclude that the company's "recent decision to split into three companies, eliminate 40,000 jobs, and bestow a pay package estimated at $16 million on its top executive has come to symbolize the sacrifice of some cherished values—security, fairness, loyalty and sense of community—to the corporate gods of competitiveness and efficiency."[54]

Civil society advocates normally do not debate the wisdom or necessity of these changes from an economic point of view.[55] Indeed, it would be difficult to claim that there is *no* connection between these changes and the robust health of the American economy. These advocates prefer to table questions of efficiency and productivity; they are rather concerned with the social ramifications of these changes. They believe that the cherished values noted above are in serious decline in our society. Changes in corporate culture are thus lamented because they have furthered the decline of American social life. Michael Sandel's concern with the growing disparity between economic classes makes the point. "As affluent Americans increasingly buy their way out of reliance on public services, the formative, civic resources of American life diminish. . . . [M]arket forces, under conditions of inequality, erode those aspects of community life that bring rich and poor together in public places and pursuits."[56]

Civil society advocates also lament the demands corporations make on employees whose jobs are not in jeopardy. In polling data, employees commonly express the belief that there are more demands on their time, that they must deal with increased expectations on the part of their employers for overtime, overnight travel, and a willingness to relocate.[57] The civil society debate has brought a heightened awareness of the strain these demands make on families. In the summer of 1996, the *Wall Street Journal* reported polling results that showed that 62 percent of parents "believed their families had been hurt by changes they had experienced at work, such as more stress and longer hours."[58] In a society that connects a declining moral environment to a decline in family stability, these findings are very disturbing and very significant. The Council on Families in America includes many individuals associated with the civil society debate (e.g., David Blankenhorn, Jean Bethke Elshtain, David Popenoe, Mary Ann Glendon, and William Galston). In its report *Marriage in America,* the council offers three policy suggestions to employers that directly address these concerns:

- Create personnel policies and work environment that respect and favor the marital commitment.
- Reduce the practice . . . of continually uprooting and relocating married couples with children.
- Create personnel polices and work environments that permit parents to spend more time with their children, thus helping to reduce the marital stress that accompanies childrearing.[59]

Thus, just as civil society advocates are primarily concerned with the family as a social institution, so are their concerns about the market specifically focused on the way in which it undermines that institution.

The operation of a capitalist economy is not irrelevant to the rest of society. And because civil society advocates believe we are approaching a social crisis, these changes in economic behavior become fair game.

There is one more manifestation of unchallenged capitalism that worries civil society advocates. That is the perception that the social values associated with a healthy democracy have been truncated, if not outright upended, by advertising. David Popenoe argues that "through advocating a social structure in which consumer choice and pleasurable consumption are the highest values, through promoting high rates of mobility, a gambler's mentality, income inequality and materialism, the market is certainly no friend of civil society."[60] Jean Bethke Elshtain approvingly quotes John Paul II's lament that rampant consumerism not only belittles the individual but stifles "solidarity," that is, "a determination to 'commit oneself to the common good.'" She then drives home the connection. "To the extent that John Paul's words strike us as utopian or naive, we have lost civil society."[61] Here again, the concern is not with advertising per se. Almost everyone accepts the idea that advertising is a given in our economic system. The point is rather that the ethos of the marketplace is less contested and less constrained than it once was. Families, neighborhoods, and churches no longer instill a competing, even at times contradicting, set of values. It is the undiluted, unchallenged encouragement of rampant consumerism, of advertising appeals to the lowest common denominator, that concerns civil society advocates.

The desire that drives the public debate, that is, the drive for moral consensus, is born of a belief that people are insufficiently civil, insufficiently committed to a common enterprise. Civil society is seen as the means for restoring a moral consensus. Despite all the differences between the two institutions, then, distaste for the state and distrust for the market are both driven by the belief that these institutions, by their very size and complexity, undermine that effort. Benjamin Barber makes the connection explicit. "Americans currently face an unpalatable choice between an excessive, elephantine and paternalistic government and a radically self-absorbed, nearly anarchic private market."[62] Thus, just as the state is understood to have compromised self-reliance in the individual and the community, the market is seen as excessively egocentric.[63] In the market, self-interest is seen as the sole motivating factor; unchallenged, it exacerbates many of our contemporary social pathologies. In all the issues outlined above, an unfettered market both reflects and aggravates the decline of civil society, and of a society that is civil.

Just as the prevailing distrust of the state was driven by conservative ideology, the distrust of the market is driven by the progressive camp. Conversely, just as liberals are less inclined to dismantle the welfare state, it is fair to say that conservatives are even more likely to pass over any serious criticism of free enterprise. Again, this condition may simply reflect a contemporary climate in which Republican ideas dominate. That is, Democrats feel more urgency to sound Republican than vice versa. In any event, the silence is often quite glaring. Dan Coats's nineteen-point plan for reinvigorating American civil society does not even mention the effects of the market on those institutions, let alone offer public policy initiatives in this regard. The same can be said of the Hudson Institute's booklet, *Is There Life after Big Government?: The Potential of Civil Society.*[64] Adam Meyerson's "Letter to Our Readers" welcomes them to a publication newly dedicated to the principles of citizenship and civil society. In it, he trumpets the idea that "the most creative answers to social problems often come from businesses that can profit by solving them."[65] But about the negative impact of business decisions on community and citizenship, Meyerson says nothing.

Ultimately, this glaring and fairly widespread silence may undermine the claim that distrust of the market is a common feature. Possibly. But I remain convinced, for two reasons. It seems to me that conservative silence on this question does not result, or does not result entirely, from their unshakable faith in the market. Indeed, I think many conservatives associated with the civil society movement share at least some of the concerns voiced by the left. But these conservatives are so convinced of the damaging effects of big government that they are unwilling to voice any concerns that might be interpreted as a vote for governmental control. George Will reflects this belief in his generally favorable review of Michael Sandel's book *Democracy's Discontent.* Will notes that Sandel "laments the 'impersonal' economic forces that shape the lives of individuals and communities." But Will argues that "personal forces—political forces—are not necessarily preferable. Indeed, often they are more bitterly resented."[66] In other words, it is precisely the right's abiding distrust of government that induces its silence on market effects.

If and when one hears voices on the right decrying the activities of business, they most often claim that the businesses in question need to regulate themselves. Recall William Bennett's campaign against TV talk shows, or Robert Dole's 1996 campaign speech denouncing the corrosive effects of movies on popular culture. Both surely decry the deleterious effects of an unfettered market. The only difference—and it is a sizable one—is that the right is adamant that such controls come from the businesses themselves, or from the culture at large, and not from any sort of governmental oversight.

It must also be noted that the issue of economic control is virulently partisan. Therefore, it is predictable that persons well connected to the Republican Party are unlikely to broach these issues. Among some conservatives who are fairly removed from partisan objectives, however, there is a greater willingness to engage these themes.[67] Don Eberly, who surely affirms the virtues of the free enterprise system, is one notable example. "The good life is explained almost entirely as the pursuit of pleasure, not purpose. The highest end of life advertised by the economic marketplace is, simply, making a purchase, by credit card if necessary."[68] David Brooks, writing in the conservative journal the *Weekly Standard,* rejects the civil society movement as inappropriate to the inbred dynamism of American cultural life. But in the process, he offers this summary:

> Civil-society theorists tend to value stability over what Joseph Schumpeter called the "creative destruction" of capitalism. They believe the things that are destroyed—close communities—are more important than the things that are created—new companies, new wealth, new opportunities.[69]

One must admit, finally, that the distaste for the unfettered market is most closely associated with the left end of the debate. What's more, to the degree that this distaste is shared by the right, it manifests a significant and oft-noted tension within the Republican Party between economic conservatives—who claim that the best economic system is the least encumbered—and social conservatives, who are most concerned with the apparent evisceration of many of their most dearly held cultural values. Nevertheless, the very strength of the civil society movement is changing the landscape of American conservatism. A 1997 *National Journal* article entitled "Rethinking Capitalism" concluded that "something big is happening in American conservative circles."[70] As with any political debate, the condition is fluid, but it appears quite clear that the civil society movement is changing both the questions and answers typically associated with American conservatism.[71] Brooks's comments reveal that there is more of Burke than Reagan in the civil society movement. It is a conservatism that is more traditionalist than entrepreneurial. Finally, it is difficult to deny, and therefore never argued, that the concerns that drive the public discussion about civil society are negatively affected by the operations of the market. For all the rhetoric, the debate is not over that fact; it is rather over how a society ought to address those concerns.

Partisanship

The fact that, for political reasons, one of the two enemies of civil society is decried while the other receives short shrift is, for civil society advocates, further evidence of a declining social order. In his book *Why American Hate Politics,* E. J. Dionne argues that while Democrats stand ready to employ the vast, powerful (and sometimes oppressive) resources of the state against the machinations of corporations and other economic institutions, they are free-marketeers in the cultural realm. When it comes to individual beliefs, tolerance rules. No one has a right to restrict, challenge, or even morally condemn the way I choose to exercise my rights. The Republicans are equally inconsistent, but in the opposite way. They are eager to affirm the virtues of the free market, and to discourage any governmental oversight, but they are all too willing, the argument goes, to decry any behavior that does not measure up to their conception of family values. Americans perceive that these positions are at best inconsistent. At worst, they reflect a duplicitous kowtowing to special interests. They have therefore grown to hate politics.[72]

The discussion of the state and the market shows that the public discussion of civil society, predictably perhaps, reflects this partisanship. Conservative and liberal thinking on this issue is subject to these very same inconsistencies. Some of this is inevitable. The ideas outlined above prevail not just among civic society advocates, but in the society at large. The civil society debate has clearly tapped into a broad and potent stream of political and social discontent. Not surprisingly, politicians of all stripes, and with varying degrees of authenticity, seek to exploit that convergence to their own ends. But without separating true believers from apostates, it is nevertheless true that this discussion also professes, often in adamant terms, that the Americans who hate politics are right: partisanship has grown stale and unproductive. Thus, the disparity noted above should not obscure the more basic point that the civil society movement reflects a widespread dissatisfaction with the condition of American politics. Putnam, for example, notes that contemporary Americans evince "an understandable disgust for politics and government."[73]

Even more importantly, the movement also exhibits a common willingness to look beyond partisan loyalties to the state or the market for solutions. Bill Bradley argues (in words that directly recall Dionne) that the turn to civil society is premised on and driven by the entrenched and empty character of contemporary politics.

> Our contemporary political debate has settled into two painfully familiar ruts . . . Republicans . . . are infatuated with the magic of the "private sector". . . . At the other extreme, Democrats . . . instinctively turn to the bureaucratic state to regulate the economy and address social ills . . . [T]hese twin poles of political debate—crudely put, government action versus the free market—utterly dominate our sense of the possible, our sense of what is relevant and meaningful in public affairs. Yet the issues that most concern Americans today seem to have little direct connection with either the market or government.[74]

The civil society movement thus manifests a widespread dissatisfaction with traditional labels and distinctions, even as it transcends the traditional objectives, language, and constituencies of the traditional right and left in American politics. Don Eberly notes that "[p]eople are not moving so much to the Left or to the Right as they are moving out of old categories and old ways of looking at problems. Civic renewal is a different enterprise from that of winning elections for one's ideological or partisan point of view."[75] Throughout the discussion, one hears talk of a third way.

Thus, the rejection of partisan politics is related to, and even presupposes, the rejection of both the state and the market. Following Dionne, the civil society debate accepts the idea that each of the two parties is the principal advocate for one or the other of these two institutions. Partisanship of either sort lauds and supports the very institutions that civil society advocates understand as the enemy. Insofar as the civil society movement concerns itself with the third leg of the stool, it is likewise constrained to reject a political choice that boils down to one of the other two legs: "If that is the choice you offer, then a pox on both their houses."

Yet for all the importance attached to ineffectual partisan commitments, it is even more important to note that it is the demand for community itself that leads civil society advocates to disparage partisanship. Thus, it is not that partisanship is inherently deleterious to the civic realm. Civil society advocates routinely affirm the lively contentiousness of American politics. Rather, partisanship becomes unacceptable when it causes a group to be so concerned with its own goals and objectives that it disconnects itself from the greater community, even to the point of advancing its own specific objectives at the expense of the common good. This belief is reflected most commonly in the movement's harsh rejection of what has become known as *identity politics.* As with partisanship generally, the problem with identity politics is not that one group bands together to further its own ends (and often, to combat a legacy of prejudice and oppression). Indeed, how could someone who lauds the fabric of autonomous political associations be against that? Rather, the problem is that in identity politics, this objective often becomes exclusive. At its extreme, identity politics means that the common good ceases to exist because the group's definition of the good does not and cannot extend past its own boundaries. "Your identity," in Jean Bethke Elshtain's words, "becomes the sole ground of politics, the sole determinant of political good and evil."[76] So constituted, identity politics nullifies the fabric of democratic civility. For anyone who is not a member of the tribe is excluded a priori from the conversation. Politics in this understanding is nothing but a battle between interests groups, unable to agree on anything but that the established procedures are better than war. Indeed, at its very worst, identity politics undermines even this agreement. As Todd Gitlin has argued, "The danger of playing identity politics is that everyone can claim one. If there is nothing holding people back and nothing holding them together, then you are on your way to Bosnia."[77]

Identity politics is thus partisanship taken to its logical and most destructive extreme. And the fact that this form of politics has come to dominate the contemporary political climate reflects a greater breakdown in a sense of common purpose and common obligation. Reactions to the O. J. Simpson trial and the Rodney King verdict revealed yet again the racial fault line in American society. But the problem, and its disturbing implications, is also manifested in relations between ethnic groups, between generations, and between classes. Civil society advocates often decry what Arthur Schlesinger calls "the disuniting of America."[78] In Bill Bradley's words, our contemporary culture suffers from "a profound human disconnection that cuts across most conventional lines of class, race, and geography."[79] *Partisanship,* at least in its contemporary usage, is a broad term that describes this disconnection. But partisanship is also a social phenomenon that helps to foster it.

Partisanship, therefore, is part of what must be overcome if we Americans are to fashion a better society.

In every instance, then, these three social institutions undermine the goals of the civil society movement. In the case of the state and the market, the problem is direct. These naturally acquisitive social institutions are seen as civil society's enemies. There is only so much room, and as these institutions grow, extending beyond their limited yet legitimate roles, civil society must inevitably diminish. To restore civil society is therefore necessarily to seek to restrain, and perhaps fight off, the infiltration of the state and the market. The problem with partisanship is related but distinct. Partisanship does little to undermine the institutions of civil society. Indeed, the idea that an autonomous group of individuals would come together in the pursuit of their common self-interest is constitutive of civil society. Rather, here again the issue is one of imbalance. Partisanship has swamped the boundaries of civility and the quest for building a common good.[80] In every case, however, the goal of the civil society movement is to limit the offending institution—to restore it to its proper, and for that matter, former, role.

Conclusion

The object of this chapter has been to show both that there are distinctive features associated with the concept of civil society in America, and that those features are driven by the perceived problems with American society. Thus, social capital institutions are desired because they are understood to be the essential and (to say the least) preeminent means for constructing or reconstructing a more moral, more civic-minded society. Just so, the state, the market, and partisanship are rejected, or at least feared, because they undermine both the end of civic and moral renewal, and the means for achieving that end, namely social capital institutions. I do not maintain that all civil society advocates manifest every aspect of this broad characterization. But I do argue that this concept dominates the American public debate. That is to say that the civil society debate, with its neoconservative and even traditionalist aspects, is yet another reflection of the conservative turn in American politics.[81] It is also to say that even those participants who, like myself, applaud the interest in civil society, yet dispute all or part of this conception, are constrained to argue in terms of it.[82] Having therefore laid out that conception, this book will outline my argument.

Chapter Two

The Concept of Civil Society and the Modern Problematic

> . . . this strange disease of modern life,
> With its sick hurry, its divided aims.
> Matthew Arnold, "The Scholar-Gypsy"

The burden of the last chapter was to show that the concept of civil society in America is driven by the perception that our contemporary age is plagued by a kind of civic and moral atrophy. The institutions of civil society, particularly those that I have called social capital institutions, are likewise understood to be in a state of decline. Indeed, for civil society advocates, the latter condition is the cause of the former. Just so, the revival of these social capital institutions is seen as the preeminent means by which this moral and civic decline might be remedied.

I believe it is necessary to view this analysis in a broader historical context. In this chapter, then, I want to show that this contemporary feeling of cultural breakdown is properly seen as a response to some problems that are endemic to the modern condition. I also want to show that the modern concept of civil society developed as a means for addressing these very problems. In other words, just as the problems with modernity have a perennial nature, so, too, does the specifically modern strategy of attending to them through the institutions of civil society.

A Historical Conceit

First, it must be said that the expression of moral and civic breakdown associated with the civil society debate often manifests a kind of historical conceit. Many critics seem so focused on the here and now that they appear unaware of the long history associated with their concerns. For all the protestations about negative campaigns and simplistic advertisements, for example, it is simply incorrect to view such phenomena as new to the American body politic. American history is full of vitriolic campaigns, not to mention politicians who were wholly motivated by personal and partisan objectives. This nostalgic rendering of America's past undermines the value of the movement's analysis of contemporary social life.

Similarly, in their lament about contemporary society, critics frequently appeal to the solid community standards and values that pervaded in the status quo ante of pre-1960s America. To be sure, this age does indeed evince many of the social characteristics that seem so absent in contemporary life; Ehrenhalt's *The Lost City* makes that question almost moot. Nevertheless, Ehrenhalt also shows that this nostalgic longing for the stability of the 1950s is selective, and ignores the trade-offs that are inevitably associated with a stable social world. In other words, it is one thing to pine for community, but it is another to ignore the authority and restrictions on choice that are an almost inevitable concomitant. Moreover, even if such standards did indeed prevail in the 1940s and 1950s, it is historically inaccurate to believe such unanimity stretches back uninterrupted into America's past. The 1920s and the 1890s were periods of widespread social and cultural disagreements. By our standards, their conflicts may evoke an innocent, even innocuous quality, but they certainly did not seem so at the time. On the other hand, while the spirit of community that characterized the 1940s and 1950s may present an unhappy standard of comparison to the 1990s, the unifying force of a world war and a four-term president and the subsequent worldwide dominion of American politics, economy, and culture make that period unique in American history. In other words, one must at least consider the possibility that the relevant past, and not the present, is the aberration.

This critique of the critique, as it were, leads to a more fundamental argument. For a variety of reasons, our contemporary society is dealing with a host of problems that the preceding generation was largely able to avoid. Yet a broader outlook shows that these problems are not new at all. Nor are we the first Americans who have felt compelled to address them. Indeed, a sufficient accounting of the historical context for the concept of civil society reveals that the problems and solutions identified with the civil society debate in America have an even longer history. For they are problems that emerged pari passu with modernity itself. To make this case, it is necessary to outline, however briefly, the long and variegated history of the term.

Civil Society and the Modern Problematic

It is worth remembering that the concept of civil society has been around a long time. Beginning with the Greeks, the term has been articulated with more or less frequency in every major historical epoch and, in one way or another, by almost every major political thinker in the Western tradition. Theoreticians almost universally note that the term *civil society* originates with Aristotle. Using it as a synonym for the word *polis,* Aristotle defines it as a community of individuals (the relevant subset of whom are free and equal) who not only live together, but who have developed rational institutions for the use, maintenance, and transfer of power. Just as importantly, these institutions are understood, in however broad a sense, to serve the commonweal. In its classic form, then, civil society simply means political society. It is an all-encompassing term in which there is no relevant distinction between the state and society. Equally importantly, a society manifesting these features could properly be called civil. A civil society is made up of citizens, who actively affirm and participate in the ordered affairs of the state, and who can expect others to behave likewise. To be sure, Aristotle argues that this state of affairs is natural; the term describes how humans ought to live. But if civil society is a natural form of human association, it is also the highest. Aristotle is quite adamant that not all societies have achieved this level of civility; thus, a civil society is also properly understood as the opposite of barbarism. It is the rule of law over and against rule by brute force.

It is universally agreed that this understanding of the concept prevailed until fairly recently. Despite a host of important differences, the basic idea that civil society is synonymous with political society continues up into the early modern era. A line of thinkers extending from Cicero, Augustine, and Aquinas up to and including figures like Locke, Kant, and Rousseau all reflect this broad understanding. John Keane notes that "[w]ell into the 18th century the influence of this classial understanding of civil society remained unchallenged in Britain, France and the German States."[1]

Between 1750 and 1850, however, this remarkable and long-standing consistency begins to break down.[2] The change is as early and as gradual as the change from a feudal to a capitalistic economic order or from prevailingly monarchic to prevailingly democratic forms of government. For the development of the modern conception of civil society is tied to the emergence of modernity itself. The rise of the Enlightenment, the growth of the cities, the development of industry, the move from feudalist and mercantilist economic organizations to a capitalist organizing principle, the rise of the individual and the breakdown of the church-state synthesis, and the replacement of the aristocracy with various forms of democratic republics; all of these related and roughly concomitant developments are constitutive of modernity. Whatever the benefits associated with these changes, all challenged and to some degree undermined the established social order. And social thinkers were constrained to address this issue.

With the advent of modernity, the old social patterns either were dying or were being destroyed. The virtues that corresponded to the old order—a sense of one's place, of being bound and obliged to the past, the land, and one's community, a feeling of stability through time—all of these were slowly dying as well. Society becomes comparatively peripatetic and rudderless, more individualistic, more driven by self-interest and the quest for possessions.[3] At the same time, a more middling, if more commensurate, set of virtues emerge. At best, many felt that this emergent society would be less worthy and less humane. But the rumbling fear was that the social order that was coming was destroying hard-won social goods. The old world was more confident in the ineradicability of the worst aspects of human nature, and they believed that the features of premodern society lent a sort of stability and metaphysical certainty that bridled these instincts. At worst, then, these critics worried that the coming social world would not be moral enough to sustain itself. This is what I mean by the modern problematic. Throughout Europe, thinkers endeavored to respond to the incipient social reality by identifying social institutions that would ameliorate or soften the atomizing, centripetal effects of democracy and capitalism.

The modern concept of civil society developed as a distinctively modern way of counteracting these fears. Interestingly, just as the classic conception saw civil society as the opposite of barbarism, the modern conception grows out of the effort to counteract fears that the necessary foundations for social order were being whittled away. Theorists disagree somewhat about which thinkers are important in setting the stage for this transition. But the birth of the Enlightenment, the decline of the aristocracy, the rise of industrialism, and the democratization of all forms of social life all challenged the established social order;

throughout Europe, thinkers endeavored to respond to the new terms of social life. They often appealed to the concept of civil society in the effort.

Adam Ferguson: The Modern Concept and the Modern Problematic

Just as the advent of industrial capitalism (and, as most would acknowledge, democracy) has its beginnings in Britain, so too do the social changes brought on by this new economic order. As a result, no matter how long these rumblings went on, and how widespread they were, it is generally acknowledged that they reached something of a critical mass with the Scottish Enlightenment. This term, too, is amorphous and often overlooks serious distinctions. It is nevertheless possible to outline the basic points. Standing at the apex of the eighteenth century, these thinkers (most notably, Francis Hutcheson, Adam Ferguson, Adam Smith, and David Hume) outline for the first time the modern social problem. They saw that the community life that characterized a feudal and aristocratic order was dying, and an emergent modern world—the world of the Enlightenment and capitalism and democracy—was coming. Their task was to help society respond to this new social reality: either by embracing it and finding new and more appropriate forms of civic virtue, or by finding ways to preserve the best elements of the older forms of social order. The Scottish Enlightenment thus presents two broad strategies for confronting the effects of the emerging modern age. Its task was to find a way for modern society to preserve the felicitous changes of political freedom and economic growth while either maintaining former sources of civic virtue and cohesion or finding new ways to do so.

In a recent introduction to Adam Ferguson's classic text, Fania Oz-Salzberger notes this distinction:

> [T]he traditional republican discourse had no answers for the new respectability of wealth and social refinement, which eighteenth-century Scots came to associate with the modern age. A choice had to be made: the civic values had to be radically readjusted to the new ethics of sociability, commerce and freedom under the law; or else new proof was required for their relevance to the modern state. David Hume, and more decisively Adam Smith, chose the first of these solutions. Adam Ferguson opted for the second.[4]

Among the major figures of the Scottish Enlightenment, then, Ferguson was most concerned to preserve elements of community and civic virtue from the waning feudal/aristocratic era, and therefore, not coincidentally, he was also most explicitly concerned with the topic at hand. His work, *An Essay on the History of Civil Society,* is therefore a critical historical resource. It also presents interesting and important parallels to the contemporary discussion.

The first point is that Ferguson fully adheres to the ancient idea that *civil society* is another term for political society. Ferguson's use of the term did not betray any effort to distinguish between the state and the civil society. What's more, his understanding of the term coheres with the ancient Aristotelian idea. Ferguson argues that while society is, in some sense, natural—humans have always lived together in affective, communal bonds—in another sense, a truly civil society is a rare human achievement. For it reflects the citizenry's active and ordered participation in, as well as their spirited attachment to, the health and well-being of the state. For Ferguson, true civil society was not a modern creation; in fact, he continually turns to Sparta as the epitome of what he has in mind, and he often laments the lost camaraderie that was part of ancient social life. Ferguson clearly did not see history as a straight-line progression (in this, as in many other ways, he shows the influence of Montesquieu), nor did he think true civility was an inevitable concomitant of economic development.

Yet Ferguson was not a reactionary; he did not want, and in any case, knew it was not possible, to return to a previous social order. He saw that the new economic system was powerful and beneficial. Nevertheless, like many associated with the contemporary public debate, Ferguson believed that some central features of his age were leading to, at least, the decline of citizenship—at worst, he believed the new order resulted in a diminished human existence. And this led him to employ the concept of civil society in ways that dramatically altered its meaning.

Ferguson's world was run by men; women were peripheral to the matter at hand. And that world operated at its best when men were allowed and encouraged to be men. Capitalism undermined this objective, for it engendered a taste for luxury. Material things had become the dominant means by which a man showed his status, and that spawned a self-absorbed, even effeminate lifestyle. Relatedly, while the challenge of economic competition to some extent feeds the spirited, combative playfulness that is innate to human flourishing, men ultimately require a sense that their strivings are connected to shared and noble ends. In capitalism, ambition was wholly oriented around self-interest, and that compromised one's responsibilities and feelings toward the whole. A proto-sociologist, Ferguson argued that the division of labor had an unintended downside. It allowed, even encouraged each individual to ignore any consideration regarding the interest of the whole, in effect, to lose the forest for the trees. Ultimately, Ferguson held, this new economic system would lead to

> a fatal dissolution of manners, under which men of every condition, although they are eager to acquire, or to display their wealth, have no remains of real ambition. They have neither the elevation of nobles, nor the fidelity of subjects; they have changed into effeminate vanity, that sense of honour which gave rules to the personal courage; and into a servile baseness, that loyalty which bound each in his place, to his immediate superior, and the whole to the throne.[5]

This enervation has one particularly important, particularly dangerous, manifestation. If the citizen becomes acclimated to a life of luxury and self-indulgence, he then becomes unwilling to take up the burdens of self-governance—most importantly, he would not do his share to defend the state when necessary. This task would then be undertaken by the state and by mercenaries—individuals whose motivation is not patriotism but employment. (Ferguson's book was published in 1767. One thinks of the Hessians used by the British some ten years later in the American Revolution.) If the state controls the military, it thereby becomes a potential power that could be used over and against society.

> But to separate the arts which form the citizen and the statesman, the arts of policy and war, is an attempt to dismember the human character, and to destroy those very arts we mean to improve. By this separation, we in effect deprive a free people of what is necessary to their safety.[6]

Ferguson believed that capitalism encouraged a life fully oriented around the pursuit of one's self-interest; such an orientation eviscerated one's identity as citizen and as a man.

Those who valued their freedom had to do something to preserve it from the state. Therefore, Ferguson suggests (and in the *Essay*, he really does no more than suggest) that the proper avenue is for the elite male citizens to form militias. Such a movement would thwart any power grab of the state. For, as Ferguson notes, "when a people is accustomed to arms, it is difficult for a part to subdue the whole."[7] (One wonders if the framers had Ferguson's argument in mind when they drafted the Second Amendment.) Just as importantly, it would reinstill the connection between virtue and virility and the strength of character that emerges when one struggles with others to achieve a worthy goal. Finally, it would resuscitate the abiding sense of regard for the other, "the love of the public," upon which the state depends.

Many of Ferguson's complaints and prescriptions have, to say the least, not aged very well. While few would dispute his appeal to the special camaraderie that emerges in a challenging and shared enterprise, few would be willing to limit this experience to half of the human race. And surely none would restrict citizenship in such a manner. Even more importantly, Ferguson frequently writes as if he thinks that war is a good thing for a society—it provides a healthy and constructive outlet for spirited adolescents. Yet for all that, there is much in Ferguson's writings that is resoundingly familiar. The public discussion is likewise premised on the belief that the new social order no longer manifests a shared commitment to one another, nor to a set of higher ideals. While the focus now centers on the deleterious effects of the state, many also decry the prurient impact of advertising, our culture's inability to see success or achievement except in monetary terms, and what might be called the dominant narrative of self-obsession. It is very unsettling to recognize that, in many ways, Ferguson's problems are our own.

All of this not only manifests Ferguson's continued relevance, it also shows his more immediate importance in understanding the historical development of the concept. In the first place, Ferguson follows John Locke in advancing an implicit distinction, even an implicit animosity, between the society and the state. In this way, both figures unconsciously undermine the idea that civil society = political society even as they explicitly affirm it. At the same time, one can see in Ferguson the need to redevelop a public spirit among the elite to counteract this trend—to, in effect, reunite consumer and citizen, society and state. Ferguson suggests that this can be accomplished through the development of citizens' associations—and especially through the development of citizens' militias. The dual role associated with the modern concept of civil society—the idea that there are institutions formed and maintained by citizens that are independent of the state, and also serve to cultivate, maintain, even restore a spirit of civic virtue—is hinted at here for the first time. What's more, Ferguson appealed to institutions that we would identify as part of civil society to achieve both of the concept's modern functions: he sees them as a way to both maintain a check on governmental power and redevelop a sense of civic virtue.

Insofar as Ferguson implicitly outlines two functions for civil society, he sets the stage for the confusion associated with the modern understanding of the concept. Keane notes that "the traditional, increasingly moribund meaning [that is, civil society = political society] coexists and overlaps with the new, incompatible distinction between the state and civil society, whose meaning becomes subject in turn to pluralization through interpretation and disputation."[8] In just this way, Ferguson also sets the stage for the contemporary discussion in America.

The emergence of modernity created a society that is generally more atomistic, less cohesive, more materialistic, and less secure in its beliefs and values. Much of the greatest political and sociological thought of the modern era can be seen as responding to this new social order. Since the eighteenth century, therefore, civil society was understood to have a task. The role of the independent social associations came to be seen as a mechanism that might undo, or at least soften, some of modernity's harsher side effects. For most, the task was synthetic: to try to accommodate the powerful achievements of the new order, while maintaining some of the best elements of the old. The concept of civil society emerged as a crucial mechanism whereby this synthetic end might be achieved.

The relevant point is that this synthetic task remains operative. That is, for all the talk about the new and distinctive troubles appearing on the social horizon in America, those troubles have a perennial dimension as well. The same social phenomena that have been buffeting the social order since the beginning of the modern age—namely, the rise of the individual, a skeptical attitude toward established patterns and values, the atomizing effects of capitalism and technology—all of these changes are still with us, and they continue to affect the social order. Perennial, too, is the synthetic objective: to combine the undeniable benefits of modernity with the more humane elements of the former social order. Thus, the movement's ardent call for a community and consensus that incorporate, transcend, and thus rein in the individual; the belief that freedom is more a matter of shared governance and responsibility than unbounded individual expression; the belief that a

well-ordered society requires a sense of commitment that extends beyond self-interest; the fear that changes in traditional social institutions
will unintentionally endanger society's essential foundations—all of
these objectives reflect a conservative heritage and disposition that ultimately go back to the first rumblings of the modern era.

To be sure, the concept of civil society in the public American debate
remains distinctive. Part of this distinctiveness is cultural. For one
thing, the American concept is decidedly more populist than the European model. The "little platoons" that Burke celebrated, and to which
civil society advocates repeatedly refer, were under the tutelage of the
aristocrat who exercised dominion over his little corner of English society. The contemporary discussion, in contrast, highlights informal
interactions like church picnics, chats with neighbors, and family dinners. David Brooks has made the same point: "The civil society movement . . . looks to local communities to provide moral renewal, not to
elites. . . . But most important, the content of its morality is populist.
It revolves around the day-to-day virtues involved in neighborliness,
self-restraint, and childrearing."[9] Similarly, the European model does
not profess the ardent distrust of the state that is also seemingly innate
to American souls. It is also true that while we, like Ferguson, live
with the benefits and travails of modern social life, our context is much
different. Indeed, I will show that the thinkers who follow in the
Tocquevillian tradition believe that our society has come to manifest
many of the grave problems that Tocqueville himself only foresaw.
In other words, these thinkers believe the stakes are much higher and
immediate. Finally, I argue that the contemporary American context is
centered on the concept of social capital. There might be a number of
reasons for this feature; indeed, it is certainly yet another manifestation of the populist dimension of American political thought. But the
point here is simply that having the neighbors over for a barbecue is
a long way from having one's fellow aristocrats over to form a militia.

For all this, the points of contact between the contemporary concept
and that outlined by Ferguson are undeniable. We, too, are troubled
by the apparent insouciance with which citizens deal with their fellows
and with society at large. We, too, see ourselves relating to each other
less and less, approaching each other more as potential combatants
than as allies in some shared enterprise. Our world has become coarser
and less commodious. Just so, we appear less interested in bearing the
responsibilities of democratic life. To be sure, our respect for our government and governors continues to wane. Yet as we close the door

each night and turn on the TV, we are confident that others are assuming those burdens, and we are content to let them do so. At the most basic of levels, our problems and Ferguson's fears are the same. So, too, is the putative solution: civil society.

I am aware, of course, that many in the academic community dispute any meaningful affinity with Ferguson and reject the characterization of our world as "modern." Our time is postmodern, and while the term is inherently transitional and diffuse, it reflects the adamant belief that whatever we are living through, it is no longer modernity. As must be apparent, I do not share this view. Indeed, one could view this chapter as an argument against such a conception. On the other hand, there is an understanding of postmodernism that sees our time as different in degree rather than in kind. This conception holds that modern categories remain, but they have been exposed and thereby compromised. The moderns set us out to sea, but we are left without their deep harbors. Again, I argue that there are reasons for believing that our generation confronts these modern problems with more exigency and fewer resources. This conception is therefore not incommensurate with the argument I present here. But I do not want to speculate more about the point. My intention is to show that there are common features to the modern concept of civil society. That concept developed as a modern solution to a set of distinctively modern problems. It remains so to this day.

The perennial dimension of the civil society debate, as well as its historical conceits, means that the discussion must expand its frame of reference. In order to understand the contemporary public concept and its objectives, it is necessary to understand its historical sources; in order to understand where we are, it is necessary to understand where we came from. The writings of Hegel and Tocqueville, like those of Ferguson, further reinforce the notion that our problems are not new, nor is the turn to the eminently modern phenomenon of civil society. The thought of these two thinkers, and their followers, continues to echo in the contemporary debate. In part 2, I show how this is so. I also show why it is incumbent upon us to attend to their legacy.

Part
Two

The Progenitors of Civil Society

Chapter Three

The Tocquevillian Tradition

Within the modern period, the concept of civil society has developed along two lines: the Hegelian and the Tocquevillian legacies. Both strains concern themselves with the same broad categories of analysis, and overlapping influences are commonplace. What is more, both can be seen as responses to an emerging modern world, especially the threatening forces of capitalism and democratization. Yet the movements are distinct. While both address the same basic issue, they are not talking to each other. As a result, using terms outlined in chapter 1, we might say that the two paths outline distinctive conceptions of what civil society is and what it is for.

Both strands inform the modern concept of civil society, and both find their place in the contemporary American discussion. Indeed, their combined influence accounts for much of the dissonance within the contemporary movement. In chapters 5 and 6, I recount the Hegelian legacy. This chapter and the next focus on what I am calling the Tocquevillian tradition. I claim that after many fits and starts, the thought of this central historical figure has developed into a historical, intellectual trail—one that employs a specific concept of civil society to address deep concerns regarding the features of modern life. Tocqueville's thought has left an important legacy—one culminating in a series of recent events that directly inform the modern concept in America. Tocqueville is the theorist who is by far the most important to the self-understanding of contemporary civil society advocates. It is therefore essential to outline the wellspring of that tradition, and show how it has come to play such an essential role in the ongoing discussion.

The Inexorable Fact of Democracy

Tocqueville came to America in the spring of 1831, ostensibly to review the American penal system for possible adoption in France. But despite his relatively short time here (less than nine months), Tocqueville's reasons for coming far transcended this rather limited purpose. Tocqueville saw the whole of America as a giant experiment. America was the world's fullest expression of democratic government and democratic society. He therefore believed that what he saw in America was of almost indescribable importance for France. His sweeping account, *Democracy in America*, was an attempt to make clear to his fellow citizens why it was that America thrived, thereby offering important lessons and insights for a struggling French society.

Tocqueville, like Ferguson before him, saw clearly that the old social patterns were dying. A more democratic order was slowly replacing the aristocracy. He also believed that there were profound losses, and dangerous risks, associated with this change. Yet Tocqueville's assessment is not one of simple condemnation. In *Democracy in America*, Tocqueville recounts that over the last several centuries, at every historical turn, the forces of history have furthered the cause of human equality. Even those groups that were most adamantly opposed to popular rule and individual freedom acted in ways that, despite their intentions, ultimately helped secure democracy's advance. Tocqueville therefore concludes that democracy, and the accompanying "equality of conditions," is providential; it reflects God's will and God's action in history. This being the case, the "effort to halt democracy appears as a fight against God Himself, and nations have no alternative but to acquiesce in the social state imposed by Providence."[1] The rise of modernity may present grave problems, but like it or not, modernity is coming.

The will of God cannot be unavoidably bad for humans. And indeed, it is clear to Tocqueville that democracy is a political expression of the ideal of human equality long advanced by Christianity. But while providence might set the broad patterns of history, it did not negate human freedom and responsibility. Humans could respond well or badly to the possibilities God provides.[2] Tocqueville acknowledges that the fears of his fellow aristocrats are far more than simply the bitter complaints of a vestigial social anachronism. The advent of democracy is by no means an unalloyed good. It destroys old established ways of keeping nasty human proclivities under lock and key, and thus creates possibilities for social evil that the world has not seen before. But none of this legitimates efforts to "keep the past upon its throne." The question, rather, is how best to direct and accommodate this inexorable reality. How might human beings respond to the new social order in a way that was most likely to achieve God's own ends, and most likely to prevent social disaster? The change from aristocracy to democracy requires "a new political science" (12), and that is the task that Tocqueville sets for himself in *Democracy in America.*

For Tocqueville, democracy is more than simply a political system in which the people rule. Democracy defines a kind of society—one grounded in the belief in and affirmation of human equality. The first sentence in this very long book is: "No novelty in the United States struck me more vividly during my stay there than the equality of conditions" (9). Democracy is thus a pervasive reality that makes America a unique society and culture. Likewise, equality is more than just a political condition, born of popular sovereignty; it is "the basic fact," "the creative element" that either colors or outright transforms all features of social life.

> In the United States the dogma of the sovereignty of the people is not an isolated doctrine, bearing no relations to the people's habits and prevailing ideas; on the contrary, one should see it as the last link in a chain of opinions which binds around the whole Anglo-American world. . . . That is the great maxim in which civil and political society in the United States rests. (397)

The idea of popular sovereignty is the coupling of political freedom and political equality. But while freedom is impossible without equality, the opposite is not true; citizens can suffer equally under political oppression. What is more, while political liberty requires effort, even vigilance, the advantages of equality are immediate and easy. For Tocqueville, all this means that the two terms are united, yet unequal: "The first and liveliest of the passions inspired by equality is . . . love of that equality itself" (503). This is why Tocqueville sees 'equality of conditions' as both pervasive and novel, and why equality becomes the focus of his work. The fact of popular sovereignty has bred within American culture a passionate devotion to human equality.[3]

The Unanticipated Dangers of Equality

This ardent love of equality leads to two conditions that are new to the democratic society. In the first place, equality engenders a sense of independence, even self-sufficiency in its citizens. "In all matters that concern himself alone he [each individual] remains the master; he is free and owes an account of his actions to God alone. From this derives the maxim that the individual is the best and only judge of his own interest and that society has no right to direct his behavior unless it feels harmed by him." (66). This feeling of autonomy and self-mastery lends a dignity to everyday life that would have been unthinkable for the commoner in aristocratic society. Tocqueville also avers that this equality more adequately reflects the truth of the matter; humans do possess a basic (if hardly pervasive) equality. Democracy is therefore more just than aristocratic society. Yet as is so often the case with Tocqueville, the change is ambiguous. In aristocratic society, people were not equal, but their very inequality served to link everyone together. The aristocrat had some responsibility to the peasants in his fiefdom, and they to him. In a democracy, each individual is equal and free, but as a result, people are also made more separate. "Equality puts men side by side without a common link to hold them firm" (510).

For Tocqueville, this separateness ultimately manifests itself in a way of living that is unique to democracies. He calls it individualism: "a calm and considered feeling which disposes each citizen to isolate himself from the mass of his fellows and withdraw into the circle of family and friends; with this little society formed to his taste, he gladly leaves the greater society to look after itself" (506). Because of equality, each individual's frame of reference tends to constrict. People are not inclined to look ill upon their neighbor so much as they are inclined to ignore them. Of course, this isolation is likely to make social life less agreeable. But the problem goes far deeper than that. Rather, the issue is what this isolation does to the very democracy that engendered the problem in the first place.

If people are less inclined to concern themselves with the problems of society at large, then patriotism, along with a sense of public spirit and public virtue—that is, the very virtues that make a free society possible—inevitably decline. As we shall see, this decline can become so great as to leave open the possibility of despotism. Moreover, the insouciant disregard for all things public is corrupting. At first, Tocqueville believes, individualism "only dams the spring of *public* virtues, but in the long run it attacks and destroys all the others too" (506–7). Ultimately, individualism develops into a misguided and inadequate conception of self-interest, indistinguishable from egoism, i.e., from selfishness. At that point, the condition is no longer ambiguous; it is a vice; and it is a sorry foundation from which to maintain a democratic polity.

The other major problem born of equality of conditions is the tendency for individuals to focus on base and materialistic concerns. Here too, Tocqueville draws his comparison to the aristocratic order. In the aristocracy, one either has significant wealth and is strongly discouraged from striving to acquire more, or else one is socially proscribed from attaining it. In either case, humanity's innate acquisitiveness— the drive to both define oneself and to allay life's disquiet through ever more possessions—is restrained. In the democracy, there are no such constraints, and therefore, equality "lays the soul open to an inordinate love of material pleasure" (444). As with individualism, Tocqueville's complaint is measured, if not outright ambiguous. The freedom to pursue one's desires, to strive without arbitrary limits, affirms justice and human dignity. What is more, the materialism that is characteristic of democratic regimes is not morally obscene. Indeed, Tocqueville calls it "decent." Yet while it "will not corrupt souls," it does become the individual's sole orienting focus.

Thus, while democratic materialism is effectively benign, Tocqueville worries that the striving for wealth and possessions is wholly absorbing, leaving little room for any other pursuit. What's more, as with individualism, the emergence of this mild defect is not the end of the story. If materialism is not restrained, it can come to dominate and disorient one's life. For Tocqueville, the drive for possessions is incessant, and it is incessant because it is inherently unsatisfying. It cannot get at the itch that needs scratching, yet we continue in a vain quest, disoriented and dissatisfied, ceasing only when we die.[4] Tocqueville continually marvels at the frenetic pace of American society and the dramatic contrast it offers to his experience in France. Life in the aristocracy is centered on one's name and one's land. Thus, everyone is more aware and respectful of what Tocqueville felicitously calls "the woof of time." (507) "Democratic man," by comparison, "does not know how to orient his life. Material goods are the sole fixed point, the sole incontestable value amidst the uncertainty of all things."[5]

It is this disorientation, bred by materialism, that Tocqueville fears. Here again, the mediocre faults associated with democracy can eventually degenerate into something far worse. The social fact of human equality does not extinguish and even increases the desire for anything that might distinguish the self over against the herd. This struggle for distinction, combined with unleashed acquisitiveness, encourages people to focus on the near term and draws them to conspicuous, even ostentatious displays. Even society's best minds are increasingly led to a truncated and debased notion of success, focusing on trivial and even degrading concerns. Finally, materialism and individualism feed off each other. The freeing up of innate human greed only accelerates and renders more likely the move from individualism to egoism: the spiral downward only intensifies. Of course, all of this only furthers the decline into isolation and self-centeredness—the public good fades even further into oblivion. Even when citizens are constrained to focus beyond themselves, their decision-making capacities have been corrupted; the inbred focus on the short-term leads to "a contempt for tradition and formalities" (459) and an inability to make hard choices. Again, democracy's innate tendencies undermine the long-term viability of democracy.

For Tocqueville, democracy and its effects are indeed more natural, more true to the human condition, than the aristocracy is. But in radical contrast to his sometime mentor Rousseau, Tocqueville rejects the premise that nature is good and artifice is bad. On the contrary, Tocqueville believes, with Pascal, that original sin has left its mark on all humanity. The failures of individualism and materialism are social manifestations unique to a democracy, but they are based on innate human proclivities. The aristocracy—with ties to land, name, and people—moderated those proclivities. Democracy may be more just and more natural, but the unnatural injustices associated with the aristocracy were very useful indeed. Now that they are gone, Tocqueville fears, human failings are unleashed to wreak havoc on human society.

If these problems grow unchecked, they will continually compound each other, and ultimately, two future possibilities will emerge: anarchy or tyranny. Of these, the former is rather easy to anticipate: the lack of socially induced rules and norms, the ever more competitive drive for immediate wealth, and, most obviously, the decline of any meaningful concern for anyone outside one's tiny circle of family and friends, all combine to create an environment in which the center cannot hold. Democracy does indeed more closely echo humanity's natural state. And as the innate tendencies of democratic society work themselves out, the democratic order degenerates back into a state of nature, that is, a Hobbesian state of war of all against all.

Tocqueville's other concern is harder to foresee: despotism is, of course, the opposite of too much freedom, and it is difficult to see how a people accustomed to and proud of their freedom would allow it to be taken from them. But recall that for Tocqueville, Americans' attachment to liberty and equality, while passionate, is not equal.

> I think democratic people have a natural taste for liberty; left
> to themselves, they will seek it, cherish it, and be sad if it is
> taken from them. But their passion for equality is ardent, in-
> satiable, eternal and invincible. They want equality in freedom,
> and if they cannot have that, they still want equality in slavery.
> They will put up with poverty, servitude, and barbarism, but
> they will not endure aristocracy (506).

Again, Tocqueville believes that while Americans love and celebrate their freedom, equality of conditions is the central fact of American life. It is this fact that makes tyranny possible.

The decline into tyranny is similar to the decline of individualism into egoism, and of the decline of decent materialism into vice: it is gradual and almost imperceptible. The innate tendencies of individualism and materialism lead people increasingly to value creature comforts. Left free to enjoy the consolation of hearth and home, they are willing to ignore any other aspects of their freedom. In addition, as equality of conditions evaporates distinctions between individuals, any sign of inequality, whether wealth or genius or eccentricity, is looked upon with increasing envy and resentment. Those in the majority are thus all the more willing to prevent such signs, and will increasingly turn to the state to advance that end.[6] Finally, the rising tide of individualism leaves people feeling isolated and helpless. If and when a crisis should arise, individuals may very well be left with no one to turn to. They are thus naturally inclined to see the state as a savior. In the abstract, they do not want the state to take on such a role, but faced with their own dire circumstances, abstract concerns go out the window: they want and indeed demand that the state alleviate their misery, fix their problems, and restore their former lives.

The state, for its part, is made up of humans. Therefore, like all humans, it is naturally acquisitive, ever and always striving to increase its power. That means that the state is all too willing to accommodate these middling steps to despotism. It is happy to meet the citizenry's demands in order that it might restrain and ultimately eliminate their ability to make future demands. To be sure, Tocqueville acknowledges that because it is born of democracy, the kind of despotism he foresees is unique in human history. Indeed, Tocqueville is not even sure what to call such a state. For unlike tyrannies throughout history, this one is simply giving the people what they want. The democratic dictatorship is despotic, but it is a benign, paternalistic form of despotism. As democratic society reveals natural, albeit unfortunate human proclivities, the state appears as an "immense, protective power which is alone responsible for securing their enjoyment and watching over their fate. . . . It would resemble parental authority if, fatherlike, it tried to prepare its charges for a man's life, but on the contrary, it only tries to keep them in perpetual childhood" (692). The people have offered their freedom for the price of comfortable, untroubled existence, and the state is happy to pay it. And by fulfilling its end of the bargain, the state also takes the citizenry's dignity and humanity.[7]

Tocqueville is at a loss to say which one of these dangers is most likely. "One cannot state in any absolute or general way whether the greatest danger at the present time is license or tyranny, anarchy or despotism. Both are equally to be feared, and both could spring from one and the same cause, that is the general apathy, the fruit of individualism" (735–36). But he also thinks the very question misses the point. "We should . . . direct our efforts, not against anarchy or despotism, but against the apathy which could engender one or the other almost indifferently" (ibid.). Again, Tocqueville believes the tendencies he sees in America are endemic to democracy. Yet at the same time, he does not see American society as doomed. On the contrary, while he is fearful of its future, he regards its present as an amazing success. American society proves that democratic society need not inevitably sink into either catastrophe. Because Tocqueville sees that democracy will inevitably come to France as well, his task is to determine how America is able to avoid these problems.

Democratic Solutions to Democratic Problems

If democratic society is to survive, it is clear that it must somehow duplicate the achievements of aristocratic society. That is, it must at once instill a set of behavioral norms that combat the failings that human beings are naturally heir to, and it must likewise temper the naturally acquisitive tendencies of the state. America proves that democracy can do just that. What is more, America shows how that can be done. The secret is to acknowledge that with the death of the aristocracy comes the ineffectiveness of aristocratic conventions. America succeeds because it has constructed a distinctively democratic set of countervailing institutions and conventions. Specifically, Tocqueville believes that Americans have used the innately democratic tendencies toward self-interest to secure democracy and to advance the cause of liberty.[8] As we have seen, Tocqueville believes that democratic society is more natural, often to its peril. The irony is that that naturalness extends to the solutions. Even democracy's social conventions are more natural.

Tocqueville's account is exhaustive. He recounts even such apparently innocuous features as geography to account for the preservation of liberty. He also spends a good deal of time recounting the formal features of American self-government, including federalism, an independent judiciary, the jury system, and the Bill of Rights. Yet he also believes that in any effort to account for America's success, laws are more important than geography, and mores—the whole moral and intellectual state of a people—are more important than laws.[9] To be sure, the laws of any society have, for good or ill, an important pedagogical role. I will note later that Tocqueville by no means discounts it. Nevertheless, Tocqueville believes that the primary responsibility for the inculcation of this moral and intellectual state falls on three social institutions that are separate from the state, that is, part of American civil society: political and civil associations, religion, and the family. In light of my focus here, I will concentrate on these elements in Tocqueville's analysis.

Associations

Tocqueville contends that democracy needs to develop social conventions that run counter to egoism and rampant materialism, and it needs a political mechanism that limits the naturally acquisitive reach of the state. Associations, that is, individuals (otherwise strangers) freely coming together to pursue a common interest, do both.

Though he does not always make note of it in his discussion, Tocqueville distinguishes between two kinds of associations: political and civil.[10] The difference between civic and political associations centers on their object. There is obviously overlap, but civil associations are not directly concerned with matters of law, while the effort to develop political power and effect change through the political process is the primary, if not sole focus of a political association.[11] Thus, political associations include everything from town meetings and other forms of local government to political parties, partisan newspapers (in mid-nineteenth-century America, there really was no other kind), and community groups. The neighbors who come together to effect some legal remedy for their common problem have organized themselves into a political association.

Civil associations, on the other hand, more closely conform to the common contemporary conception of civil society. They include just about every other instance in which individuals associate. In a famous discussion, Tocqueville writes,

> Americans of all ages, all stations in life, and all types of dispositions are forever forming associations. There are not only commercial and industrial associations in which all take part, but others of a thousand different types—religious, moral, serious, futile, very general and very limited, immensely large and very minute. Americans combine to give fetes, found seminaries, build churches, distribute books, and send missionaries to the antipodes. Hospitals, prisons, and schools take shape in that way. Finally, if they want to proclaim a truth or propagate some feeling by the encouragement of a great example, they form an association. In every case, at the head of any new undertaking, where in France you would find the government or in England some territorial magnate, in the United States you are sure to find an association. (513)

Civil associations thus constitute the much larger group. Tocqueville also clearly believes that both types of associations, considered together, form the backbone of American society and political culture.

Just as these associations are distinct yet related, so, too, is the role they play in society; political and civil associations have both a common social function and one that is characteristic of one or the other. By their very nature, all associations are a training ground in democratic action and thinking. They bring democracy down to a face-to-face level. In a neighborhood or community meeting, popular rule is readily accessible. The issues, stakes, and opponents are clear to all. So, too, are the imperatives and niceties of democratic culture. Individuals must learn and accept a common set of procedures in order to advance to their common end, and they must accept the rule of the majority. In this sense, all associations are schools for democracy. "Local institutions are to liberty what primary schools are to science; they put it within people's reach; they teach people to appreciate its peaceful enjoyment and accustom them to make use of it" (63).[12]

Tocqueville thus concludes that associations allow Americans to perceive their self-interest in a more realistic way. The teaching that goes on in all associations moves individuals to realize that their self-interest requires that they not remove themselves to their private homes and ignore the world outside. Their private interests can be satisfied only if they are willing to work with others with similar interests, according to fair procedures. "As soon as common affairs are treated in common, each man notices that he is not as independent of his fellows as he used to suppose and that to get their help he must often offer his aid to them" (510). What is more, through their common enterprise, citizens come to learn that their fellows are not much different than they are. They learn that all have a common set of objectives and interests and that no one wishes ill for the other. I will note later the importance of this issue for civil associations, but for now, it is important to note that all associations start and end with self-interest. But along the way, Tocqueville believes, self-interest is educated in a way that is beneficial to democratic society at large.

Yet while all associations train individuals in the procedures and demands of political liberty, and in determining where their real interests lie, there is also a distinction regarding the effect these two types have on society at large. Tocqueville believes that political associations are more likely to check the power of the state, whereas civil associations are more likely to inculcate feelings and dispositions that work against the isolative tendencies of democratic life.

A political association is a collective of individuals—a whole that is greater than the sum of its parts—operating with a level of effectiveness that no individual could reach. Moreover, that association has internally trained itself in the manners and mechanisms of democratic rule. It is thus more savvy and experienced; it is far better able to maneuver through the real world of democratic politics and achieve its desired ends. Because of these effects, political associations give individual citizens the means and the insight to challenge tyranny. First, they enable the citizens who find themselves in the minority to hold back the tyranny of the majority. (By doing so, associations also serve as a defense against the leveling of tastes and manners that Tocqueville believes is inherent in democratic society.) Second, political associations build up independent sources of political power that stand on guard against any encroachment of their interests. Thus, they check the naturally acquisitive tendencies of the state.

In the past, the aristocracy served these purposes. Its irrevocable loss therefore increases the possibility of despotism. Tocqueville's concern, therefore, is to find something within the democratic social fabric that can act as the functional equivalent of the aristocracy.[13] Associations fill this purpose, and that is why they are so central to Tocqueville's analysis and to the success of the American democratic republic.

> [N]o countries need associations more—to prevent either des-
> potism of parties or the arbitrary rule of a prince—than those
> with a democratic social state. In aristocratic nations secondary
> bodies form natural associations which hold abuses of power
> in check. In countries where such associations do not exist, if
> private people did not artificially and temporarily create some-
> thing like them, I see no other dike to hold back tyranny of
> any sort. (192)

By freeing self-interest to form political associations, it is both schooled
and directed so that it becomes a social phenomenon that is able to
stand up against the power of the majority and the power of the state.
Tocqueville says that political liberty is "the only effective remedy
against the evils that equality can cause" (513).[14] It is a democratic solution to a democratic problem.

Again, civil associations are likewise oriented by self-interest. The
impetus that brings an individual to join a choral society is not fundamentally different from the impetus to take part in a town meeting.
Consequently, civil associations, too, function as independent sources
of political power.[15] But here, political power is not the immediate goal.
The burden is lighter in civil associations; thus, Tocqueville believes
they pave the way—ease the move—to political ones.[16] More importantly, this distinction means that while civil associations, too, are
driven by self-interest, they also provide a mechanism for moving beyond self-interest. As Pierre Manent notes, the goal of these associations "is to incessantly re-knit the social fabric that equality of conditions continually tends to unravel."[17]

Tocqueville believes that appeals to self-sacrifice died along with the
aristocratic era. The equality of conditions that underlines democratic
life means that any appeal not grounded in self-interest is bound to
fail. But if selfishness is what brings individuals to associate, that is
not the end of the matter. As a simple by-product of their interaction, Tocqueville says, "[f]eelings and ideas are renewed, the heart en-
larged, and the understanding developed" (515). It is primarily in civil
associations, then, that the famous "habits of the heart" are fostered
and nurtured. To say this, however, is not to contradict the claim that
associations produce enlightened self-interest. For Tocqueville, the development of these habits only reflects the truth of the matter. By conforming to that truth, individuals live a life that is fuller and happier.
Thus, the development of those habits is indeed more commensurate
with one's self-interest.

In its least appealing visage, Tocqueville's "self-interest rightly understood" is still fundamentally selfishness; it is merely smarter selfishness. Ambition is advanced by attending to, or at least appearing to attend to, the interests and concerns of others.[18] At best, however, the selfish need for others leads to a consideration for, and ultimately a regard for, others. William Johnston puts the point very well. By means of associations, he notes, "greed become self-conscious may become concerned beyond itself, thereby ceasing to be only greed. A sense of rights may lead to a sense of rightness; a sense of duty to oneself to a sense of duty to 'this collective being.' "[19] Again, the problems inherent to equality require solutions that acknowledge and accommodate that condition. Civil associations start in selfishness, and in some fundamental sense they remain there, yet they also able to create social conditions that temper and arrest the decline of individualism into egoism.

Religion

If Tocqueville believes that associations are essential to the continued health and viability of democratic society, he does not understand them to be sufficient to that task. Tocqueville believes that self-interest—even self-interest rightly understood—is not enough to ensure a moral order. Tocqueville believes that morality often dictates behavior that self-interest, no matter how well understood, cannot prescribe. Yet society depends upon just this sort of behavior. Every society, for example, from time to time requires the self-sacrifice of soldiers going into battle. What's more, Tocqueville believes that a democratic society is especially needy of religion's felicitous effects. Tocqueville worries that civil associations will not be enough to keep individualism and materialism from degenerating into destructive vices. Religion, by its very nature, counters humanity's worst proclivities, and moves us to self-sacrifice and a regard for others that self-interest alone is unable to achieve. American democracy depends upon mores, and mores require religion. Tocqueville therefore insists that no matter how successful its associations, a democracy must possess a common religious foundation.

There is another reason democratic society requires religion. As I have said, the establishment of political freedom means everyone is left his or her own master. This leads to greater dignity and independence, but it also leads to the decline of any sense of metaphysical bedrock. In a democracy, the individual alone is ultimate judge of good and bad, right and wrong, correct or incorrect. Yet the mere fact of what one might call metaphysical individualism does not negate, and indeed only strengthens, the need for some kind of foundation. Tocqueville believes that we humans must possess a set of beliefs that allow us to make sense of the world, and quell the disquiet that comes with chronic incertitude. Dogmatism, of one sort or another, is thus both necessary and inevitable. Indeed, if democratic society tries to function without a religious foundation, a demagogue will inevitably step into the existential void. Therefore, because of what aristocracy and democracy respectively engender, democracy needs religion more. Tocqueville is so convinced of this that he says, "[I]f he [humanity] has no faith he must obey, and if he is free he must believe" (444).

So America, more than any other country, requires the salutary effects of a common religious belief. Yet with its multitude of sects, dogmatism would appear impossible. What's more, democracy is somewhat unreceptive to religion. True, Tocqueville believes that democracy's grounding belief in human equality grows out of and confirms Christianity. But aristocratic society was more equipped to accept the ideal of self-sacrifice and concern for the needs of others—ideals commonly associated with (if not constitutive of) religion. Tocqueville thus acknowledges that the very reason America needs religion—namely to cull the tendencies toward individualism and materialism—would seem likely to negate the very possibility that religion would have any social utility.

Tocqueville says that America illustrates once again how the problems of democracy are to be solved: here, too, America has developed democratic solutions to democratic problems. America is able to achieve a workable (indeed, a remarkable) level of religious dogmatism by accepting and acquiescing to the realities of democratic society. Just like associations, religion works in America by working within the natural realities of self-interest.

Tocqueville believes that all religions frame their arguments in the language of self-interest; they merely extend the point of reference from this life to life after death: i.e., "if you knew what was going to happen to you after you die, you would come to this church and follow its strictures."[20] But not only do Americans accept and confirm this kind of claim, they also bring the objective out the next life and back into this one.

> [T]he better to touch their hearers, [preachers] are forever pointing out how religious beliefs favor freedom and public order, and it is often difficult to be sure when listening to them whether the main object of religion is to procure eternal felicity in the next world or prosperity in this. (530)

Church members are thus instructed that their faith is consistent with the social order, and that the former mandates their concern for the latter.

Religion, Tocqueville notes, is different in democratic society, and one of the ways it is different is its acceptance of, even focus on, the here and now. As we have seen, Tocqueville believes that the drive for acquisition is endemic to democratic society. The passion for well-being is "the most lively of all the emotions aroused or enflamed by equality" (448). This passion is innately human; democracy did not invent it, it merely released it. But it has been released, and this changes religion's position within society. If religion were to wholly delegitimate this passion—if it were to attack and seek to destroy these basic features of democratic life—it would not only fail, it would assure its own destruction as a relevant social institution. Tocqueville writes,

> [T]he main business of religions is to purify, control, and restrain that excessive and exclusive taste for well-being which men acquire in times of equality, but I think it would be a mistake for them to attempt to conquer it entirely and abolish it. They will never succeed in preventing men from loving wealth, but they may be able to induce them to use only honest means to enrich themselves. (448)

Religion in America does not reject materialism; it is satisfied merely to moderate it, direct it, and keep it honest. Religion thus remains a viable social force in a democracy because it has, in effect, cut its losses and modified its demands.

This strategy is also manifested in, and required by, the innate condition of religious pluralism. America would appear to present an insoluble dilemma. Democracy needs dogmatism, but democracy creates religious pluralism. How can you have dogmatism when no one professes a common creed? Tocqueville believes America has solved this problem as well. In the first place, religion is strong in America because it is separate from political institutions. Religion maintains its dominance over society by relegating itself to the social realm. In the second place, by removing itself from politics, it (or rather, the many different religions) has allowed itself to be changed into a kind of overarching civil religion. Christianity comes to operate less as a revealed doctrine and more as a key element of common opinion. Religion is turned into democratic religion, i.e., a civil and natural religion that preserves, legitimates, and sanctifies the prevailing social order. Thus, even in the midst of a vast array of competing sects and denominations, a common moral authority is preserved. For "all preach the same morality in the name of God" (290).[21] Here too, Tocqueville believes, self-interest sets the terms for the solution. Everybody intuitively knows that democracy needs religion, so the moral thread common to almost all religions is magnified, supported, and ingratiated into the public social realm. Democratic vices are thereby controlled, and religion thus maintains its social utility.

In both instances, religion achieves the goal of social control by accommodating the new features of democratic life. Just as the rise of equality reveals the need for a new science of politics, America has shown that this is true for religion too. Tocqueville writes, "[B]y respecting all democratic instincts which are not against it and making use of many favorable ones, religion succeeds in struggling successfully with that sprit of individual independence which is its most dangerous enemy" (449). Religion thrives in democratic society by bargaining with it. Yet it is worth noting that democracy sets the terms of the bargain. The price for the continued existence and social relevance of each individual denomination is that it loses its distinctiveness. Each denomination functions in the public realm as nothing more than a common set of moral beliefs—moral beliefs that check democratic excess while affirming the democratic ethos. "I have seen no country in which Christianity is less clothed in forms, symbols, and observances than it is in the United States" (448). Again, Tocqueville is quite clear about the effectiveness of this strategy. Nevertheless, to the degree that a specific religion (Methodism, say) functions felicitously in society, to that degree it becomes something less than the unique system of doctrines and practices by which it formerly distinguished itself. Ernest Gellner reiterates the point: "In North America, religious attendance is high, but religion celebrates a shared cult of the American way of life, rather than insisting on distinctions of theology or church organization."[22] Recall the almost ubiquitous contemporary phrase 'Judeo-Christian ethic.' The differences between Judaism and

Christianity are, to say the least, significant—even if we limit the discussion to questions of social ethics. Nevertheless, as far as the culture is concerned, those differences are papered over. The problem is that while this evisceration of difference begins in the culture at large, it does not end there. Tocqueville wants to show that democracy changes religion within and without the church doors.[23] Tocqueville's great respect for the social utility of religion clearly informs the vigorous advocacy for religious institutions and religious speech among civil society advocates. But here, as is so often the case, Tocqueville's analysis is not straightforward, and we must question whether contemporary advocates (especially advocates who profess religious convictions) would or should so willingly accept the bargain Tocqueville outlines. (I say more about this question in chapter 9.)

Marriage, Family, and Women

There is one more essential link in the chain. I have shown that for Tocqueville, democracy requires mores. That is, the vices that are released by equality require a set of moral beliefs that are supported and inculcated by the culture at large. The maintenance of these mores, in turn, cannot be achieved by the workings of civil society alone. Free society needs a moral sense that transcends self-interest and personal choice; free society, therefore, needs religion. But religion, in turn, is severely undermined by the very features of democratic society that it naturally seeks to contain. The heady world of democratic society produces values and habits (materialism, egoism, an almost ardent orientation toward the here and now) that run counter to the ethos of almost any revealed religion. It therefore cannot maintain its place in the culture without the active support of those who are the most removed from this world, namely, women. "Religion reigns supreme in the soul of women," and for Tocqueville, that means that "it is women who shape mores" (291). Following this trail, we therefore come to the conclusion that, for Tocqueville, the viability of American democratic society depends decisively upon the efforts and status of American women.

In a democracy, Tocqueville believes, the family naturally reflects the social changes brought on by the equality of conditions. In contrast to life in the aristocracy, "the relations between father and sons become more intimate and gentle; there is less of rule and authority, often more of confidence and affection, and it would seem than [sic] the natural bond grows tighter" (587). Democracy also means the abolishment of primogeniture; therefore, democracy produces a similar effect in the relations between siblings; the first born does not rule, and all siblings approach each other with equality and more genuine affection.

Yet it is significant that when Tocqueville describes the relationship between husband and wife, the effects of democratic life are not so clear. Tocqueville readily acknowledges that the equality of conditions effects the status of women as well. Democratic society affords girls the same educational opportunities as boys; what's more, it takes very seriously women's "feminine chastity," both within and without the institution of marriage. Yet within the marriage relationship itself, equality is constrained by what Tocqueville regards as the natural distinction between the sexes. As a result, the same woman who found her father's house "a home of freedom and pleasure" finds her husband's home to be "almost a cloister" (592). Women are universally absent from the world of commerce and self-interest and focus their efforts and interests wholly on hearth, home, and raising the children.

Without question, Tocqueville celebrates this combination of equality and distinction. He believes that within the American form of marriage "the highest and truest conception of conjugal happiness has been conceived" (291). Yet his analysis causes one to wonder whether that happiness is somewhat one-sided. He describes the home as "a perfect picture of order and peace," a haven from "the turmoil of politics" (ibid.), but since the latter is a world that women are not a party to, they can hardly experience the need for such a haven. In contrast, Tocqueville describes the women he sees as "sad and resolute" (594). I frankly doubt that Tocqueville believes both parties are equally satisfied with the operative state of affairs.

Now, this apparent difference and a number of other questions regarding the role and status of women in democratic society are controversial matters among Tocquevillian scholars.[24] But the basic point is very important. For Tocqueville, the family is an indispensable social institution. It is, in effect, the first place one learns how to be an American. As a child (quite literally, at mother's knee), one learns about the expectations, values, and beliefs—again, in Tocqueville's terms, the mores—that sustain democratic life against the atomizing forces of democratic vices. And mother is able to perform this task precisely because she is separate from the public world of individualism and materialism, and is therefore more open to the countervailing claims of religion. Again, Tocqueville says that the social norm of women in the home while men are sent out into the cruel world is grounded in the uniquely American acceptance of human equality on the one hand along with the affirmation of the natural distinctions between the sexes on the other.[25] Thus, the family preserves once again the American wisdom of finding natural solutions to democratic problems.

Here again, Tocqueville's analysis provides support for the contemporary conception. The public debate about civil society focuses heavily on the essential social role, and the troubling contemporary condition, of the American family. But, once again, there is something to make us pause. Our world, to say the least, is quite different. Tocqueville's ostensibly natural distinction is clearly not what it used to be in American society. Therefore, for those who would appeal to Tocqueville's analysis for our contemporary problems, two questions immediately arise. First, would Tocqueville say that we are experiencing the deleterious effects of the love of equality to the degree that contemporary American society denies this distinction? Is it possible that our condition results primarily as an unintended consequence of the sexual revolution? And second, given the extremely unlikely restoration of this strict separation of sexual roles, how are we Americans once again to reinvigorate the mores upon which democratic society depends? If we are now all part of the tumult of democratic life, then where is the haven to which we can repair? Where is the foundation upon which alternative narratives may be sustained?

Summary: The Key Features

Tocqueville, for civil society advocates, is surely the most important theoretical source. All analytical development of the concept effectively begins here. Before continuing, it is worth summarizing the features of Tocqueville's thought that inform and conform to the dominant public conception.

Tocqueville sees three social institutions as crucial to the maintenance of democratic society: associations, religion, and families. Whatever concerns Tocqueville's analysis might present, the point here is simply that this compendium is directly reflected in the triumvirate of institutions associated with the contemporary analytical concept. The latter's insistence that family and religion are indispensable supports for the democratic social order is a direct legacy of Tocqueville's thought. Moreover, modern civil society advocates see these institutions as Tocqueville did: the means by which democratic society culls the acquisitive tendencies of the state, while simultaneously training individuals for citizenship and for democratic community.

Finally, Tocqueville gives theoretical ground to the more modest, populist goals of the civil society movement. Tocqueville is quite forthright that there is something middling and mundane about democratic society when compared to the aristocratic order. Nevertheless, he also believes that the democratic world is more just, and therefore, more benign.

> [I]f your object is not to create heroic virtues but rather tranquil habits, if you would rather contemplate vices than crimes and prefer fewer transgressions at the cost of fewer splendid deeds, if in place of a brilliant society you are content to live in one that is prosperous, and finally, if in your view the main object of government is not to achieve the greatest strength or glory for the nation as a whole but to provide for every individual therein the utmost well-being, protecting him as far as possible from all afflictions, then it is good to make conditions equal and to establish a democratic government. (245)

For Tocqueville, while popular rule ensures that democratic society will not be great or noble, it does allow for the construction of a society that is more basically decent. Summarizing the contemporary movement, David Brooks closely echoes this quest for, and celebration of, decency. He notes that civil society advocates "tend to emphasize community more than the heroic individual, organic structures more than dynamic change, local serenity more than national greatness, authority more than freedom, stability more than change."[26] Tocqueville informs this emphasis. His thought accounts for the movement's affirmation of human equality and the everyday lives of ordinary citizens, and for its belief that this affirmation is constitutive of a well-ordered liberal democratic society.[27]

Tocqueville's analysis is also reflected in what I am calling "the antitriumvirate." Most importantly, Tocqueville affirms the typically American distrust of big government. This idea hardly originates with Tocqueville. Nevertheless, the idea that the state is inherently disposed to grow and usurp power, the idea that by its growth the state has co-opted social roles normally associated with the institutions of civil society, and the idea that this process is killing the American spirit of self-reliance—all of this is commonly associated with the civil society debate—and all of this is distinctively Tocquevillian. "The more government takes the place of associations, the more will individuals lose the idea of forming associations and need the government to come to their help. That is a vicious circle of cause and effect" (515).

Tocqueville is similarly concerned about the effects of rampant, unbridled consumerism on democratic practices and political liberty. The contemporary debate is perhaps more focused on the behavior of large corporations, whereas Tocqueville is more concerned with the effects on individuals. In addition, I have noted that Tocqueville includes businesses and corporations among civil associations. That means that those corporations instruct (or at least can instruct) self-interest in the same way that noneconomic institutions do. Nevertheless, Tocqueville and the contemporary movement are united by a more fundamental concern that economic decisions, and a strict (i.e., unenlightened) economic rationality, can undermine the civic and social dimensions of the polity.[28]

The resonance between Tocqueville and the civil society debate is clear and, for that matter, largely uncontroversial. Yet it is not so clear how this came to be so. In the next chapter, I show how the trail of thought first articulated by Tocqueville finds its way, over 150 years later, into the public debate about civil society in America.

Chapter Four

The Tocquevillian Legacy

Along with myriad other effects, Tocqueville's analysis of democratic society, and his careful attention to the modern problematic, set the stage for the modern discipline of sociology. One can find clear resonance with Tocqueville's thought in the work of French sociologist Emil Durkheim, for example. Durkheim, too, believes that the little communities within the larger society support and sustain the moral unity that any society requires. What's more, he also agrees that these little communities are far more difficult to sustain in the modern world. Durkheim believes that rampant consumerism and the modern rejection of revelation have undermined traditional sources for meaning and identity; we end, he says, up "like so many liquid molecules." The term *anomie,* that is, the feeling of being detached, impotent, and alone, is Durkheim's coinage, and it shows up frequently in the writings of civil society advocates.[1]

Yet for all their resonance, Durkheim does not explicitly associate himself with Tocqueville. Indeed, Durkheim is probably more commonly thought of as working out of the Hegelian tradition. Regarding the minimal points outlined here, I think it's fair to claim Tocqueville as the more important resource. But in any event, the connection between Durkheim and Tocqueville illustrates a common point about Tocqueville's legacy. Tocqueville made several dire predictions about the future of democracy, and he said those outcomes could be avoided only if democracy developed and preserved the institutions of associations, religion, and the family. Since the time he wrote, those institutions and their standing within democratic society have been increasingly stressed—by the working out of Enlightenment logic, the development of advanced capitalism, the rise of technology, and a host of similar effects. In other words, the very features of modernity that gave rise to Tocqueville's own thought have continued to advance, and thereby ingratiate themselves within the broader social fabric. Thus, the legacy of Tocqueville is found primarily in the fact that his warnings have come to show ever more prescience. Consequently, many generations after his death, political thinkers continue to return to his writings in order to find some help in turning things around.

This pattern is particularly true in America. Over the last fifty years or so, Robert Nisbet, Peter Berger and Richard Neuhaus, and, most recently, a group of neo-Tocquevillians led by Robert Putnam most directly account for the impact of Tocqueville's thought in the modern conception. These influences will be discussed in chronological order, and, not coincidentally, in the ascending order of their impact on the contemporary movement.[2]

Robert Nisbet: The Quest for Community

Durkheim offers a felicitous transition to the thought of Robert Nisbet. For Nisbet was not only a noted sociologist in his own right, he was also an accomplished Durkheimian scholar. His work *The Quest for Community* is an impressive application of Durkheim's and Tocqueville's thought to what he saw as the dire circumstances of the mid–twentieth century.[3] It is this work that establishes Nisbet as the spiritual godfather, or perhaps grandfather, of the contemporary American discussion.

In *The Quest for Community*, Nisbet offers a long historical account in which he describes the modern collapse of community. The rise of the modern, centralized state and, to a lesser extent, the capitalist economic system, Nisbet argues, have systematically compromised what he calls the "intermediate associations" of family, church, neighborhood, and local community.[4] These "modern facts of political mechanization, centralization, and collectivism" possess a unifying logic and an air of historical inevitability. And as they grow, they delegitimate and replace these pluralistic institutions.[5] The individuals who sought a larger state were motivated by an authentic desire to release humanity from "its long bondage to oppression, misery, and ignorance."[6] But the more the state grows—the more it emerges as "the sole source of legitimate power"—the more it kills off these more accessible sources of community.[7]

Nisbet, like Tocqueville, is no mere nostalgist. His concern is what the loss of these institutions means for democratic society. A paradigmatic conservative, he wants to show the unintended consequence of this policy.

> This is the area of association from which the individual com-
> monly gains his concept of the outer world and his sense of
> position in it. His concrete feelings of status and role, of protec-
> tion and freedom, his differentiation between good and bad,
> between order and disorder and guilt and innocence, arise and
> are shaped largely by his relations within this realm of primary
> association.[8]

For Nisbet, the destruction of these associations means nothing less
than the destruction of the only operative sources of human meaning
and purpose.

Bereft of these sources of meaning, the individual is left stark and
alone, alienated and impotent. Nisbet's portrait is almost Hobbesian
in its despair. Yet precisely for this reason, we cannot remain in
this condition; the need for community and companionship is innate
and overpowering.[9] The individual is therefore driven to seek other
sources. But if the state has destroyed any viable alternative, then the
only source for community is the same centralized and all-consuming
state; the only community left, in other words, is "political community." Thus, the innate tendencies of the modern state and the equally
innate needs of the human psyche combine to necessitate the community as nation—a community that can be sustained only by a warlike
ethos and can be purchased only at the price of freedom and individual
autonomy. Thus, for Nisbet, the contemporary horrors of Nazi Germany and Stalinist Russia should not be understood as bizarre historical aberrations; they were the inevitable and all too human end to a
slow historical decline. Contemporary society engenders the development of the atomistic, impotent individual—an individual who is both
amoral and susceptible to totalitarian dreams. Therefore, Nisbet believes, there are finally only two alternatives to which modern society
can orient itself: unitary democracy (totalitarianism) and pluralistic democracy, and the latter is possible only if sources of power and meaning other than the state are sustained. He argues that "the sole possibility of personal freedom and cultural autonomy lies in the maintenance
of a plurality of authorities in any society."[10]

The basic similarities between Nisbet and Tocqueville are fairly obvious. Nisbet himself says that Tocqueville "points directly to the heart
of totalitarianism . . . and the genius of his analysis lies in the view of
totalitarianism as something not historically 'abnormal' but as closely
related to the very trends hailed as progressive in the nineteenth century."[11] To be sure, there are differences: Tocqueville says despotism

will allow individuals to maintain independence, whereas Nisbet, looking to extant examples of what he has in mind, says that totalitarianism is a replacement for community. For both, however, the despotism is more benign than former varieties. Just as importantly, Nisbet also agrees that intermediate associations are essential to forestalling the decline into despotism. Nisbet, too, acknowledges that associations are born of self-interest. "People do not come together in significant and lasting associations merely to be together. They come together to do something that cannot easily be done in individual isolation."[12] But he also believes that this self-interested association indirectly produces an indispensable sense of community. "Community is the product of people working together on problems, of autonomous and collective fulfillment of internal objectives, and of the experience of living under codes of authority which have been set in large degree by the persons involved."[13]

Yet Nisbet also represents an important turning point in the Tocquevillian legacy. With Nisbet, Tocqueville's prediction is recognized, perhaps for the first time, as explanation; the former's anticipated fears are recognized as well-advanced realities. Relatedly, Nisbet also alters the question that Tocqueville's analysis begs. The concern is no longer "how do we preserve these institutions?" but "how do we restore them?"

Nisbet's analysis clearly resonates with the contemporary conception. For example, I am not aware of any other twentieth-century theorist who is so concerned with the status of the family in liberal society, nor do I know of anyone prior to Nisbet who stressed the institutions of family, church, and neighborhood as the central focus for a strategy for the renewal of American society. Nisbet epitomizes the great American tradition of the public intellectual—his work is not meant merely for fellow academics—yet one must nevertheless admit that the initial impact of this work was largely limited to the academy. Nisbet's thought did not have an immediate impact. For many years, his analysis lay fallow. For reasons about which I later speculate, the times were not yet receptive to the idea of a civil society movement.

Berger and Neuhaus: To Empower People

Berger and Neuhaus, too, wrote their relevant work many years before the civil society movement really began. Yet their analysis and prescription likewise resonate with the modern concept. What is more, they confirm that the turn to civil society is yet another manifestation of what I am calling the modern problematic. That is, they explicitly acknowledge the modern effort at finding a synthesis between modernity and that which came before. "Our argument is not against modernity, but in favor of exploring the ways in which modernity can be made more humane."[14] Yet because they took up this task in 1977, in the midst of the Cold War, as American society rode the hard wake of Watergate and Vietnam, their take on the modern problematic reflects many of the same concerns outlined by Robert Nisbet. In addition, whatever development we may see in their work can perhaps best be explained as the working out, the coming to fore, of Tocqueville's predictions.

Whether they take more from Nisbet than even their explicit reference acknowledges or they are assessing the same underlying dynamic, it is quite clear that Berger and Neuhaus are strongly indebted to Nisbet. Their booklet (a pamphlet really, only forty-five pages long) *To Empower People* is even more focused on the ostensibly unchecked growth of the state, the creeping despotism that they believe is robbing American society of its vitality, its plurality, and ultimately its freedom. Berger and Neuhaus also reflect Nisbet's belief that the most hopeful strategy for dealing with this problem is one that frees and encourages what they call "mediating institutions."

They readily acknowledge that this trail of diagnosis and prescription is hardly new. "What is new is the systematic effort to translate it into specific public policies."[15] That is, Berger and Neuhaus believe that just as the state is largely responsible for this condition, the state can orient itself in such a way as to reverse the decline of mediating institutions. At the least, the state can agree no longer to harm civil society; at the most (not necessarily the best), the state can carefully and with circumspection endeavor to nurture and build up these institutions. Berger and Neuhaus's booklet, therefore, is concerned to isolate a few key mediating institutions—namely, family, church, neighborhood, and voluntary associations—and develop a new approach to public policy regarding these social institutions.

Berger and Neuhaus's list is also clearly commensurate with Nisbet's and, not incidentally, with the modern conception. Their list does not purport to be exhaustive, but for our purposes their selections are instructive. They were chosen because they were judged "most relevant to the problems of the welfare state with which we are concerned."[16]

What are those problems? The growth of the state and other 'mega-structures' have compromised the mediating institutions that stand between the individual and the state. We are left to face the state alone. As a result, private life is anxious and uncertain, listless and directionless. The contemporary effect of this unchecked growth, for Berger and Neuhaus as well as for Nisbet, is alienation and impotence: an "anomic precariousness."[17] More important, however, is the fear that because of this condition, we are also all the more willing to give up even more freedom to the state. This downward spiral of expectations is for Berger and Neuhaus (as for Nisbet) straight out of Tocqueville. The search for direction, meaning, and purposiveness is the proximate concern, yet the fear of the despotic state is what drives the argument.

Berger and Neuhaus start with two underlying moral propositions: first, the "everyday lives of Americans" have inherent, inestimable worth and dignity,[18] and second, in order to preserve that worth and dignity, human beings require freedom and self-governance. The authors maintain that Americans are uneasy and distrustful because they are aware that the growth of the state ultimately jeopardizes this moral status, and it is a judgment that they affirm. "[T]he current anti-government, anti-bigness mood," they contend, "is not irrational."[19] Berger and Neuhaus hold that since the New Deal, the state is grown ever more distant, ever more alienating, and ever more hostile to the mediating structures that form people's lives. Behind this characterization of the welfare state, one can clearly sense an unstated Tocquevillian premise: namely, that the state is innately covetous of power; without formidable constraints, it will act (albeit most often unintentionally) in ways that threaten human freedom.

This is an argument that is adamantly populist and pluralistic. For part of recognizing the moral imperative of human dignity is recognizing that the people know best where their best interests lie. "Our belief is that human beings, whoever they are, understand their own needs better than anyone else—in, say, 99 percent of the cases."[20] Government cannot understand, and hence cannot respond to, problems better than the affected individuals themselves.[21] They also say that mediating institutions are where most people find meaning. They find their values, and concretize them, in "the little platoons" of their own lives.[22] Thus, Berger and Neuhaus reflect the Tocquevillian claim that civil society (or, in their language, mediating institutions) achieves two essential social functions: it wards off the state and instills democratic citizenship. The task of public policy, in turn, is to empower these everyday people and the institutions that are most significant in their lives.

To be sure, this policy choice means that there is going to be a great deal of pluralism among social norms. But Berger and Neuhaus are comparatively unconcerned about the need for some kind of overarching moral consensus. In fact, they say that the democratic idea of tolerance and fairness is strong enough to allow free play of pluralism. They appear fairly confident that minimal unity will remain, and that even a newly revitalized pluralism will not significantly undermine this minimum. While Berger acknowledges that perhaps they "might have spelled out more fully how other limits are to be conceived . . . the essential point . . . is that our understanding of the American experiment precludes the establishment of a politically defined moral authority to which the various communities of meaning have, as it were, to apply for ethical certification."[23] Neuhaus reiterates this point, even more strongly: "Berger and I would encourage a robust skepticism toward the political empowerment of anything that claims to be normative. . . . [O]n the questions treated in *To Empower People,* the bias in favor of pluralism includes a pluralism of norms."[24]

But Berger and Neuhaus are also adamant that the only way to make political values real (or at least the only way that respects human freedom) is through mediating institutions. For Berger and Neuhaus, as Jay Mechling puts it, "[i]n modern times, abstract patriotism is attached to the nation-state" but "this abstract sort of patriotism is not viable unless it is rooted in the concrete experiences of every American community."[25] Thus, the inculcation of citizenship is, like tempering the power of the state, dependent upon pluralism. Mediating institutions are, for Berger and Neuhaus, the only salient way both to make people moral *and* to connect people to the overarching mores of the state. "Mediating structures are *the* value-generating and value-maintaining agencies in society. Without them, values become another function of the megastructures, notably of the state, and this is a hallmark of totalitarianism."[26]

Now it is not the case that the state has no role to play. The very idea that their work outlines a new set of public policy objectives means that the state is not irrelevant to achieving their goals. Even if the state's only task is to get out of the way, the state is involved. What's more, the determination of whether the minimum or maximum strategy is more appropriate, and the idea that social policy must distinguish between good and bad mediating institutions,[27] implies that the state is not wholly incompetent, nor are its actions wholly incorrigible. But the fact remains that the role they envision for the state is a decidedly, passionately minimalistic one. Berger and Neuhaus aver that they are not enemies of the welfare state (indeed, in 1977, at least, they say that it "ought to expand the benefits it provides").[28] But the only point where they spell out an active role for the state is with regards to securing human rights. In particular, they are most concerned with the issue of race. The authors are particularly sensitive to the idea that mediating institutions, if truly free, will sometimes abet discriminatory beliefs and practices. Given this fact, the state has a formative role in educating against "racial bias." Apparently, the claim is that the American dilemma of race is a unique problem. Few other moral questions approach this level and therefore, given the danger of totalitarianism, the state must, to say the least, give a very wide berth. But race is different: perhaps because of their own experience with *the* American dilemma, they are not willing to assume the wholesale resiliency of the democratic ideals of tolerance and fairness.[29]

There are, quite clearly, significant similarities between *To Empower People* and the contemporary civil society debate. Like Nisbet before them, Berger and Neuhaus echo, almost precisely, the triumvirate: neighborhoods, families, churches. They also build on Nisbet's conception, identifying the family as first among equals: it is "the major institution within the private sphere."[30] They also reflect, in no uncertain terms, the nation's growing dissatisfaction with government. Again, coming off the shattering experiences of Vietnam and Watergate, Berger and Neuhaus start with the assumption that government action is fraught with unintended consequences. Not only is it often unable to solve problems, it often only makes things worse. The current problems are thus understood to have begun with the rise of the federal government in the twentieth century, and the concomitant decline in civil society. Whatever the intentions, the absolutistic, unifying dynamic of modern federal government is responsible for much of the current dissatisfaction. Moreover, this feeling of distrust leads to an explicit nervousness regarding the "maximalist" strategy. Berger and Neuhaus continually express "the real danger" of co-option by the state. Any time the government and government money are involved, "institutions reshape themselves to continue receiving government largesse."[31] Thus, while they generally accept the welfare state and modern society's New Deal character, they are more concerned about what they call "fatal embrace of the state."[32]

Again, perhaps it is fair to say that, as with Nisbet, their approach to the state reflects life in which Tocqueville's fears are more fully realized. But the central point for our purposes is to note that these remain exigent and inform the contemporary civil society movement. The state is almost universally understood to be of only minimal utility to the task at hand, and most frequently it is judged to be antithetical thereto. This aspect of the movement finds its clearest and most relevant expression in Berger and Neuhaus; and it is ultimately indebted to Tocqueville.

At the same time, it is difficult to judge the direct impact of this work. Michael Novak notes that it "really did change the course of public policy analysis."[33] President Reagan, in particular, continually expressed the language and themes of the work in his call for a new federalism, etc. Yet even Berger and Neuhaus say the climate was not right; twenty years later, in 1997, it is "much more auspicious."[34] And even though every president since Reagan has felt compelled to laud mediating structures, Novak also notes that "they only mentioned the idea in speeches, painfully little in practice."[35] Surely the work is important, surely it informs the contemporary debate—especially the more libertarian wing of the movement—yet the very fact that the ground was much more receptive in the 1990s causes one to question whether and to what degree Berger and Neuhaus can be understood as causal agents and how much of the impact of their ideas is only viewed in retrospect.

The features of the emerging movement are not precisely the same as those articulated by Nisbet and Berger and Neuhaus. The intervening years have led to the rise of another strain within the Tocquevillian legacy. Fear of the state and loss of freedom are now viewed against, and often in comparison to, a fear of moral collapse and social atomism. The difference, to be sure, is subtle, and both ideas ground themselves in Tocqueville's thought. Regardless, the difference is real and significant. We have moved from a world in which we are concerned with empowering people to one in which people are bowling alone. In light of the equally ubiquitous contemporary concern for moral breakdown, there are evidently other sources that account for the contemporary civil society movement. It remains for me to recount the differences between Nisbet and Berger and Neuhaus on the one had and the contemporary movement on the other.

Putnam and the Neo-Tocquevillians

Tocqueville's most recent, and most relevant, legacy is found in a group of contemporary social critics and social scientists who explicitly follow his analysis. Alan Wolfe, Jean Bethke Elshtain, Michael Sandel, and Robert Putnam are all academics, more or less public intellectuals, all of whom explicitly claim to be examining the contemporary social climate in terms of Tocqueville's analysis; thus, all can be fairly characterized as neo-Tocquevillians. I will not outline the niceties of each of these thinkers. Rather, in what follows, I will try to present the most relevant features of the group as a whole by offering a sustained commentary on Putnam's work, and especially his pivotal essay, "Bowling Alone."

Putnam's work in this arena began with an exceptionally important twenty-year study in Italy. Employing a host of methods, Putnam compares the different regions within the nation. His objective is to determine why the northern regions were almost universally more successful than those in the south—more efficient, more responsive, more professional.[36] His conclusion is that democracies (and, for that matter, economies) work better when there exists an independent and long-standing tradition of civic engagement. For reasons that go back almost a millennium, the north has such a tradition, and the south does not. The north has more soccer clubs, more choral societies, more voting, more newspaper readership, etc. These institutions create social capital,[37] and social capital, in turn, leads to an engaged citizenry, a citizenry that plays by the rules and trusts that others will as well, a citizenry that possesses a vague but pervading sense of equality, accountability, and solidarity. The south lacks the former institutions, and therefore it also lacks a successful democracy. Putnam insists that his is not a counsel of despair, but he acknowledges that anyone hoping to build the institutions upon which democracy depends must be willing to wait decades, even generations, for results to manifest themselves.[38]

Putnam compellingly notes that his analysis effectively repeats the conclusions of modern-day game theory. The north has instituted social norms and expectations that allow individuals rationally to trust each other. The south has no such institutions; therefore, rationality demands a different kind of behavior. In brief, citizens in the south have no reason to trust their neighbors, no reason to expect neutral behavior from elected officials, no reason not to seek to develop a dependent relationship with a source of independent political power. Game theory can be arcane and confusing, but the key point is simple. For Putnam, as for Tocqueville, self-interest remains the underlying basis for making decisions. In terms that explicitly echo Tocqueville's, Putnam argues that the social institutions of the north train the individual's self-interest. Thus, whatever its ultimate derivation, social capital is a concept that, to say the least, resonates with Tocqueville's analysis. Whether we are talking about associations or informal get-togethers between neighbors, the beneficent effect of these meetings transcends their explicit function or goal. In both instances, the social benefit centers on the fact that the interaction moves individuals beyond the indisputable rationality of mistrust and suspicion, and develops among the participants "self-interest which is alive to the interests of others."[39]

In 1995, Putnam took his conclusions and applied them to the American context. In his breathtakingly famous article "Bowling Alone: America's Declining Social Capital," Putnam begins with the same Tocquevillian thesis: that "the quality of public life and the performance of social institutions [including the performance of representative government]" is "powerfully influenced by norms and networks of social engagement."[40] He then goes on to examine many of the same empirical indicators of civic engagement: voting, political participation, newspaper readership, and participation in local associations. He concludes that in every case, these indicators are down, sometimes precipitously so. Americans do not participate in the democratic process like they used to, nor are they taking part in the associations that defined the social lives of previous generations of Americans (PTAs, the Red Cross, Kiwanis, etc.). Without these kinds of institutions, social connectedness, neighborliness, and social trust all decline. Just as importantly, Putnam's study of Italian government showed that democracy does not work without the social capital these institutions produce. Therefore, in the terms of his analysis, contemporary America risks turning into a contemporary Palermo. Acknowledging that much work remains to be done, Putnam notes that there is reason for grave concern here. He concludes that the question of reversing "these trends in social connectedness" needs to be "high on America's agenda."[41]

The astonishing response to Putnam's article—a response that has transcended the academy, let alone the normal readership of the *Journal of Democracy*—reveals that Putnam has struck a very raw, very sensitive nerve. His case offers a clear and apparently convincing explanation for the unease Americans were already feeling. Americans who have lived long enough sense (and decry) a decline in social connectedness; the neighborhoods in which they now live are qualitatively different, less neighborly, then those in which they grew up. Putnam gives them a place to hang their hat regarding these concerns. Irrespective of the question of deficiencies within Putnam's work, this fact goes a long way toward explaining its widespread significance.

Yet the question of deficiency is also important, and it, too, is reflected in the deluge of critical responses to Putnam's piece.[42] More often than not, this criticism asserts that Putnam is wrong about his empirical claim; while older and effectively obsolete forms of civil society have indeed declined, the innate American desire to join remains as vibrant as ever.[43] Yes, PTAs have declined, but youth soccer is growing astronomically. Similarly, while mainline Protestantism may be declining, evangelical churches like the Willow Creek Community Church in suburban Chicago pack them in every Sunday. These critics therefore conclude that Putnam's angst is, at best, overblown, if not wholly misplaced: civil society may have changed, but it is not defunct.[44]

I believe that much of this criticism is accurate, but largely beside the point. For it fails to acknowledge the functional distinction that is at work here, and indeed that has been operative from the very beginning of the modern history of civil society. Once again, civil society has perennially been understood to perform one or more specific social functions. That being the case, the question is not one of mere numbers. Let us grant that new forms of civil society are arising that are replacing older forms. Let us even stipulate that participation in these newer forms of association is, numerically speaking, roughly equal to or even superior to former, more established, forms. Yet even if civil society is not decaying, not dying, the question remains whether or not civil society continues to perform the tasks of culling political power and, more importantly, developing a more enlightened self-interest. Putnam himself notes that organizations like the AARP and the Environmental Defense Fund do not seem to develop "social connectedness" the same way that a PTA group does (or did).[45] As a member of the Commission on Civic Renewal, Jean Bethke Elshtain reflected a similar point. In response to an empirical analysis about the condition of American civil society, she asked whether there was not a "qualitative distinction between playing in squash clubs and going to church."[46] The question of whether newer and more vital forms of civil society—youth soccer, evangelical churches like Willow Creek, book clubs, and the like—are similarly effective in inculcating enlightened self-interest is, to be sure, far more difficult to measure empirically. What's more, I would acknowledge that it remains, at this point, largely open.[47] But to my mind, the almost wholesale failure to even note the distinction constitutes an inadequate understanding of the concept.

The Stages of Tocqueville's Dire Predictions

Putnam can surely defend himself. The point here is to note that Putnam's concerns are not identical to those outlined by Berger and Neuhaus. To make clear the distinction I want to draw, I need to begin by recalling Tocqueville's analysis. Tocqueville argued that democracy in America succeeded because of the network of social institutions that controlled democracy's dangerous effects. But Tocqueville worried that the permanence of these institutions could not be assumed. Without them, democratic society would become ever more materialistic and ever more isolated. Finally, the growth of these all too human vices would ultimately endanger democracy itself; unchecked, a heretofore unknown form of benign despotism would be the end result.

In broad strokes, Nisbet, Berger and Neuhaus, and the neo-Tocquevillians are united in the belief that Tocqueville was largely right about his prediction. Therefore, they all express serious concern regarding the status of the institutions of civil society. Yet within this agreement, there is a subtle distinction. Berger and Neuhaus and (perhaps to a lesser degree) Nisbet are primarily concerned with Tocqueville's ultimate prediction: the collapse of democracy into despotism. Putnam and the neo-Tocquevillians are less convinced that the state is an enemy and more concerned with Tocqueville's penultimate prediction: namely, that democratic tendencies would turn vicious, and life would become ever more egocentric, ever more materialistic, and ever less decent, civil, and commodious.

Berger and Neuhaus focus on the belief that individuals feel alienated from government and each other, and they feel powerless to do anything about it. The primary cause for this state of affairs is the ethos underlying the New Deal. Modern liberalism has adhered to its own rigid logic, taken on ever larger social projects, and has thereby killed off the local institutions that manifested both a limited state and an innate propensity for pluralism. For Putnam, the problem is a loss of social trust, a loss of neighborliness.[48] He does not deny that we trust government less, but more important is the fact that we trust each other less as well. Life in America is not as neighborly, not as friendly as it once was. We are producing less social capital than we once did, and this condition is undermining the very fabric of our democratic society. More importantly, even if these facts are related, as Putnam believes, that does not mean that government bears primary responsibility for the current state of affairs. For Putnam, it is television that bears primary responsibility.[49] Television takes up the bulk of our leisure time. We have fewer opportunities for interaction, and as a result, we are left ever more disconnected, ever less trustful. My objective here is merely to note this debate—not to adjudicate it. While both are operating within the broad Tocquevillian tradition, Putnam's understanding of the problem and the cause thereof is distinct from Berger and Neuhaus's.

Finally, this distinction finds its way into their respective descriptions of central social institutions. Berger and Neuhaus note that "there is little evidence that the family is in decline."[50] For Putnam, "evidence of the loosening of family bonds is unequivocal."[51] For Berger and Neuhaus, the objective of public policy reform vis-à-vis neighborhoods is not to change neighborhoods, but to "empower our own places."[52] For Putnam, the problem with neighborhoods is not a loss of power, but a loss of neighborliness. We have noted that Berger and Neuhaus see associations as "schools of democracy": they are mechanisms in which citizens are trained to resist the encroachment of the state. For Putnam, as we have seen, associations primarily function as mechanisms for producing social capital: their operation produces trust, neighborliness, a sense of reciprocity.[53] In every case, then, while both are looking at the very same institutions, they are not seeing the same problems.

There is no point in straining this distinction too far. As I have noted, Berger and Neuhaus speak of alienation and anomic precariousness. So, too, Elshtain most clearly reflects the universal neo-Tocquevillian belief that nothing less than the future of American democracy is ultimately at issue. (Though even here, the feared rise of dictatorship is seen as the inevitable filling of an anarchic vacuum. Here again, the state is not a significant agent of decline, nor is it the principal focus of concern.) Nevertheless, while both sides of this distinction are reflected in the contemporary debate, there is a subtle but real difference with regard to the contemporary understanding of the modern problematic. In Martin Marty's words, that problematic is now "less fear of despotism—though one always has to keep despotic possibilities in mind—than of individualist anomie and intergroup anarchy."[54]

The concept of civil society that emerged in the 1990s reflects two concerns: that the state is growing ever more powerful, and, more importantly, that the American citizenry has become significantly more atomistic, disconnected, disaffected, and immoral. And it understands the revitalization of the family, neighborhood, churches, and voluntary associations as the most important strategy for addressing both problems. This dual function is perhaps the best illustration of the concept's profound debt to the Tocquevillian legacy and, more broadly, to the liberal tradition as a whole. But it also shows that the movement is especially attuned to the neo-Tocquevillians' reading of that legacy.

The End of the Cold War

In chapter 7, I show how the Tocquevillian and Hegelian strands come together to inform the American concept, and how both strains reveal the inadequacy of the civil society solution. For now, I want to explain why the earlier works of Nisbet and Berger and Neuhaus had little immediate impact, and why some central features of the movement differ from the analysis presented in those two works. Ironically, the argument that I believe best accounts for these two conditions is found in the work of Robert Nisbet. For I believe the primary explanation for the change is found in the end of the Cold War.

From time immemorial, political thinkers have exploited the unifying power of war. The urgencies of war readily provide the leader with a unifying goal, a common sense of meaning and purpose. Whatever else it is, social life in wartime is more exciting, less mundane, more focused, and more unified.[55] Nisbet argues that in the contemporary world, the unifying effects of war are enhanced even as the demand is heightened. War is, in effect, the modern answer to the modern problem. The bureaucratizing and centralizing tendencies innate to the modern era are particularly suited to, and are particularly rife within, the military. What's more, it is uniquely suited to fill the void modernity causes. "[W]e should be blind indeed if we did not recognize in the war state, the war economy, and in war morality qualities that stand in the most attractive contrast to the instability and the sense of meaninglessness of modern . . . life."[56]

In the twentieth century, many nations have exploited the effects of a war mentality to achieve an otherwise out-of-reach level of community and patriotism. In modern American history, several presidents have even tried to adopt this effect to nonmilitary problems. Arguing for 'the moral equivalent of war,' they attempted to conjure through martial rhetoric a new, prevailing ethos—a moral turning of the tide—for seemingly intransigent social problems like inflation and drug abuse. It is also difficult to avoid connecting Nisbet's portrayal to the Cold War. By so doing, my point is not that that forty-odd-year struggle was somehow contrived or inauthentic. (Sometimes it surely was; most often it was not.) Rather, I simply wish to note that, willy-nilly, the Cold War functioned this way in America. The United States (and other Western nations) may not have always been able to articulate a substantive and common moral vision—indeed, with few exceptions (the civil rights movement and the environmental movement come to mind) such common articulation often seems beyond the pale. But while any common sense about what we Americans were for might have been comparatively thin and insubstantial, we were quite united in our opposition to the Soviet bloc, Marxist-Leninism, etc. This common enemy, Nisbet shows, provided our nation with "the intoxicating atmosphere of spiritual unity that arises out of the common consciousness of participating in a moral crusade."[57] Different in degree but not in kind from the martial consciousness of Nazi Germany, the Cold War thus provided America with a typically modern substitute for community—a source of social union, and a common sense of meaning and purpose. In the modern age—at once pluralistic and atomistic—that is a significant social desideratum.

Yet Nisbet also persuasively argues that there is more to it than that. He says that in the modern era, the bureaucratizing and centralizing tendencies associated with the military expand to "widening areas of social and cultural life."[58] This means that not only did the Cold War provide a viable, if ersatz and unsustainable, sense of community, it also greatly increased the destructive effects of centralized government on the institutions of real community.[59] The need for bureaucracy and centralized control thus furthered the evisceration of the intermediate institutions upon which true community depends.

The Cold War strengthened national identity, and gave our society a sort of martial tenor. This source of community allowed Americans to ignore more traditional sources of meaning and identity. Indeed, except for instances like the civil rights movement, it allowed Americans to direct their attention outward, away from the internal dynamics of American society. Despite the fact that our attention was focused elsewhere, we Americans simply assumed that sustaining institutions could endure. When the war finally ended, so, too, did society's preeminent source of community and meaning. When people returned to the old sources of meaning, they found that the same Cold War had left them severely, sometimes irreparably, depleted. In Michael Sandel's words,

> [F]or a time, the special circumstances of American life in the two decades after World War II obscured the passing of the civic conception of freedom. But when the moment of mastery subsided—when the rigors of the early Cold War eased and the economy faltered and the authority of government began to unravel—Americans were left ill equipped to contend with the dislocation and disempowerment that they confronted.[60]

Here, then, is an explanation as to why, even in victory, Americans felt a disquieting undercurrent of anxiety. It also explains why the civil society movement came so quickly on the heels of 1989. It took the collapse of the war community to bring the realization that the other sources of community had already collapsed, and that meaning, purpose, and a common sense of national identity were not to be found.

The same explanation can account for the change in the concept of civil society between Berger and Neuhaus on the one hand and Putnam on the other. By Nisbet's logic, the state's need to take on more power, to grow ever more centralized and bureaucratized, grew proportionately to the perceived threat. Thus, one would expect that the federal government would take on more of the acquisitive tendencies Tocqueville feared during the height of the Cold War. Just so, with the end of the war, the need for, and legitimacy of, an extensive federal bureaucracy diminishes, and the state inevitably appears less dangerous. The account is admittedly speculative. Nevertheless, one can plausibly claim that the end of the Cold War also accounts, in large measure, for the change that took place within the concept of civil society itself, from Berger and Neuhaus to Putnam—the change, that is, from a concern over the tyrannical tendencies of the state to one over an atomistic, amoral social order.[61]

This argument should not be seen as conflicting with the claim that the repeated appeal to Tocqueville in the twentieth century reflects a society in which his predictions are proving ever more accurate. If I am correct in claiming that the end of the Cold War is responsible for a more fertile climate, it is in large measure because it has revealed rather suddenly a process of deterioration that has been going on for decades. In *Making Democracy Work,* Putnam notes that while institutional change happens very slowly, there are "historical turning points" that "can have extremely long-lived consequences."[62] Perhaps the end of the Cold War constitutes one of those turning points. Perhaps the nervousness of many Americans, and the concomitant rise of a civil society movement, stems from a sense of this very point.

Chapter Five

The Hegelian Tradition

The preceding chapter showed that Tocqueville provides the theoretical grounding for much of the contemporary discussion. In this chapter, I want to make a more controversial point. I want to argue for the significance of the thought of G. W. F. Hegel to that same discussion. To that end, in this chapter I will seek to outline the essential features of Hegel's political thought and then trace the development of that thought through his successors, Karl Marx and Antonio Gramsci. In the next chapter, I will show the conceptual legacy of the Hegelian-Gramscian tradition in the Solidarity movement.

Hegel: The Emergence of the Modern Concept

After Ferguson and the Scottish Enlightenment, there were, of course, a number of other figures whose thought proved to be seminal to the developing understanding of civil society. Keane argues that Thomas Paine represents an important developmental stage; for he rigidifies and radicalizes the emerging English-inspired separation of state and society.[1] Arato and Cohen note that Immanuel Kant and Johann Fichte combine this separation with a new, democratic understanding of society itself. In contrast to the orders of society that characterized the feudal age, Kant and Fichte reflected the intellectual excitement of the French Revolution, and applauded a set of universal rights that obtained in the individual.[2] They thus affirm the new order in much the same way Ferguson condemned it. Yet for all the different paths taken by these historical analysts, they all seem to end up at the same place. There is almost universal agreement that Hegel most clearly understood the rumblings of early modernity and, by synthesizing them, most dramatically changed the concept of civil society. As Manfred Riedel notes, "[O]ne might well say that before Hegel the concept of civil society in its modern sense did not exist."[3]

Yet while Hegel is critical to the emergence of the modern concept, the path that I want to draw between Hegel's work and the contemporary American concept of civil society is by no means self-evident. Indeed, the historical connection between Hegel and Solidarity and thus, I will argue, America, appears to be entirely absent. Nevertheless, I argue that the conceptual legacy remains, and this conceptual connection both accounts for the Hegelian elements within the American concept and reveals the contemporary relevance of his writings. Arato and Cohen argue that

> several important theoretical traditions that emerged after Hegel, with or without conscious reference to him, continued to move within the terms of analysis that he has brought together. For this reason, we would like to present Hegel . . . as the most important theoretical forerunner of several later approaches that have preserved their potential to provide more global, intellectual orientation even in our own time.[4]

To be sure, my objectives are not entirely commensurate with Arato and Cohen's. I also reiterate that Tocqueville's legacy is more relevant than Hegel's, at least to the American concept. Nevertheless, my use of Hegel is quite similar to theirs. In this chapter I show that Hegel is indeed one of the most important theoretical forerunners to today's civil society movement. In the next, I show that the Solidarity movement emerged from Hegel's legacy.

Hegel, Modernity, and Civil Society

Hegel, of course, saw himself as the philosopher who was finally able to break the code of history. Coming along at the right time, standing on the shoulders of giants, he was able to discern the working out of history's underlying, unifying and transcendent logic. He therefore adamantly maintains that he can speak only in the past tense, for the philosopher is able to discern historical patterns only after they have happened—in his famous phrase, "the owl of Minerva spreads its wings only with the falling of the dusk."[5] Yet Hegel also exhibits, and at times even acknowledges, a detailed normative agenda. Hegel's project—or at least that portion that concerns us—is driven by the same concerns that occupied Tocqueville and the Scottish thinkers. Hegel, too, is attempting to address the specifically modern problem.

Like Ferguson, Hegel respects, admires, and even pines for the ethical authenticity and immediacy of bygone worlds. In his case, he assigns these virtues to ancient Greek life. This legacy, now irretrievable, stands in stark contrast to the atomism and base materialism that Hegel, too, associates with the modern, capitalist age. Yet Hegel also acknowledges the awesome complexity of modern life, and, like Tocqueville, he cautiously affirms and celebrates the distinctively modern expression of freedom and respect for the rights and status of the individual. Indeed, Hegel regards the latter as the singular achievement of the modern age. For it expresses a level of consciousness, an awareness of our humanness, that was simply unavailable to the Greeks. *The Philosophy of Right* is Hegel's most explicit attempt to preserve the best elements of the ancient and modern world—to synthesize these competing and apparently contradictory social conceptions, and thereby offer a social and political order in which freedom and community, rights and duty, individuality and ethics, are both expressed and affirmed.

Again, Hegel's history begins with the ancient Greeks. His analysis of ethical life, on the other hand, begins with the family. There are rich similarities between the two. In both, individuality is left unexpressed. Rather, each individual's wants and interests are submerged in a powerful, emotional, and immanently laudable attachment to the common unity. The family is thus unconscious, undifferentiated ethical life.[6] But according to the strict terms of Hegel's logic, its expression necessarily leads to its transcendence, its *Aufhebung*. The married couple naturally seeks to express their union, their newly formed ethical identity, through children. But children grow up, and eventually the very thing that expresses the unity of the family leads to its dissolution. The individual child inevitably leaves the security and the loving embrace of the family, and becomes simply one individual among many. He (Hegel, like Ferguson and Tocqueville, sees the external world as decidedly, even exclusively, male) enters the largely heartless world of competition and self-interest, and this is for Hegel the world of civil society.

Civil society thus begins, logically, with the isolated, self-subsistent individual, who seeks both to express his individuality and to concretize his existence by acquiring and possessing things: in a sense, I have, therefore I am. At this level, each individual is the same—acquisitive, with unlimited wants, turning everything into a commodity for personal consumption. Yet each individual slowly comes to realize that this quest requires the active cooperation of others, and the introduction of social institutions—initially the principles and institutions of supply and demand, and eventually welfare agencies and a criminal justice system—that can establish a series of ground rules. Hegel refers to this level of social organization as the system of needs, or the external state. It defines a group of individuals who, as a result of perceived common interest, agree to, contract to, a set of practical institutions and procedures to aid in their common but individual pursuits.[7]

The story is by no means over, but it is important to note that, to this point, Hegel is employing a definition that reflects his indebtedness to Adam Smith. The capitalist order can thrive first because it accepts and even fosters a minimal, even subsistence level of civic virtue and second because its very operation brings in its wake the development of the bourgeois state—that is, institutions that develop in order to preserve the economic order, but also preserve the social and political order.

Yet at the same time, this first stage in Hegel's conception also recalls the classic understanding of the concept. Hegel uses the term "civil society" to describe a kind of society. Civil society effectively means nothing more or less than the classic liberal state; we might call it bourgeois society.[8] To be sure, Hegel believes this conception is ethically wanting. Hegel is the first to use the term "civil society" to mean anything less than the pinnacle of human social ordering. As we will see, Hegel believes that this bare-bones conception of the state is incomplete without the state's higher political organs, and, more importantly, the flesh and sinew of a real ethical community. But it is also important to remember that as with the classic conception, we are talking about a fairly complete social world. Moreover, while he clearly judges it inadequate and inferior, Hegel also echoes the normative assessment characteristic of the classic conception. The freedom and respect for the individual that characterize this moment of ethical life are a singular moral advancement. Hegel calls civil society "the achievement of the modern world."[9]

Hegel to this point is reflecting a position that recalls Adam Smith's 'invisible hand.' The pursuit of private ends inevitably leads to the market, and within the market, the most single-minded selfishness positively affects both the lives of others and society as a whole.

> In the course of the actual attainment of selfish ends . . . there is formed a system of complete interdependence, wherein the livelihood, happiness, and legal status of one man is interwoven with the livelihood, happiness, and rights of all. On

this system, individual happiness, etc., depend and only in this connected system are they actualized and secured. This system may be *prima facie* regarded as the external state, the state based on need, the state as the Understanding [i.e., reason that stops short of Hegel's insight into the unifying logic of history] envisages it.[10]

Like Gordon Gekko in the film *Wall Street*, Hegel acknowledges that "greed is good. Greed works."

But Hegel goes further than Gordon Gekko, let alone Smith's invisible hand. Like Ferguson, Hegel believes that at its core, the modern problem is the result of the capitalist economic order. Greed works, but its very success undermines some of the most essential features of a shared social existence. But unlike Ferguson (and for that matter Tocqueville), Hegel believes that the resolution of that problem lies nascent within that economic order as well. He argues that the activity of the market does more than simply produce wealth. It also socializes individuals. In their interactions, they come to recognize their commonalty with others. Eventually, their conception of self-interest becomes more sophisticated. They learn that their wants cannot be achieved, nor even reasonably considered, independently of others. In his notes to the *Philosophy of Right*, T. M. Knox offers the following able summary:

> [T]he member of civil society . . . is . . . like the subject in consciously pursuing his own private ends. . . . He differs from the subject in gradually coming to recognize himself as a member of society and to realize that to attain his own ends he must work in with others. Through working in with others, his particularity is mediated; he ceases to be a mere unit and eventually becomes so socially conscious, as a result of educative force of the institutions of civil society . . . that he wills his own ends only in willing universal ends and so has passed beyond civil society into the state.[11]

This movement from crass self-interest to a more civil, more enlightened social sense leads us to the more important, more morally substantive, conception of civil society. For Hegel argues that one of the central means by which individuals begin to recognize their common interests is through the Corporation.

Hegel's Corporations exist for the same reason the external state does. They are an inevitable outgrowth of the recognition that cooperation leaves individuals better able to achieve their self-interest. Given our own understanding of the term, we are inclined to assume Hegel is referring simply to large, organized businesses. And, indeed, this is perhaps the best representative of Hegel's meaning. Though Hegel was referring to trade guilds and the like, he explicitly associates corporations with the business class, as opposed to agricultural workers or bureaucrats. But this does not exhaust Hegel's meaning. Because people's desires are endless, and because civil society is the expression of "the endlessly growing complexity and subdivision of human ties,"[12] the Corporation is a vague but expansive concept, which also "includes religious bodies, learned societies and sometimes . . . town councils."[13] Corporations are diverse and multitudinous because they reflect the naturally boisterous expression of human freedom.

Hegel's concept of Corporations forms the backbone of the modern conception of civil society. For it refers to any one of numerous independent associations that are made up of individuals who have no affective relationship to one another, who are brought together by their common self-interest. But the Corporation is not only a legacy to our contemporary analytical understanding of civil society, it also reflects the modern notion of its normative function. Hegel's Corporations thus articulate the modern understanding of what civil society does, as well as what it is. In line with the innate dynamism of Hegel's project, the Corporation is especially significant in uniting individuals behind a common purpose. As a result, it becomes "like a second family for its members."[14] The purposes of the Corporation are always limited; so, too, therefore, are its virtues. The ethical expression of the Corporation is merely a partial, restricted representation of the complete unity of the state. But for that very reason, it also performs an essential educative function that at once leads to and supports the state.[15] Again, within the internal dynamism of the Hegelian dialectic, each moment contains the seeds of its own inevitable dissolution. In Hegel's words, the particularity of civil society "destroys itself." But by destroying itself, it leads to the union of the universal and the particular, the ethical sufficiency of the state.

In contrast to the Corporation, the state is certainly a more fully realized ethical unity. In that sense civil society is left behind. Yet in typically Hegelian fashion, while civil society is transcended, it is also preserved. Hegel says that civil society and the family are the two ethical roots of the state. As stages in Hegel's logic, civil society represents the particular, the individual, the abstract; the family represents the universal, the community, the concrete. The specific features of the state can be postponed until later. Suffice it to say that the celebration of the individual, the recognition of pluralistic interests, and even the acceptance of some measure of serious disagreement are all maintained in the state, and thus reflect the continued presence of civil society within the state.

Yet while the pluralism and particularity of civil society are preserved, it is also the case that it depends upon the state for its status and its orientation. In one way, Hegel is making a rather obvious point (although it is one that the current public discussion would do well to recall): a flourishing civil society depends on a system of rights and freedoms, and these can be secured only by the state. That state is surely limited—not the least by civil society itself—but it cannot be so limited as to be unable to protect pluralism. But Hegel goes further than this, arguing that the institutions are oriented toward, and have a certain status because of, the larger state. He makes an important distinction between associations and Corporation, noting that "it is only by being authorized that an association becomes a Corporation."[16] Again, there is something of the feudal guilds in Hegel's concept. (To anticipate, both Marx and Gramsci complained that Hegel's concept was hopelessly anachronistic.) Alternatively, one can understand the idea in light of the Corporatist thought of fascist Italy and Spain and its long-standing history in Latin America. But in either case, the dominant oversight and interest of the state is clear. For Hegel, the purpose of the Corporation is to develop, foster, and uphold the ethical unity of the state.

> They [the Corporations] are, therefore, the firm foundation not only of the state but also of the citizen's trust in it and sentiment toward it. They are the pillars of public freedom since in them particular freedom is realized and rational, and therefore there is implicitly present even in them the union of freedom and necessity.[17]

This purpose clearly sets limits to the legitimate or even legal expression of civil society.

Hegel's understanding of the role of civil society within the state thus reveals an extremely significant and commonly acknowledged statist dimension to his thought. Anyone who accepts the necessity of some social order will also accept that there is a limit to just how far pluralism can go. But Hegel often takes this necessity further than most; he is emphatically not a liberal democrat. For example, Hegel only grudgingly tolerates the existence of religious communities (like the Quakers and the Mennonites) that will not accept military service. With a singularity of purpose reminiscent of Rousseau, Hegel argues that "genuine" religion "does not run counter to the state in a negative or polemical way. . . . It rather recognizes and upholds it."[18] Religion, like any Corporation, is made legitimate by, and is understood to be in service to, the state. Hegel thus anticipates the contemporary understanding of civil society as a means for inculcating a common moral core, a source of unity and identity, for society. As Arato and Cohen argue, "For Hegel, undoubtedly the highest purpose of public life is to generate a rational universal identity that he equates with the patriotic ethos of the state."[19] Civil society is, finally, an indispensable means to this ultimate end, but it must also be understood that, for Hegel, it is merely a means.

Hegel articulates both the ancient and modern understandings of what civil society is. He uses the term to describe a specific kind of society, and he also uses it to explicitly identify a specific subset of society. But in contrast to Ferguson and his precursors, Hegel, like Tocqueville, does it consciously and deliberately. Moreover, Hegel reflects the modern concept's dual functional dimension. He acknowledges the cacophonous expression of interests and objectives, and he even lauds this pluralism as a pillar of public freedom. Civil society, Hegel says, serves as "a barrier against the intrusion of subjective caprice into the power entrusted to a civil servant, and it completes from below the state control which does not reach down as far as the conduct of individuals."[20] Yet, just as importantly, these pluralistic institutions simultaneously cultivate an inclination to accept and affirm common purposes, and thus to affirm a common civic and moral identity. Here again, what Ferguson and others merely suggested, Hegel made explicit. Considering both the analytical and normative aspects of the concept, then, it is clear why Hegel is almost universally regarded as the first modern theorist of civil society. He identified civil society (specifically, the Corporation) as a subset of society that was at once part of society, but not under the direct supervision of the state, and argued that it was responsible for inculcating, even in the midst of its own particularity, a common moral identity.

Marx: Civil Society Is a Fraud

As everyone knows, Marx strove to construct and foster a radically new social order—one grounded in the public ownership of the means of production. Unlike his most important predecessor, Marx argued that the object of philosophy was not merely to understand the world, but to change it. Yet many commentators have noticed that there is also a distinctively conservative element to his thought. While offering measured affirmation of the freedom and respect for the individual that comes to fruition in the modern era, Marx, like Hegel before him, sought to recapture the universality, the commonalty, and the connectedness of the days gone by. The complete absence of this former sense of belonging was a result of the contemporary economic order. Its restoration (albeit in a radically superior, radically more human way) could be achieved only through revolution. In order to destroy the alienated modern world, humans must transcend the modern capitalistic order and create the conditions that would usher in the communist system. For all his revolutionary zeal, then, Marx is driven by the same broad concerns that orient the modern interest in civil society. As Peter Berger has noted, "the socialist myth derives much of its power from its unique capacity to synthesize modernizing and counter-modernizing themes."[21] In that sense, at least, Marx is another representative response to the modern problematic. He follows naturally in the legacy of Ferguson, Tocqueville, and Hegel.

Speaking narrowly, Marx accepts the Hegelian understanding of civil society. His own definition of "a member of civil society" could be taken directly from Hegel: "an individual separated from the community, withdrawn into himself, wholly preoccupied with his private interest and acting in accordance with his private caprice."[22] Marx also affirms Hegel's belief that this social order is a modern invention and that it is therefore of a piece with the newfound respect and political standing of the individual. But the similarities effectively end there. In particular, Marx does not share his mentor's high opinion of civil society and its standing within the state.

Marx says that for all his genius, Hegel wallows in idealism. As a result, he inverts the terms of his analysis. Hegel makes the Idea—the quasi-mystical ground and end of history—into the subject and active agent of history, and the concrete events, places, people, and things of real life are taken as mere predicates; they are the acted upon; they are the raw stuff of history. In his critique of *The Philosophy of Right*, Marx writes,

> The fact is that the state issues from the multitude in their exis-
> tence as members of families and as members of civil society.
> Speculative philosophy expresses this fact as the idea's deed,
> not as the idea of the multitude but as the deed of the subjective
> idea different from the fact itself.[23]

On one level, this is an arcane argument between philosophers. But it is not simply that. Marx argues that Hegel's idealism required that he look for a solution to the isolation and anomie of the bourgeois world from within: Hegel thus believed that the pathologies of civil society ultimately produce their own vaccination. It is this mistake that causes Hegel to equate the ideal state, i.e., the condition of actual, real ethical unity, with the contemporary state, i.e., the political order as it is now. Such a conflation, Marx argues, ignores and obscures the alienation (in a very Hegelian sense) that remains at the very core of the contemporary state. The idealism in Hegel's thought caused him to substitute the ideal for the real, and to equate the ideal with the present. To achieve real human freedom, this element had to be purged—in his famous phrase, Marx had to turn Hegel on his head. The real solution to Hegel's problem lay in the future, and it required that human beings radically change the present.

Marx argues that Hegel had failed to see that the underlying explanation for social organization, and the real force for change, is not found in a mystical-logical historicism; it is found in the economic modes of production. In "The German Ideology," Marx writes,

> Civil Society embraces the whole material intercourse of indi-
> viduals within a definite stage of the development of produc-
> tive forces. It embraces the whole commercial and industrial
> life of a given stage and, insofar, transcends the State and the
> nation. . . . Civil society as such only develops with the bour-
> geoisie; the social organization evolving directly out of produc-
> tion and commerce, which in all ages forms the basis of the
> State.[24]

The rampant individualism that characterized Hegel's civil society was the product not of the working out of the Idea in history, but the result of a specific social ordering of economic forces. Because civil society is born of and reflects this basic reality, it, and not the state, is the commanding feature of the social order. For Marx, the state is simply the superstructure, the elaborate outgrowth, of bourgeois economic organization. Hegel was wrong to argue that civil society is subsumed into the state. On the contrary, the former dominates and defines the latter. "[P]olitical life [that is, the life of the community, the life of the citizen] declares itself to be only a means, whose end is the life of civil society."[25]

Like Hegel, Marx accepts the idea that civil society has brought about the conditions that anticipate the real ethical community, but for Marx, the transcendence, the *Aufhebung*, of civil society does not begin within civil society. The achievement of real ethical community can come about only with the destruction of the extant economic order by those who are at once its product and its victims: the proletariat. Only when they have achieved the communist revolution will the alienation that underscores the bourgeois world wither away, and only then will the truly ethical community be possible.

One might notice that this discussion appears to undermine my claim that the concept of civil society inevitably has an analytical and normative dimension, and that the latter drives the former. For while Marx accepts Hegel's conception of what civil society is, he denies Hegel's normative objectives. How can this be? The answer is that Marx accepts only part of Hegel's analytical definition. Hegel says that while civil society certainly includes bourgeois life, it is not limited to this conception. As Kumar states, "Hegel also includes within it the impulse to citizenship, the passage from the outlook of civil society to that of the state. That is why the sphere of civil society contains not just economic but social and civic institutions."[26] Because Marx accepts only part of Hegel's analytical description, he cannot stomach his normative understanding: civil society cannot do what Hegel wanted it to do.

So while Marx accepts the idea of civil society as derivative of the economy, he accepts nothing more. Therefore, he says that this economic order not only is the root cause of civil society; it is the root cause of the state too. In radical contrast to Hegel, Marx avers no meaningful distinction between the two. With Marx, the modern idea of civil society hits a dead end. Marx echoes, albeit in a Hegelian way, the ancient conception of civil society is a unified whole, but he has little more than contempt for such a society. He also denies that civil society can achieve any normative end. This is how Ernest Gellner begins his book,

> [O]ne way of summarizing the central intuition of Marxism is to say: Civil Society is a fraud. The idea of a plurality of institutions—both opposing and balancing the state, and in turn controlled and protected by the state—is, in the Marxist view, merely the provision of a facade for a hidden and maleficent domination.[27]

The institutions of civil society are not independent, so they do not and cannot temper the power of the state. On the contrary, the institutions of the state, like the institutions of civil society, are merely buttresses for an oppressive, coercive, and vapid economic order. The state is merely superstructure, manifesting and maintaining the real source and foundation for the social order—the economic institutions of civil society. The ethos that is fostered by those institutions is likewise in service to that order. If they provide any truly moral service at all, it is that the institutions of civil society drive home the abject failure of modern social life. Only when civil society dies—or more accurately, when it is killed by the proletariat—will the opportunity for an ethical life, the epiphany of real freedom and real community, emerge.

Gramsci: The Marxian Return to Hegel

Marx was a revolutionary philosopher. Antonio Gramsci was a partisan who saw philosophy as an indispensable revolutionary tool. His only goal was revolution, his magnum opus a series of disconnected pieces, clandestinely written while he was slowly dying in prison at the hands of Mussolini. This overarching concern, combined with his all-too-concrete personal experience, made him a Marxist who was contemptuous of Marxist orthodoxy. He derisively rejected positivistic currents within Marxism that held that the revolution was a theoretical inevitability. To be sure, Gramsci wanted to advance a new social order that eliminated class structures and the private ownership of the means of production. With Marx, Gramsci sees the bourgeois state as the enemy of true liberty, the obstacle to a truly human society. Yet Gramsci knew from experience that subverting, let alone replacing, the capitalist order was no easy task. It required, above all else, a willingness to dispense with Marxist theory when it conflicted with the hard realities of modern social life. In particular, it required that Marxists rethink the Marxian understanding of civil society.

Gramsci believes that as far as civil society is concerned, Marx is either simply wrong or his analysis is historically obsolete. For civil society is both more and less than Marx says it is. It is less than the whole foundation for modern society, the base upon which the whole edifice of the state rests. Yet, in what amounts to the same thing, it is also more than, indeed, something other than, the sum total of economic relationships.

As we have seen, Marx argued that his understanding of civil society was largely commensurate with Hegel's. The same may be said of Gramsci. The difference centers on the developmental dimensions of Hegel's concept. Marx focuses on the first stage of Hegel's civil society, "the system of needs." At this level, it is indeed equivalent to bourgeois society; it is the sum total and the sum effect of economic relationships. Yet as I have tried to show, Hegel's conception does not end there. Civil society develops and creates within itself the seeds of its transformation. Civil society starts with a crass, egocentric ethic, but by and through its functioning, it creates a higher ethical standard, and finally becomes, in Hegel's words, "the ethical root of the state." Gramsci's understanding of civil society is oriented around this fact, and is most closely associated with the third stage of Hegel's concept: Corporations.

Yet Gramsci expands and alters Hegel's notion dramatically. In the first place, while the contents of Hegel's Corporation were vague, anachronistic, and centered around economic relationships, Gramsci explicitly includes the vast array of religious, cultural, and political institutions that he believes express, affirm, and cultivate the values and beliefs of modern capitalist society. Similarly, he rejects Hegel's contention that civil society grows out of economic institutions and relationships. On the one hand, Gramsci thinks that Hegel's economism once again reflects the medieval elements of his thinking. More importantly, however, Gramsci sees the economic system as the core of the modern problem; he therefore can hardly expect to find the means for toppling that system within the system itself. Yet whatever the importance of these differences, there are key points of continuity between Gramsci and Hegel. Most to the point, Gramsci believes that civil society is independent and dynamic; it is the arena within which the class struggle continues and it is the means by which society can construct a new, shared civic identity. Similarly, Gramsci agrees that this new identity—fully realized—would constitute a synthetic combination of the best elements from the former social orders: it would thus constitute a more unified, more ethical, and more fully human social world.

To be sure, Gramsci believes with Marx that civil society in the capitalist society is, along with the state, a mechanism of social control; the two work together to achieve the total dominance of the propertied classes. But while both serve the needs of the exploiting class, the method of control is very different. The following is a key passage from Gramsci's prison notebooks:

> What we can do, for the moment, is to fix two major superstructural "levels": the one that can be called "civil society," that is the ensemble of organisms commonly called "private," and that of "political society" or "the State." These two levels correspond on the one hand to the function of "hegemony" which the dominant group exercises throughout society, and on the other hand to that of "direct domination" or rule exercise through the State and the juridical government.[28]

The institutions of civil society that create the reigning cultural ethos work in lockstep with the coercive powers of the state. As Marx also believed, liberal political theory is, indeed, deluded. The independence of the political and economic realms is a mirage; they are but two sides of the same apparatus—the bourgeois, liberal-democratic state. But while both the state and civil society are institutions of class control, the state's apparatus is coercive, martial, and domineering. Effectively speaking, it has no ethical content; it is raw power. Civil society, on the other hand, does not dominate—it seeks consent and, to that end, uses ideology, religion, and culture to produce a milder, yet very effective form of control; it is control by persuasion. Gramsci writes that "[i]n this multiplicity of private associations . . . one or more predominates relatively or absolutely—constituting the hegemonic apparatus of one social group over the rest of the population (or civil society): the basis for the state in the narrow sense of the governmental-coercive apparatus."[29] Civil society is thus the noncoercive means by which the ruling class extends and cements its power. And when the institutions of society are combined with the coercive apparatus of the state, that is, when domination and hegemony are working in tandem, they create a formidable, almost unbeatable foe.[30] But in contrast to Marx, Gramsci argues that even though both state and civil society serve the same master (the dominant class), there remains a meaningful distinction between the two. The institutions of civil society possess some measure of independence and autonomy. And that autonomy is the key to his revolutionary strategy.

Gramsci follows Hegel in the claim that civil society is the basis for the transition to the new, fully realized state. It is for this reason that Gramsci sees civil society as dynamic—as a social construct capable of instituting social change. In Gramsci's understanding, civil society and the ideologies that flow therefrom are, in Noberto Bobbio's words,

> no longer seen merely as a posthumous justification of a power whose historical formation is dependent on material conditions, nor merely as rationalizations of a power which already exists, but as forces capable of shaping and creating a new history and contributing to the formation of a new power which will progressively emerge.[31]

Therefore, if the objective is Marxian, i.e., to overthrow the dominant economic order, these institutions can be seen as the point of attack. Infiltrating and changing these institutions that buttressed the established social order, and constructing new institutions that could challenge the ideological hegemony of the ruling class, is thus an essential and surely primary element in fostering the workers' revolution. Indeed, the dominance, reach, and power of the capitalist system make this the only effective revolutionary means yet available. If revolutionary forces were able to ally themselves, infiltrate the institutions of civil society, and build alternative ones, they could perhaps one day form a collective revolutionary force, and subvert the state's monolithic control.

To that end, Gramsci stressed the importance of trade unions and factory councils, for these institutions would advance the principal goal of reeducating the oppressed. Gramsci wrote that "the immediate task of the proletariat, therefore, must not favor the extension of state power and state interventions; instead, its goal should be to de-center the bourgeois state and to create the autonomy of local and trade union bodies beyond the reach of regulatory laws."[32] By participating in these councils, the worker would come to see for himself that he was being led by the nose; he would learn the truth of his condition. He would further come to understand his own worth and inherent freedom. Finally, by joining with others, he would learn for himself the redemptive power of collective revolutionary struggle.

For Gramsci, the revolutionary's job was not to incite the masses to the barricades. It was rather the more arduous and *almost* hopeless task of creating a collective will, a new way of thinking, a new way of perceiving (Gramsci called it a *forma mentis*), within and among the oppressed. This effort required not just that the oppressed come to recognize and understand their condition. By creating independent forms of culture and education, they begin to overcome it; they begin to train themselves for freedom. For Gramsci, then, civil society is the weak point at which Marxists ought to apply the crowbar of revolutionary action.

This was, to say the least, no easy task. The capitalist system was singularly adept at conceding just enough power to the oppressed classes so that they might buy into their own oppression. It was far too entrenched to expect a revolution any time soon. On the contrary, revolutionaries had to gird themselves for the long haul, accepting that they themselves might well be "the manure of history," planting seeds that might take generations to bear fruit and might not flower at all. Languishing in prison, Gramsci had little reason for optimism. But with a determined realism born of hard experience, he argued that this patient "war of position" marked out the facts of the matter. "[T]he most intelligent phase of the struggle . . . consists in the effort to re-enrich culture and heighten consciousness. And this effort cannot be postponed until tomorrow or until such time as when we are politically free. It is itself freedom, it is itself the stimulus and the condition for action."[33] Here, then, was the only salient strategy for achieving revolutionary ends. Just as importantly, it is the only alternative to despair. Gramsci offers his revolutionary tactics as the sole means by which one could reconstruct a meaningful life and reclaim human dignity amidst the antihumanism of the capitalist state.

At this point along our Hegelian trail, we can offer this short summary: Hegel gave birth to the modern concept of civil society, Marx killed it, and Gramsci resurrected it. What's more, not only did Gramsci remake civil society into something more than a mere fiction, a facade that hides the workings of exploitative economic relationships, he also recaptured the Hegelian idea that civil society is an indispensable mechanism for achieving a more vibrant form of social unity. Indeed, Gramsci built on the dynamism inherent in the Hegelian understanding to argue that civil society can and should be seen as a means for effecting radical social change.[34] For this reason, Gramsci, perhaps more than any other figure except Tocqueville, is the theoretical figure most important to understanding the contemporary concept of civil society—including the public concept in America. It is a startling irony: for all its conservatism, even traditionalism, for all the support it receives among Republicans, and even Libertarians, the public concept in America relies on civil society to partially create and partially restore a more moral and civic-minded social world. And thus, the concept of civil society in America bears an unmistakable conceptual resemblance to the writings of an Italian Marxist. In the next chapter, I show the path by which this resemblance finds its way into the contemporary American debate. I will argue that the Polish Solidarity movement is the lynchpin that accounts for this conceptual affinity.

Chapter Six

Civil Society in the Polish Solidarity Movement

Imagine yourself a leftist intellectual living in Poland during the 1970s. The latest of several promises of reform from within has, once again, come apart. Your hope is, once again, shattered. In March of 1968, under a cloud of violent repression and often virulent anti-Semitism, the Polish government purged the elite institutions (that is, any institution controlled by the Communist Party) of anyone calling for social reform. Only the most confirmed totalitarians were left in control. A few months later—in a blow that was felt throughout Eastern Europe—the Soviet bloc's invasion of Czechoslovakia crushed the Prague Spring. As if more reason for hopelessness were needed, in December 1970, police fired upon protesting Polish workers.[1] The state, it was all too clear, would not tolerate the slightest hint of authentic freedom, and would crush anyone who failed to heed its stern warnings.

It appears that you are left to live out your days in a crude and ruthless, violent and manipulative society—relentless, consuming, stultifying. The ruling political class, having achieved complete control of the social network, having extinguished or merely co-opted just about any social institution not under the direct control and tutelage of the state, is occupied merely with its own self-perpetuation. You may very well be no fan of the free market, you may indeed be a sort of socialist, but you recognize that the state is a crass and empty shell of Marxism. It maintains the facade of its official ideology only to mask an ever more stifling sense of cynicism and soullessness. What is there to do but despair?

The astonishing events of the late 1980s are already fading into memory, and as they do, they take on an air of formality, even inevitability. Even limited distance makes it easy to forget that the past was not always merely prologue. From the vantage point of 1970, the efforts of a few lonely and stalwart Eastern Europeans were anything but the first faltering kicks that would bring down a world empire. On the contrary, their actions could only be seen as vainglorious and almost criminally foolhardy. Yet the story of their triumph is quite relevant to our purposes. For it is precisely the environment and circumstances described above that caused Eastern European leftist intellectuals to turn, almost in desperation, to the concept of civil society. Indeed, it is here that the concept reemerged from its Marxian irrelevancy. While Gramsci's strategy obviously had little direct impact in pre–World War II Italy, the events of the 1970s and 1980s presented a new opportunity for the application of a Gramscian revolutionary strategy. This application, and its breathtaking success, informs the current debate in America about civil society. I therefore want to try to lay out this remarkable history, focusing most directly on events in Poland. My objective is to illustrate that Solidarity was, at bottom, the audacious if unknowing application of Gramscian social thought and that a unique concept of civil society emerged out of these events.[2] It is a concept that continues to influence the emerging movement in the United States.

The New Evolutionism

After the events of 1968, a number of Polish intellectuals began to confront their despair, and, out of necessity, to develop a new strategy. Any hope for reform of the Polish Communist Party was indeed dead, and even if it were not, the "fraternal partnership" with the Soviet Union would quickly and ruthlessly kill it. But precisely because reform from within was no longer a viable political strategy, resistance from without—resistance that strove to ignore the state—began to emerge as the only acceptable alternative. Similarly, if the state was effectively permanent and immovable, then the only alternative point of attack was to be found in that which was not the state. Indeed, as we have seen, orthodox Marxism rejects the idea that there was any meaningful separation between the state and civil society. Therefore, any effort to identify and construct an independent social world was de facto a political act; it was an act of resistance.

The drama of Cold War Poland produced an astonishing number of truly admirable human beings, but I want to focus on Adam Michnik, Jacek Kuroń, and Lesek Kołakowski as the three bright lights of the early Polish resistance. All three had once been loyal, even ardent Marxists, and even after wholly rejecting Marxist-Leninism, all still described their leanings as decidedly leftist. All three had had their hopes dashed by the events of 1968. All were, in Michnik's words, "mind[s] in search of hope."[3] In their effort to develop a new strategy, none explicitly attributed his thinking to Gramsci[4] (nor, for that matter, to any major intellectual figure), but while the debt is neither acknowledged nor even conscious, the resemblance is striking. While there is no meaningful historical connection between Gramsci and the Solidarity movement, the conceptual connection is evident and, to my mind, important. In this section, then, I describe that conceptual connection. I hope to make clear as well that this connection is also decidedly relevant to the American debate about civil society.

Hope and Hopelessness

Kicked out of the country in the aforementioned purges of 1968, Lesek Kołakowski wrote a seminal essay in exile called "Hope and Hopelessness."[5] In it, the former revisionist accepted the claim that reform from the inside was now impossible. But that did not mean that minimal improvement could not be achieved; this immediate failure did not justify complete "hopelessness." Despite the state's ardent desire to control all aspects of society, the replacement of real Marxist ideology with the empty pursuit of self-perpetuation was obvious to all. Marxist-Leninism had been reduced to "a political system which has lost everything except divisions (no mean thing to be sure), [and] which does not know how to believe in anything apart from divisions."[6] This change had lent an even grimmer visage to Polish society, but it also made it possible to construct alternative forms of social life. The terms of that construction were left vague, and, in any case, one should not be under any delusions that such efforts could significantly alter the state; Kołakowski was not offering the pathway to a social democracy. But his essay was among the first efforts to carve out a new strategy that might make life more bearable and that allowed for the possibility of a more dignified human existence.

Six years later, Jacek Kuroń presented a similar argument. Kuroń claimed that the only viable strategy for political change was to ignore the state and to concentrate on the ostensibly independent institutions of civil society. Kuroń's piece has not been translated, but in his book *Solidarity and the Politics of Anti-politics*, David Ost offers this summary:

> Because state socialism rejects the state-society distinction, and society is therefore thoroughly politicized by the state, re-

jecting state domination over society is therefore a thoroughly political act. And so all of those people who engage in any form of social activity that the party-state does not control— a sports team, for example, or a political discussion club—are necessarily a part of a political opposition insofar as they are counteracting the totalitarian tendencies of the system. . . . The strategy of the opposition, therefore, should be to reconstruct social ties. The social is the political.[7]

Finally, in 1976, Adam Michnik began to develop these ideas into a strategy for political opposition. Michnik agreed that the status quo was, for the foreseeable future, unalterable: "To believe in overthrowing the dictatorship of the party by revolution and to consciously organize actions in pursuit of this goal is both unrealistic and dangerous."[8] But whereas the revisionists sought evolution by appealing to the party, he argued that dissidents ought to address their appeals directly to the working classes. He therefore called for the establishment of "authentic workers' institutions" as a way of instilling "a vision of a new evolutionism." Again, Ost offers a valuable summary:

Michnik calls on society to reject the state's ascribed monopoly on public life by simply engaging in independent social life, by creating an independent public square and accepting the risks incurred. This is a call for the reconstitution of civil society. The new theory of opposition thus asserts that democratization is the reconstruction of independent civil society.[9]

Here, at last, and at the least, was something other than a counsel of despair. Here was a counsel of realistic, yet strategic resistance. Kołakowski, Kuroń, and Michnik were hardheaded realists. They had experienced the power and ruthlessness of the state firsthand. They had little reason to think that this strategy would significantly change things. Indeed, it was likely that the efforts of the latter two, at least, would accomplish little except to ensure their own further suffering at the hands of the state. And even if by some unforeseeable fluke their strategy were to succeed, it would take years for it to do so—most likely after they and their comrades were long dead. Nevertheless, their new approach was indeed strategic, it was indeed resistance, and it offered at least the possibility of hope. For these reasons, it gave meaning to one's days.

In Poland in the 1970s and 1980s, just as in Italy in the 1910s and 1920s, a group of leftist revolutionaries—certainly more partisans than philosophers—were faced with a monolithic, oppressive, and apparently incorrigible state. The established pattern for trying to achieve the goal of political freedom had been thwarted, compromised, and ultimately crushed. These revolutionaries were therefore forced to develop a new strategy: one that rejected the Marxist orthodoxy, a strategy that claimed that the state and civil society were not always one and the same and strove to develop the latter as a separate and independent source of revolutionary social power. The hope was that slowly, through much suffering and infinite patience, their efforts might one day create new forms of independent and freethinking association. Taken together, these associations might act as a counterweight to the state and thereby make a workers' revolution truly viable once again. It is no small matter that these Polish revolutionaries were responding to a communist, rather than a capitalist, dominion. But the commonalties are surely more compelling. Consciously or not, Kołakowski, Kuroń, and Michnik began the development of a revolutionary strategy that can properly be described as Gramscian. What's more, insofar as these Polish thinkers serve as the seminal theoretical source for Solidarity, this movement, too, bears strong connections with Gramscian revolutionary theory. The difference is that in the Solidarity movement, against all odds, this Gramscian revolutionary theory actually worked; it achieved the overthrow of the state.

Again, these three authors do not explicitly attribute their thinking to Gramsci. Of the three, Kołakowski was likely the only one who had read Gramsci's work directly.[10] Yet while Solidarity owes no direct debt to Gramsci, the conceptual connection is nevertheless striking. How is such a thing possible? How is it, in other words, that Polish dissidents developed a revolutionary strategy that bears so many remarkable similarities to Gramsci's without any sign that the former were influenced by or even aware of the latter? Perhaps, as David Ost has said, Gramsci was simply "in the air."[11] In other words, perhaps these children of the 1960s simply reflected a worldwide antiestablishment movement, which was, in turn, vaguely informed by Gramscian ideas (along with a surfeit of others). Arato and Cohen similarly speculate that "the intellectual world and even political culture of post-Marxism (and perhaps of 'post-Gramscianism')" inform a variety of contemporary social movements, including the democratic opposition in Poland.[12] I certainly do not wish to dispute such claims, but I am inclined to think that much of the answer lies in the similar circumstances that confronted both groups. In both instances, leftist revolutionaries came to recognize their utter impotence against a ruthless state. They therefore had no choice but to focus on that which was not the state, and to develop a new, more patient revolutionary strategy. In either case, it was either that or submitting to hopelessness. The connection between Gramsci on the one hand (and Hegel, too, for that matter) and the Polish resistance on the other thus centers on the fact that for all, civil society was understood as the only means left by which they could even hope to effectuate the goal of social transformation.

KOR

In June 1976, Poland endured yet another round of violent suppression of worker protests. But, as Rupnik notes, these events were not merely more of the same; they precipitated a dramatic change within and among the opposition. In 1968, the workers stood by while the ranks of the intellectuals were purged. In 1970, the intellectuals were equally quiet while workers were being killed by police. This time, the intellectuals realized they had to form an alliance with the workers.[13] To this end, fourteen noted intellectuals (including Kuroń and Michnik) met to form KOR—the Workers' Defense Committee. With the founding of this group, the strategy outlined by Kołakowski, Kuroń, and Michnik was implemented and concretized; it would serve as the group's grounding ethos. KOR's primary task was to help protect workers against the actions of the state apparatus—by bringing money and food to the worker who was fired for political reasons, for example, or by offering legal counsel to the arrested striker. Others in the resistance movement derisively referred to the KOR members as "social workers"—but it was a term they accepted with pride. At the same time, the very notion of worker support was understood to be part of a more general mission.[14] The founding members of KOR argued that the only politically viable response to state oppression was to act as if they lived in a free society.[15] Personally, that meant that they chose to act with an amazing degree of truthfulness, nonviolence, and openness.[16] (Along with their signatures, the members brazenly listed their addresses and telephone numbers.) In terms of concrete actions, it meant that the members would strive to build or rebuild the independent social institutions that characterize a free society.

In light of this concrete agenda, KOR responded to the extant social order with a number of rather startling social initiatives. Because the state university was censored and cowed by Marxist orthodoxy, KOR formed an alternative: the so-called flying university. (The university was "flying" because it could never safely stay in one place. Dates, times, and meeting places were passed by word of mouth.) KOR members, along with others recruited for the cause, presented lectures and minicourses that sought to correct the lies that littered the official account. Since the presses were similarly censored and chained to the party line, the only alternative was to form independent presses—ones that sought not only to provide reliable information but also reflected the interests and objectives of different groups within society. Finally, since the official unions were mouthpieces for the state, laughably unresponsive to the needs of their ostensible constituency, their challenge was to form free trade unions.[17]

In every case, KOR was not expecting any major changes. The chronicler of the KOR movement, Jan Lipski, notes,

> I think that no one in KOR believed that the possibility of regaining full independence was near. . . . What was important was to preserve in the nation—and especially, among its young people—a will to "break through to independence," and yet at the same time not to encourage hopes and moods that would threaten the security of the country.[18]

Yet while their expectations were, to say the least, both minimal and long term, it was nevertheless precisely here that Solidarity had its beginnings. For while, as Ost reports,

> the strikers of 1970 may have first proposed the creation of new unions, it was KOR and its supporters that sponsored the first "Free Trade Union" committee in 1978. It was just a hope at the time, and Lech Walesa joined the KOR mavericks without much conviction that they would succeed.[19]

Solidarity

As most will recall, the Solidarity movement began with the strikes at the Lenin Shipyards in Gdansk in August of 1980. At that point, it had many of the features of a true trade union. The strikes constituted a collective action by members of a specific industry, even a specific workplace, against the employer in order to pressure the latter to undertake needed reforms. Yet because of its roots in KOR, the Solidarity movement from its inception concerned itself with the condition of Polish society at large; the leaders of Solidarity saw the trade union movement as a way to move toward a free society. The demands of the Gdansk Interfactory Strike Committee concerned itself with issues of wages, hours, and jobs, but it also demanded the release of political prisoners, the relaxation of state censorship, even the broadcasting of the Roman Catholic Mass on state radio. This broad outlook was also reflected in the diverse initiatives begun under the auspices of the union. Ost notes that "in its first months of existence [Solidarity formed] discussion clubs, political forums, independent social organizations, diverse newspapers, numerous ad hoc organizations."[20] Here, too, Solidarity reflected its roots in KOR, and ultimately in the theories of Kołakowski, Kuroń, and Michnik. The trade union movement and worker advocacy were understood by all as part of a broader strategy of restoring independent civic institutions and building a free Polish society.

Yet if Solidarity followed KOR in its philosophy and tactics, there were also at least two fundamental differences. First, the members of Solidarity were not content to serve as historical manure. Michnik writes, "We [the leadership of KOR] knew that independent, self-governing trade unions were impossible in a communist system, but the workers didn't know. That's how Solidarity arose, without us and against us, although we always considered it to be our child. An illegitimate one, you might say."[21] Thus, behind Solidarity's demands was the firm belief that those demands were achievable, and that they could, through united action, force the state to concede.

The other difference stems again from a difference in strategy. KOR felt that the way to combat the state was to foster the growth of a pluralistic civil society. The institutions normally associated with civil society are naturally, even inherently pluralistic. While they were hardly oblivious to the need for unity in the face of governmental oppression, they also hoped that by letting a thousand flowers bloom, they might help to undermine the reach and power of the state. The genius of Solidarity was to unite all disparate expressions of civil society under the overarching ethos of a trade union movement. Timothy Garton Ash notes that "[a]lready in October 1980, if one was asked, 'What is Solidarity?,' one could not accurately reply 'a new trades union.' It was, at the very least, a massive and unique new social movement, a movement which was perhaps best described as a 'civil crusade for national regeneration.' "[22] This combination was, to say the least, an uneasy one. It was perhaps incoherent and ultimately untenable. But it enabled Polish society to construct a powerful counterweight to the state. In Gramscian terms, it enabled the opposition to achieve social hegemony over and against the state's political domination.[23]

By the time martial law had been declared in December of 1981, Solidarity had grown to around ten million members, and included not only any sort of industrial worker, but also peasants, artists, and intellectuals. (Amazingly, it also included one-third of all Communist Party members.) At that point, Solidarity's roots as a trade union movement remained: its members were united against a common, more powerful foe, and their only effective means of response was collective action in the form of strikes. But it was obvious to all that Solidarity had achieved far more: it had become an alternative form of social organization, cohesion, and understanding. In its first and last national congress before the imposition of martial law, an official communiqué affirmed that

> our organization combines the features of a trade union movement and a broad social movement. . . . Thanks to the existence of a powerful union organization, Polish society is no longer fragmented, disorganized and lost, but has recovered strength and hope. There is now the possibility of real national renewal.[24]

The rest of the story is known to all. The party, claiming the immanent invasion of Soviet and Eastern bloc forces, imposed a state of war and sought to completely destroy Solidarity. Outlawed, almost decapitated, the movement was driven underground. Yet while its activities were restricted to the barest minimum, it nevertheless continued to possess the almost unanimous support of the population at large. With Gorbachev's rise to power in 1985, the era of glasnost and perestroika began. In 1986, the state granted amnesty to virtually all remaining political prisoners. In 1988, in response to yet another round of strikes, roundtable talks were held that included Lech Walesa and Solidarity. Finally, in the breathtaking year of 1989, the revolution begun in 1980 achieved its ultimate goal—the Communists were democratically and peacefully removed from power and Poland officially changed its name back to the Republic of Poland. In 1990, the electrician from Gdansk, Lech Walesa, was elected president.

Solidarity and Civil Society

The most important fact about Solidarity is that it achieved the impossible. Despite its imposed hiatus during the 1980s, Solidarity and its struggle never ended. While one cannot discount the importance of figures like Pope John Paul II and Mikhail Gorbachev, there is nearly universal agreement that the rise of Solidarity was a pivotal historical event. Garton Ash's conclusion is direct and wholly accurate. "Solidarity was a pioneering Polish form of massive social self-organization, with the general objective of achieving, by means of peaceful pressure and negotiation, the end of communism. In this, it succeeded."[25] As we have seen, Solidarity saw itself as implementing a revolutionary strategy grounded in the development of a vibrant and independent civil society. For that reason alone, its achievements must be of great interest to anyone involved with the contemporary movement. In short, we Americans want to know how such a thing could happen.

In chapter 2, I noted that civil society is commonly understood to be a disparate network of independent organizations and institutions. Civil society, in fact, is a collective noun, referring to the sum total of those institutions. Now Polish society neither is nor was monolithic. Differences among classes, religions, political leanings, geography, and interests were as innate there as they are in any society. Nevertheless, within the Solidarity movement, and, indeed, within Poland during the Solidarity movement, pluralism effectively ceased to exist. Instead, civil society was identified with a massive, united, almost univocal social movement. This fact accounts for Solidarity's uniqueness; it also accounts for its quite unbelievable success. There are, in turn, two conditions that I believe account for this monolithic conception of civil society: first, the virulent opposition of and to the Communist Party, and second, the unique status of the Catholic Church in Polish culture.

Again, for the Marxist-Leninists, there is no such thing as an independent civil society, and since Poland was a workers' state, there could of course be no naturally occurring opposition to the state from among the workers. Thus, independence was, by definition, both impossible and illegitimate; anyone advancing such a cause was a counterrevolutionary, to be dealt with accordingly. Activists knew this from the beginning. They knew that the pluralistic impulse that is endemic to civil society was, from the state's point of view, inherently unacceptable. Moreover, the state was not unaware that the development of an independent civil society was undertaken as a new revolutionary strategy. Thus, it was likely to be even more vigilant and even more ruthless.

Kołakowski and other early essayists had expressed their hope that civil society could emerge under the nose of the party precisely because any new organizations would be too small to reckon or bother with. Yet this strategy could not be sustained; indeed, it became less tenable with every passing success. Pluralism and independence thus had to be combined with, and to some degree tempered by, the security of collective action. Political effectiveness, even political viability, could be maintained only if the newly emerging associations were united by a common set of ideals and goals and by a commitment to common defense.

The inevitable response of the state to the emerging power of the institutions of civil society thus forced them into becoming a unified whole. Of necessity, pluralism, free expression, and democracy were combined with strong, centralized, sometimes even autocratic leadership. As I have noted, there is, to say the least, a tension here. Ost notes that

> Solidarity had to play a treacherous balancing act. It had to be both a centralized institution and a decentralized movement, showing the government that it always could control the workers while demonstrating that it did not in fact always do so. The union's institutionalized ambiguity allowed for both kinds of responses, each of them essential in this tricky struggle to compel the socialist state to institutionally guarantee the permanence of an independent civil society.[26]

These tensions occasionally erupted into fierce internal struggles,[27] but for my purposes the point is not historical but theoretical: the effort to develop civil society as a revolutionary strategy against a state—a state that saw the very concept as not only unacceptable, but literally impossible—forced the development of a new concept of what civil society is. In order for civil society to survive at all, it had to become something it was not. It had to change from a collection of disparate, unconnected, and often even incompatible groups and associations into one cohesive whole, made up of a variety of constituencies, to be sure, but altogether united by their common purpose and their common adversary. In effect, Solidarity turned civil society from a plural to a singular noun. The ongoing era of post-Communist politics in Poland only confirms that this unity, this solidarity, was in large measure an effect—a largely artificial effect—of Communist rule.

The Catholic Church and Pope John Paul II

The other unique feature of the Polish situation to some degree contradicts the first. For one must acknowledge that in one feature at least, Poland is not like every other country, and certainly not like America. There is, in fact, an innate connection between Catholicism and Polish identity. While not everyone in Poland is Catholic (numbers average around 90 percent), there is nevertheless a sense in which being Polish means being Catholic. To a degree virtually unparalleled in the Western world (Ireland is probably an exception), religion and culture are inseparable in Polish experience.[28] This condition placed (and places) significant restrictions on the extent of pluralism in Polish society. The church has long served as the dominant source for the inculcation and dissemination of foundational moral principles. These principles thus served as a force of social cohesion, setting, for better or worse, a cultural standard that effectively reined in the innately pluralistic proclivities of civil society. It is almost universally acknowledged that during the Solidarity movement, the importance of the Catholic Church cannot be overemphasized. Therefore, during this time its significance as a unifying institution only increased.

The historical importance of the Catholic Church as a source of cultural identity is not unique to Poland. Within the USSR and the Soviet bloc, Hungary, the Baltic republics, and Czechoslovakia had a similar heritage. What is unique to Poland is that the church was able to restore some meaningful independence after the imposition of Marxist rule. These changes began when the church reached a modus vivendi with the state in 1956. According to MaryJane Osa, this arrangement, rare in the Eastern bloc, was due to the "hard bargain" driven by Cardinal Wyszynski, a church leader of surpassing influence and respect. Long under house arrest by the state, "Wyszynski refused to leave his place of incarceration without guarantees that the authorities would allow legalization of the independent institutional activities of the Church."[29] Unlike those in the rest of Eastern Europe, then, the Polish church achieved and maintained a degree of autonomy after the death of Stalin. Polish Clubs of Catholic Intelligentsia were one of the only associations of civil society (that is, an association that was truly independent of the state) that predate the rise of KOR.

But if the church was always a moderating and often a mediating force, changes within the church were also important to the emerging opposition front. According to George Weigel, those changes began with Vatican II. In particular, the Vatican's "Declaration on Religious Freedom," in Weigel's words, "taught . . . that within every human person was a *sanctum sanctorum,* a holy of holies, into which the coercive power of the state could not tread."[30] As the church grew in its explicit affirmation of human rights, so, too, did its unwillingness to accept social peace as the ultimate good. In a climate of rising tension and oppression, the church began to declare itself against the state in defense of the workers. This move was furthered by events within Poland itself. The church had long enjoyed token representation within the ruling apparatus, but the death of revisionism forced the church to abandon this arrangement and adopt a more explicitly oppositional stance. Adam Michnik noted precisely this change in his essay "The New Evolutionism." There he notes, to his satisfaction, that "jeremiads against 'godless ones' have given way to documents quoting the principles of the Declaration of Human Rights."[31] It is thus fair to say that changes within the church itself largely created the possibility of rapprochement between the church and the secular left. But regardless of the cause, there is no doubting its existence.

As the struggle with the state developed, both parties became ever more united by a shared set of goals and principles (nonviolence, openness, truthfulness, democracy) and by a virulent opposition to the state. Lipski notes that the ideology of KOR was first and foremost "a Christian ethos." He also notes that "a decisive majority of the non-religious members of KOR also adopted [that ethos] as their own."[32] On the other side, Cardinal Wyszynski early on unmistakably communicated his support of KOR's agenda.[33] Solidarity, in turn, was likewise able to capitalize on this common moral language. It provided a moral platform that had both unifying power and ideological and spiritual profundity.

There is another key point. I have noted that in Poland, the Catholic faith was inseparable from a sense of national identity. Part of being Polish is being Catholic. But it is essential to note that during the Solidarity movement, Catholicism also became a powerful symbol of national resistance against an imposed political system. The ubiquitous presence of the Black Madonna during the Solidarity movement perfectly captures this amalgam of religious ardor and nationalism. During Solidarity, and even more so after the imposition of martial law, Catholic worship was more than merely worship, it was witness against the state.[34] What's more, the act's political nature was not merely a matter of witnessing to a competing set of ideals and values. To go to Mass, to give confession, these were acts that expressed one's fundamental identity as a Pole. Michael Bernhard makes the point very well:

> The intensity of Polish devotion to the Church is not a manifestation of exceptional faith. . . . It is no country of saints. Devotion to the church is a question of national identity. . . . [Historically] . . . the church was often the only institution that had a Polish character. Thus, Polish national consciousness came to be strongly tied to a Catholic religious identity.[35]

Obviously this factor also explains, in part, the intense devotion Poles felt for John Paul II. For the advent of a Polish pope was a source of tremendous national pride, and only furthered the connection between Catholicism and Polish identity. The pope's visit in 1979, more than anything achieved by KOR or Solidarity, broke through the state's only remaining source of control. After 1979, the state was no longer simply a common enemy; the pope made it an enemy whom the people no longer feared.

In addition, because of his inestimable moral leadership, Pope John Paul II advanced the effort to develop a common moral foundation. To be sure, the pope saw himself as expressing nothing more than the imperatives of the Gospel. Nevertheless, there is within his works and words an amazing convergence of beliefs between the secular intelligentsia and the church. The *Ostpolitik* of John Paul II, Weigel writes, assumed, in terms reminiscent of Kołakowski, Kuroń, and Michnik, that "only a revivified civil society could create the kind of sturdy, nonviolent resistance that might bring the walls of oppression tumbling down."[36] After the imposition of martial law, this sense of common purpose became the only way of sustaining the spirit of Solidarity. Indeed, it caused the church to take up Solidarity's task of building an alternative culture. Weigel notes that during the 1980s, several churches started educational programs that "tried to give the people back their memory."[37] Gramsci, who considered the church an incorrigible reactionary, would have been most surprised to see it acting to build the forces of a revolutionary hegemony.

The Catholic Church thus played a central role in advancing the cause of Solidarity—not just as a powerful and independent social institution, not only as a mediator between Solidarity and the state, but as a wellspring for a common set of moral principles.[38] These principles served the movement very well; they enabled the leaders to maintain a moral superiority that further undermined the state's position. They also gave them the courage to confront their fears and stand up against oppression. For my purposes it is also essential to note that this unified commitment to a Catholic Christian ethos also helped to moderate the centrifugal tendencies that are innate to civil society but would have meant death to the Solidarity movement.

These two features—the deep and abiding roots of the Catholic Church within Polish culture and the widespread and virulent hatred of the Communist state—enabled Solidarity to achieve a kind of oppositional, indeed, revolutionary cultural hegemony through the institutions of civil society. Ultimately, that hegemony was strong enough to bring down a weakened and illegitimate political apparatus.

Solidarity thus both recalls and transcends Gramscian revolutionary theory. The abiding sense that civil society might serve as an alternative source of meaning, an alternative source of education, and an alternative source of politics, and that this alternative structure might allow people to resist, and one day, perhaps even overthrow the state, all this bears an important and often uncanny resemblance to Gramsci's strategy. Unlike Gramsci, Solidarity succeeded. Of course, the vicissitudes of history do not allow for simple comparisons. Nevertheless, it is clear that it did so because it was able to change civil society into something new—certainly something far different from what Gramsci had in mind—namely, a united, cohesive, and organized social movement, and that it was able to do so because of unique features already present within Polish culture.

One must also recognize that Solidarity serves to highlight features of Hegelian social theory as well. Solidarity used civil society not only to advance beyond the atomistic and crass materialism that is constitutive of the modern state (be it capitalist or socialist), but also to achieve an ethical unity on a national scale. To be sure, that unity was not able to maintain itself: once the foe was vanquished, it quickly evaporated. Nevertheless, Solidarity represents the single most successful fulfillment to date of what Hegel believed the institutions of civil society could and should do: i.e., to move society from a state that is little more than a set of procedural mechanisms toward one that achieves a unifying and deeply humanizing sense of moral purpose and national identity. It is also relevant for my purposes to note that this achievement was the result of a unique set of historical and cultural circumstances.

Conclusion

As I have said, the most dramatic feature of Solidarity is its undeniable success. Solidarity was the beginning of the end for Soviet Communism. It was an extremely important, and perhaps even indispensable, part of the sweeping wave of change that brought about the downfall of the Communist Party, the collapse of the Eastern bloc, and the evaporation of Marxism as a viable political theory. And, on the part of Solidarity, all this was accomplished without nuclear war, without guns, indeed, without a single death. But there's more to it even than that. The claim that Solidarity achieved its goals relates to more than merely the political realm. It also reflects the fact that Polish society achieved the kind of moral and cultural renewal that Solidarity activists continually called for.

Both in its beginnings and at its heights, Solidarity expressed the hope for renewal and restoration. Activists saw the movement as a means for bringing back something that has been taken away and that society is worse off without. In this sense, as well, Solidarity confirms its standing as part of the legacy of civil society—a legacy that, in its modern formulation, began with G. W. F. Hegel. For Solidarity likewise expressed a conservative reaction to the atomistic forces of modernity. The values and behavioral norms associated with traditional Polish society had been undone by the imposition of Communist rule. The members of Solidarity therefore called for the rebirth of those values and norms. As Garton Ash observes, they "wished the values and teaching which had been conserved in the Polish Church, the family and the unofficial counter-culture, to be restored to their proper place in the schools and the media."[39] I have already noted that Garton Ash referred to Solidarity as a "civil crusade for national regeneration," but such references are rife in his work. Most tellingly, Garton Ash recounts hearing one Pole refer to Solidarity as a "revolution of the soul," and he concludes that he can come up with "no better phrase" to describe what he saw.[40]

But, again, it is important to recognize that this was more than merely a fond wish. Here, too, the movement was extremely successful. Ost recounts a description of Gdansk and Szczecin during the height of Solidarity as "cities in which a new morality took control. No one drank, no one caused trouble, no one woke up crushed by a stupefying hangover. Crime fell to zero, aggression disappeared. People became friendly, helpful and open with one another. Total strangers suddenly felt they needed each other."[41] Of course, such conditions are not uncommon in the rush of revolutionary ardor. Yet Garton Ash concludes that "it is hard to think of any previous revolution in which ethical categories and moral goals played such a large part; not only in the theory but also in the practice of the revolutionaries; not only at the outset but throughout the revolution."[42]

Recall the discussion from chapter 1. The civil society movement in America repeatedly decries a culture in moral decline. From the perspective of contemporary America, then, this condition of community, accountability, and moral renewal appears a consummation devoutly to be wished. In the next chapter, I show that the revival of interest in the idea of civil society in America stems from the use of the term by activists in Poland and throughout Eastern Europe. But more to the point, I also suggest that our understanding of the concept—what civil society is and what it is for—evinces clear similarities with the Solidarity movement. For the civil society movement in America seeks to employ the institutions of civil society in order to activate its own "civil crusade for national regeneration." One can claim too much, but the fact that the civil society movement in America is populist, traditionalist, and antigovernment, the fact that it sees itself as a means for moral and cultural renewal, indeed, the fact that it sees civil society as both necessary and sufficient to these objectives, all of these are common to the Solidarity movement, as well. The civil society movement in America thus evinces strong conceptual ties to the Hegelian tradition. And therefore, his thought, as well, is relevant to those who turn to civil society in order to restore a more moral society.

Chapter Seven

The Product of Two Traditions

Let me summarize the argument to this point. In chapter 1, I outlined the main features of the civil society movement in America. I argued that the movement was driven by a sense of dismay over the condition of American society. Over the past several years, Americans are increasingly convinced that our society is becoming ever more mistrustful and mean-spirited; that we have lost any sense of common purpose, or even of common expectations; that our government leaders have grown cynical and manipulative; and that government itself is impotent in the face of burgeoning social problems.

As this dissatisfaction has risen, so, too, has the search for solutions. Traditionally, social institutions like families, neighborhoods, churches, and community associations offered opportunities for interpersonal interaction; trust and the development of a general series of habits and dispositions associated with democratic citizenship were, ostensibly, the result of such interactions. The civil society movement is thus premised on the claim that these institutions have been eroding, and this condition accounts for the sorry condition of our polity. The revitalization of the institutions of civil society is therefore understood as the way for American society to revitalize itself: to achieve moral and civic renewal.

This common set of objectives led to a distinct and similarly unified understanding of what civil society is. I said that the civil society movement was characterized by its celebration of families, neighborhoods, and churches (in addition to local organizations), and that it was similarly united in its distrust and distaste for the market, the state, and political partisanship.

In chapters 3 through 6, I outlined a brief survey of the history of the concept of civil society in both the Tocquevillian and the Hegelian traditions. I showed that the Hegelian tradition echoed in the actions of the Solidarity movement in Poland. Solidarity was a broad social movement, united by a common set of moral imperatives and a virulent opposition to the state, which turned to the idea of civil society in order to both restore and transform Polish society and culture. The Tocquevillian legacy, on the other hand, was manifested in a stream of twentieth-century American authors who argued, effectively if not always explicitly, that Tocqueville's concerns about the future of American democracy have come to pass. These authors therefore maintained that America must concern itself with the revitalization of civil society in order to preserve its democratic way of life.

Having thus laid out the present and past of the concept of civil society, in this chapter I tie these two strands together. I show that the concept of civil society in America today is a combination of the Tocquevillian and the Hegelian legacies. With that argument in place, I go on to claim, by the lights of this twin legacy, that the institutions of civil society alone cannot achieve the goals associated with the contemporary movement.

The Conceptual Combination

I have noted from the beginning that the American civil society movement is uniquely and principally indebted to Tocqueville. Now that I have laid out Tocqueville's analysis, as well as the legacy of that analysis in twentieth-century American social thought, the resonances are no doubt clear. The civil society movement follows Tocqueville in attaching particular importance to families and religion, as well as civil associations. Just so, Tocqueville's thought resonates in the movement's antitriumvirate. In chapter 4, I noted Tocqueville's belief that the state is driven to aggrandize its own power and his worries about an unfettered market. Both institutions, Tocqueville believes, can undermine the possibility of democratic society if unchecked. In more or less explicit ways, the civil society movement echoes similar concerns.

Finally, and perhaps most importantly, the movement echoes Tocqueville in its claim that the institutions of civil society at once foster the development of mores—i.e., an overarching moral and intellectual social framework—and maintain the pluralism necessary to restrain the naturally acquisitive tendencies of the state. I would reiterate that the understanding of these institutions and their function is not exactly the same as it is for Tocqueville. I have shown, for example, that there are important distinctions in their respective understandings of the family and religion as cultural institutions. Similarly, while it is fair to say that Tocqueville saw the domineering state as the primary problem (as did, in the twentieth century, Nisbet and Berger and Neuhaus), the contemporary movement is more concerned with the condition of the American moral consensus. But this distinction should not cloud the fact that both Tocqueville and the contemporary movement see civil society as a means for achieving both objectives. Thus, the point remains that the latter exhibits a belief in the dual function of civil society that directly echoes the goals articulated by the former.

The connections between the contemporary American movement and Hegel's writings, on the other hand, are not nearly so clear. There are similarities, of course, between the two. As I noted in chapter 6, Hegel, too, articulates the modern understanding that civil society creates, or at least creates the conditions for, a modern form of ethical unity. But even here, the connection is strained. For while Hegel saw the family as a pillar of modern society (along with civil society), the two were, analytically speaking, utterly distinct. For Hegel, the family was grounded in affection. It was therefore the analytical opposite of civil society, which was formed out of the enlightened but wholly self-interested cooperation of strangers. More importantly, many of the most essential features of Hegel's thought—most notably, its statist dimension—run counter to some of the basic elements of American cultural experience. The contemporary movement reflects this innately American attitude. It regards the state, at best, with wary apprehension. For Hegel, on the other hand, the state is the culmination of his political system, the institution that he takes to be the fullest expression of, and the sine qua non for, ethical unity. For all this, I want to argue the contemporary concept of civil society in America bears the influence of the Hegelian tradition. But in keeping with the last two chapters, I will show that this influence is found not in the intricacies of Hegel's own writings, but in the working out of that tradition: in the thought of Antonio Gramsci, and in the concrete expression of that tradition in the Solidarity movement.

As I have noted, Gramsci argued that civil society could function as a means for building a social revolution against the oppressive state. Civil society is not merely an explanation for a given (and felicitous) state of affairs, as it is for Tocqueville. For Gramsci, civil society is a dynamic social force, capable—indeed, uniquely capable—of combating the oppressive forces associated with the status quo and of shaping and creating a more just and more moral social order. By developing institutions that were independent of the state, society could develop a new consciousness that could perhaps one day effectively challenge and eventually overthrow the state. The Solidarity movement developed a revolutionary strategy that, as I have shown, was remarkably similar to this Gramscian idea. Again, I must be clear that Gramsci's name was never invoked by Poland's striking miners, students, and shipbuilders. Nevertheless, they all saw themselves as creating a separate and independent social movement to challenge or at least fend off the state, through the revitalization of social and cultural institutions. And the common goal of this movement was the restoration-transformation of Polish society.

I argue below that the term "civil society" returned to the West via Poland and the rest of Eastern Europe. But my concern here is to outline the conceptual dimension of the American movement. And in that regard, it is clear enough that the American movement does indeed evince many concrete similarities with Solidarity. The contemporary American movement is likewise indisputably populist and traditionalist at its core. In both instances, the people themselves are the means by which a new social synthesis—a combination of the older, more humane social order at a new level of freedom—is to be achieved. Similarly, Solidarity saw religion as the civil society movement sees it: as a benign force for building social cohesion and restoring a moribund culture rather than as a dangerous, disruptive agent that must be kept out of the public square. Again, this idea is commensurate with the Tocquevillian tradition (Hegel's understanding of the relationship between religion and the state is complex; I return to that discussion in chapter 10), but there is more to the story. As I noted in chapter 7, Solidarity also brought international attention to the social thought of John Paul II and the Roman Catholic tradition. The Roman Catholic concept of subsidiarity, in particular, bears significant and quite often explicit associations with the contemporary debate about civil society in America.[1] The point, then, is not just that religion is an important example of civil society, or that it is uniquely responsible for undergirding a public moral consensus, as Tocqueville affirmed. In addition, the civil society movement ties the rejection of the state, and the concomitant affirmation of democracy, to a basic belief that, whenever possible, God wants human beings to be free and autonomous. Thus, in both Solidarity and the civil society movement, subsidiarity forms the link between its populist roots and its affirmation of religious thought and expression. It is reasonable to conclude that the events associated with the Solidarity movement account for much of the contemporary interest in the connection between democratic theory and Catholic social thought.

Related analytical connections are also found in the attitudes both movements have toward the state. I have noted that the contemporary movement in America goes beyond the claim that civil society is independent of the state. It routinely argues that the state has created or at least exacerbated many of our problems. The state has stepped ever further beyond its allotted bounds and thereby choked off private and group initiative. What's more, it is at least equally convinced that the state cannot solve these problems. Effecting the conditions for cultural and civic renewal, they contend, will require the independent yet collective efforts of citizens; the "excessive, elephantine and paternalistic government," advocates contend, stifles freedom, encourages impotency, and is, at best, almost wholly ineffective at addressing these problems.[2] While Tocqueville, too, was certainly worried about the encroachment of the state, the more specific contention that our nation's social condition cannot be ameliorated, or even addressed, through public policy, but rather and only through the restoration of civil society, finds its conceptual beginnings in the Solidarity movement.

From its inception, the Polish resistance saw itself not as a political movement, but as a social movement, wholly independent of the state. In "The New Evolutionism," Adam Michnik wrote that "what sets today's opposition apart . . . is the belief that a program for evolution ought to be addressed to an independent public, not to totalitarian power. Such a program should give directives to the people on how to behave, not to the powers on how to reform themselves."[3] Reform from within was impossible. Therefore, as much as possible, the people had no choice but to ignore politics and take matters into their own hands. This ethos is a new phenomenon within the history of the concept of civil society. Kumar summarizes the change:

> At the heart of the Solidarity experience—before the unexpected achievement of power in 1989—was seen a movement of the "self-defence" and "self-management" of society. The elevation of civil society meant not so much a new relationship between state and society as their virtual uncoupling. The state was not to be directly challenged; it was to be ignored.[4]

This feeling that civil society can spontaneously develop and thrive without any concern of and for the state is echoed in the contemporary American debate.[5] For all his libertarian notions of popular control, Tocqueville never advocated what Kumar calls the uncoupling of society from the state. The belief that the state is, at best, irrelevant to the goals of the civil society movement cannot be explained within the confines of Tocquevillian theory alone. As Kumar concludes,

> It is evident, as the example of Solidarity well illustrates, that the concept of civil society that is most widespread today is fundamentally Gramscian. . . . [A]s with Gramsci's own inclination, the right direction to move is seen in the fullest expansion of civil society—identified with the realm of freedom—and the greatest possible contraction of the state or 'political society,' identified with the sphere of coercion.[6]

Yet there is another important legacy here that has no Tocquevillian affinity. In Poland and elsewhere, the civil society movement continually averred that it was trying to find a third way, that it was allied with neither the first nor second world. Hungary's George Konrád insisted that "I am neither a communist nor an anticommunist, neither a capitalist nor an anticapitalist; if one must absolutely be for and against something, I consider a permanently open democracy to be the greatest good."[7] In his book on Solidarity, Ost quotes these lines from Konrád, and then goes on to note that

> Probably no other passage states as neatly or as crisply just how the Polish left opposition perceived its goal. . . . The goal was a political arrangement neither capitalist nor socialist, neither East nor West. . . . It is for this reason that the Polish opposition rejected being pigeonholed into Western categories of "right" and "left." This is why they scorned naive questioners asking if they favored "capitalism" or "socialism". . . . Their goal was a political system centered on neither the state nor the market, but on . . . a strong, pluralist, and independent civil society.[8]

To be sure, a good deal of this can be explained as an attempt to mollify the ever-present Soviet threat: i.e., "We dissidents may not be wild about your idea of statesmanship, Comrade General Secretary, but we are also not mindless lackeys for Western counterrevolutionaries." At the same time, these feelings were clearly genuine.[9] As with the non-aligned nations movement, Solidarity leaders saw the struggle between the Cold War adversaries as sterile and unproductive. The social and political possibilities were limited by conflict, and any new idea was inevitably crushed by the weight of ossified categories. The Cold War had settled into deep and well-fortified ideological trenches. Any new idea, or any new look at an old idea, was either commandeered to one side or the other or left to die in no-man's-land.

I have noted the constant refrain within the civil society movement regarding its distaste for the state of political partisanship. Advocates commonly express a belief that political debate has become fractious and unproductive. But the resonances on this specific point are inescapable. The civil society movement demands nothing less than the death of obsolete categories. In America, of course, the "Cold War" struggle is between Democrats and Republicans, and their respective alliances with the state and the market, but the underlying response is identical: that the debate between the two alternatives has become stagnant and unproductive, and that the civil society advocate desires to reject these labels and find a new center in between these equally unacceptable extremes. I do not want to claim that such desires are limited to civil society advocates. But I do claim that this attitude is wholly pervasive among those advocates, and that there is, so far as I can see, nothing within the Tocquevillian tradition to account for it.

The idea that democracy, and the inevitable expression of democracy through the institutions of civil society, is part of God's will for human society; the idea that the state is inherently unable to solve the central social problem of meaning and morality; and the idea that real policy solutions have to happen outside the sclerotic and mindlessly combative patterns of politics as usual—all of this is characteristic of the contemporary movement, and all of it resonates strongly with the Solidarity movement. The Tocquevillian categories are powerful, but they are not determinative. The analytical dimension of the contemporary American notion of civil society evinces the influence of both the Hegelian and the Tocquevillian legacies.

But just as with the Tocquevillian legacy, the influence of the Hegelian tradition can be found in both the analytical and normative dimensions of the contemporary movement, and in the necessary relationship between the two. The real significance of Solidarity, and its most important contribution to the contemporary American movement, is found in this normative dimension.

Again, in Garton Ash's words, Solidarity understood itself to be "a civic crusade for moral regeneration." As we have seen, Solidarity saw itself, defined itself, as Polish civil society. Thus, Solidarity offered a radically new understanding of what civil society was, and what it could do. It was not primarily a collection of disparate and pluralistic civic and social institutions. It was rather a vast and unified social movement; constituencies that were normally at odds with each other were all united in their rank opposition to the state, and in their goal of social and cultural restoration.

Most importantly, Solidarity operated under the utterly romantic notion that its strategy could work, that civil society, so conceived, could achieve these goals. The activists most responsible for the birth of Solidarity—in my analysis, Kuroń, Michnik, and Kołakowski—had no such illusions. They constantly reiterated the likelihood of suffering and the need for patient struggle. It is for this reason that Michnik calls Solidarity the "illegitimate" child of KOR.[10] But of course, the strategy (or at least Solidarity's version of that strategy) did work; against the most preposterous of odds, Solidarity brought down the Communist state, and at least set the stage for the restoration of Polish culture. Weslowski notes that the political inadequacies born of this romanticism were revealed, indeed, became relevant, only after the movement started to succeed.

> After Communism collapsed it became clear that the Solidarity ethos did not provide a workable set of principles for the future organization of society. . . . [B]ecoming a ruling movement, seemed to demand a historical switch in the perception of goals and the principles of societal organization, putting more emphasis on its competitive structures and formal political organizations. . . . For that purpose, the Solidarity ethos, and Solidarity's internal organization and methods of acting, were inappropriate, in some aspects counter-productive. Intellectual circles came to realize that Solidarity itself was in a way the swan-song of Polish Romanticism.[11]

Yet American social critics were adverse to looking beyond the heady days of 1989, and for those contemplating the anomie of American society, the achievement of the Polish people was extremely significant. Indeed, it served to reinforce the romanticism so intimately associated with the contemporary debate. Just as civil society brought down communism, it can also serve as the mechanism by which Americans might restore a morally unified and civically engaged culture. This romanticism is at the very core of the self-understanding of the contemporary American movement. First, it accounts for the fact that this restoration is premised by a largely idealized vision of the past, and by a historical conceit that limits relevant history to before and after some time in the late 1950s or early 1960s. Second, the civil society movement understands the revitalization of the institutions of civil society to be the means, indeed, the sole and sufficient means, by which this restoration can occur.

Solidarity understood itself (and thus, understood civil society) as citizens, acting independently of the state, yet united by a common goal of moral, cultural, and political restoration. This self-understanding is commensurate with the contemporary movement in America. And, here again, the Tocquevillian legacy cannot account for it. Civil society in America is not merely a device for gauging the future of democratic society, nor is it simply a paradigm for public policy initiatives, nor finally, is it merely a means for revitalizing American citizenship. It is, to be sure, all those things, but it is also and primarily a social movement, led by public intellectuals, united by the task of moral restoration—a task undertaken by the people themselves, a task in which the state is at best irrelevant, if not counterproductive—and by the romantic belief that the revitalization of civil society is both the indispensable and the sufficient means toward that end. It is thus, in large measure, the application of the legacy of Solidarity to contemporary American experience.

The Historical Combination

How did these two strands of social thought combine into the American concept? How did this conceptual amalgam take place? The historical argument is complex. More importantly, it is circumstantial; it does not constitute proof for my contentions. I cannot produce the rhetorical equivalent of "the smoking gun." Nevertheless, I believe there is ample historical evidence to support the claim that the legacies of Tocqueville and Hegel are both significant in accounting for the conceptual understanding that underlies the American civil society movement. Briefly, I submit that the concept of civil society emerged in America in two stages. The first accounted for the introduction of Gramscian-Hegelian themes, the second for the reintroduction and ready acceptance of Tocquevillian categories and objectives.

The emergence of Solidarity in the early 1980s, the imposition of martial law, and the movement's ultimate reemergence and triumph in 1989 were a startling event in contemporary world history. Americans, like everyone else, followed the movement's achievements with interest and with more than a little pride. This workers' revolution, after all, revealed in stark, indisputable terms the lie of the workers' state—it showed, in effect, who were the good guys in the Cold War. And with this movement, the term "civil society" reemerged from its Marxian torpor.

Throughout the 1960s and 1970s, it was clear enough that a significant change was taking place within the dissident movements of Eastern Europe. But despite this increase in activity and expression, the term "civil society" was referred to only periodically. George Konrad, perhaps the most important Hungarian dissident, did indeed write that his "antipolitics" centered on "the ethos of civil society."[12] Yet in Poland, at least, the term initially was rarely used. To be sure, Polish dissidents were similarly motivated. They, too, wanted to create, in Kuroń's words, "a Poland of civic concern and independent social activity."[13] But the attribution of the term "civil society" to this emerging ethos was not primarily the work of Polish dissidents. It was rather the work of scholars and other observers who were familiar with the concept and its intellectual history. Surveying the common elements associated with the broad yet disparate movement within Poland and the rest of Eastern Europe—the turn away from revisionism, the commitment to act as if one were free, and the encouragement of independent social organizations—these scholars announced "the death of revisionism and the rebirth of civil society."[14] So employed, "civil society" can perhaps best be seen as a term of art, identifying a common set of themes and objectives rather than an explicit set of categories.

Gradually, this loosely descriptive term began to filter back into the self-description and self-understanding of KOR and Solidarity. Adam Michnik wrote an article entitled "A Year Has Passed," in which he connects the actions of Solidarity with the term "civil society."

> The essence of the spontaneously growing Independent and Self-governing Labor Union Solidarity lay in the restoration of social ties, self-organization aimed at guaranteeing the defense of labor, civil, and national rights. For the first time in the history of communist rule in Poland "civil society" was being restored, and it was reaching a compromise with the state.[15]

Over time, the term "civil society" became the dominant way Poles (and other Eastern Europeans) described who they were, what they were doing, and what they hoped to achieve. Whatever else distinguished the actions of dissidents throughout Eastern Europe, they were united in a new strategy: freedom (personal and perhaps, someday, political) through civil society. David Ost notes that "[t]he term grew so pervasive under Solidarity that when one Party official in 1989 wanted to mock Solidarity's program, he did so by making derisive reference to 'His Excellency, Civil Society.' "[16]

Yet it is especially relevant to note that Michnik felt it necessary to place the term *civil society* in quotation marks. Michnik appears compelled to note that this term is not his own, and that while it refers to a movement that he wants to affirm, that movement has transcended the contribution of him and his colleagues. Thus, the adoption of the term by Poles and others reflects a filtering back of this term of art: it is a fair description of a broad social movement, but it is not wholly accurate description of who they see themselves to be and what they want to accomplish. This distinction might account for the fact that the Solidarity movement never did develop an explicit, let alone rigorous, understanding of the term. Even as late as 1989, Solidarity's parliamentary leader, Bronislaw Geremek, said that the Poles did not require a definition of civil society. "We don't need to define it, we see it and we feel it."[17] Civil society was not only a means to freedom, it was a way of expressing the goal itself. Civil society was the undiscovered country; it therefore could not but be vague.

As the term came into common usage among the Eastern Europeans, more and more scholars began to take notice. In 1991, the American political theorist Michael Walzer published an article entitled "The Idea of Civil Society," in which he acknowledges the debt. "In the West . . . we have lived in civil society for many years without knowing it. . . . Now writers in Hungary, Czechoslovakia, and Poland invite us to think about how this social formation is secured and invigorated."[18] Such acknowledgments were common throughout the West. While the term had been associated with America and Western Europe throughout its modern history, it had been revived there only because it had first reappeared to respond to circumstances in Eastern Europe.[19]

In any event, once the concept had been revived, Western writers began to consider it anew and to apply it to conditions within the West. As early as 1989, Alan Wolfe spoke of the "discontents" associated with modernity. He, too, noted the reemergence of the concept of civil society among Eastern Europeans and wrote that their use of the term spurred his consideration of the modern problematic. He noted that while "citizens of capitalist liberal democracies understand the freedom they possess, appreciate its value, defend its prerogatives . . . they are . . . unclear about the moral codes by which they ought to live." He went on to connect this problem to "the withering away of civil society."[20] Wolfe's writings were seminal in American social criticism, but they fairly summarize what was going on.[21] As of the late 1980s, the term "civil society" had begun to develop a certain standing in the West. Within the academy at least, the idea of civil society—what it was and how it functioned—began to be a subject of newfound interest. Just as importantly, scholars and social critics began to question whether there was a connection between the condition of civil society in the West and the increasingly evident long-standing social problems associated with modern Western culture.

It was within this ferment that the second, neo-Tocquevillian, wave took place in American society. Again, I have noted that a number of American scholars sought to introduce civil society to the public realm. Michael Walzer, Alan Wolfe, Jean Bethke Elshtain, and others all sought to pitch their arguments at the level of social criticism. But one publication is singularly responsible for moving civil society out of the academy, and making it part of the public domain: Robert Putnam's essay "Bowling Alone." I have already said a great deal about this piece and its evocative title in chapter 5, including the plenitude of responses and commentaries. But in this context, it is worth noting Putnam's use of "civil society."

Putnam, like Walzer, Wolfe, and others, begins his piece by noting that civil society has emerged as an important topic among post-Communist countries. Again like his forebears, he then goes on to ask whether America is as much an exemplar of civil society as previously thought. At the end of the piece, Putnam returns to this question, noting that "[t]he concept of 'civil society' has played a central role in the recent global debate about the preconditions for democracy and democratization."[22] Putnam thus ties his analysis to the first wave I identified above. Yet the very fact that Putnam's last use of the term is in quotes reveals that he does not wish to wholly identify with it. Instead, Putnam is more inclined to use similar terms like "social capital," "civic associations," and "civic community."[23] Thus, as with the dissident movement in Eastern Europe, civil society was less Putnam's own term than one already in the air when Putnam penned the article.

The other significant time Putnam uses the term is in a piece in which he responds to the groundswell of public discussion. In an article published in the *American Prospect* in 1996, Putnam refers to civil society—again, not to describe his own work, but to contrast that work with the movement that has grown up at least partially in response to it. What's more, here again, Putnam puts the term in quotes: "For good historical reasons, progressives should resist the view, now being articulated by some simple-minded reactionaries, that government can be replaced by 'civil society.' "[24] I have already argued that the idea that distrust of the state's capacities and role is not limited to simple-minded reactionaries within the civil society movement. While I acknowledge the movement's strong and natural affinities with the conservative wing of American politics, a number of centrists and left-leaning figures have expressed similar feelings. But in any event, my concern lies elsewhere. Putnam is referring to a movement, or at least an aspect of that movement, to which he does not subscribe. Indeed, he is rejecting association with many of those who have adopted the terms of his article to bolster their own agenda. Thus, just like Michnik, Putnam apparently accepts that "civil society"—both as a term and as a social phenomenon—transcends his own contribution. Yet he also wants to make clear that his position is not wholly equivalent to the burgeoning movement.

The term "civil society" is thus not only evidence of the connection between these two waves of interest, it is the very point at which these two strands unite. Events in Eastern Europe cultivated an interest in civil society among Americans. It also led them to form a certain set of fairly vague expectations regarding the relevance of the concept in their own nation. Most importantly for Putnam himself, the above quotation reveals that the emerging civil society movement was much less receptive to the restorative role of the state than he was himself. Relatedly, Putnam appears to reject the idea—one that, I have argued, characterizes the contemporary movement—that the institutions of civil society are effectively a cultural wonder drug, able to appeal to a host of political constituencies and solve a whole host of social problems.

This all serves to explain two things. First, it is for this reason that the contemporary movement is more than Putnam writ large. The first wave of interest had already begun to form a concept in American intellectual circles. As I have said, Putnam had a dramatic impact on that movement, and almost single-handedly moved the debate into the public realm. But for all this, interest in the concept preceded him and the emerging movement in America at least partially overwhelmed him. Second, the first Eastern European wave (along with the end of the Cold War) helped to soften the ground, so to speak, and increase interest in the very questions Putnam wanted to ask. Thus, the public had become dramatically more receptive to concerns about the condition of our society and culture than it had been at the time of earlier, less successful efforts by Berger and Neuhaus and Nisbet.[25] The idea of civil society was once again thrown out there, and this time, something grew. Putnam's piece is singularly important, but it does not alone account for the development of a civil society movement.

So the term "civil society" connects the two historical moments in this way: in the first, civil society described a singularly united network of social institutions that sought to, and ultimately did, overpower a totalitarian regime and move toward the restoration of a former way of social life—one that was more civic minded, more concerned with moral behavior, and more communal. In the second, civil society described a series of social institutions that appeared to be declining. This decline offered a ready and persuasive explanation for much of the anxiety that Americans were feeling about their nation, their local communities, and their shared social lives. The two-stage lineage of this concept was rarely noticed, or at least rarely made explicit, but the connection is clearly there.[26] These two stages combined to form the contemporary American concept. As a result, civil society not only described our social problems, but it offered the fairly wondrous means for overcoming them as well. Civil society was a powerful normative tool that could enable Americans to restore the best features of American democratic life. Thus did civil society become a romantic movement for social renewal.

Now that I have outlined what civil society means, how the movement manifests itself, and what it hopes to achieve, the questions inevitably arise: Are the analytical dimensions of this concept sufficient to achieve the goal the social movement sets out for itself? Granted that this concept of civil society derives from the goal of moral regeneration, can the highlighted institutions achieve it? I contend that the answer to that question is no. These institutions are indeed necessary, but they are not sufficient. You cannot achieve, restore, or maintain social unity—whether moral, civic, or any other sort—solely through the operation of social institutions that are identified and constituted by their pluralism. If you want a moral society, you need to set universal guidelines according to which civil society ought to function, and that means you must concern yourself with politics: that is, political associations, public policy, and political institutions. In the next two chapters, I begin to outline that argument. I will do so, first, by returning to the founding figures of the contemporary concept. Both Tocqueville and Hegel saw civil society as necessary but incomplete. And both also affirmed the necessity of politics. Then, in chapter 9, I go on to show that the contemporary manifestations of these two strands of thought, namely the revolutionary strategy of Solidarity and the neo-Tocquevillian idea of social capital, likewise confirm the insufficiency of civil society.

Part Three

The Insufficiency of Civil Society

Tocqueville, Hegel, and the Sufficiency of Civil Society

The question that occupies this work is whether the institutions of civil society highlighted in the contemporary debate can indeed achieve moral and civic renewal on a national scale. In this chapter, I will address the question by returning to the dual wellsprings of the contemporary concept. I show that the idea of the sufficiency of civil society is wholly inconsistent with the thought of both G. W. F. Hegel and Alexis de Tocqueville.

Hegel and the Prerequisites for Civil Society

Hegel is quite explicit: the modern era, for all its sparkling achievements, has rendered former forms of social cohesion obsolete. Modernity has achieved unprecedented and, for that matter, wholly laudable levels of freedom, personal autonomy, and wealth. Yet these very structures have also left people disconnected from each other and from former sources of meaning and common purpose. The quest to find a solution to this problem drives Hegel's project, and, by his lights, all of modern political philosophy. Thus it is that he says that "unity is the chief of all desiderata."[1] This unity is what Hegel means by ethical life, or *Sittlichkeit*. In Z. A. Pelczynski's words, a nation has achieved ethical life "when its members share certain ethical ideals and are united by a generally accepted system of social morality prescribing their duties, roles or functions in society."[2] I will show that while civil society is an indispensable means for achieving this goal, and while it remains an essential element of a well-ordered modern society, that goal cannot be fully achieved in the civil realm. For Hegel, the solution to the modern problematic also requires the state.

As we have seen, Hegel would claim that the institutions of civil society can indeed bring a society to the point under which this unity can begin to emerge; it is therefore essential to the goals of building a moral and civic-minded modern society. Hegel understands that in a modern society—that is, a society that is oriented around the individual and has spurned former ties to the land, class, and extended family—the institutions of civil society develop the feelings of common purpose and affiliation through which a social order can be sustained. Civil society is created out of the common but unalloyed self-interest of the various members, but through their interaction, each member comes to recognize that "he belongs to a whole which is itself an organ of the entire society, and that he is actively concerned in promoting the comparatively disinterested end of this whole."[3] One must never forget that Hegel includes civil society within the broad framework of the nation's "ethical life." He thus agrees with Tocqueville that civil society is the means by which self-interest becomes enlightened, and whereby society's common moral language and identity are constructed and advanced.

Nevertheless, while civil society is an essential means by which the modern individual is oriented toward ethical unity, it is not sufficient. Civil society is identified, indeed, constituted, by particularity, that is, self-interest, and as long as we remain in the realm of civil society, that particularity remains inescapable. The culmination of civil society for Hegel, the Corporation, does indeed develop a common—i.e., unified—interest among its members. But it is a *particular* common interest, limited only to its members. Bona fide, operative, sustainable unity can obtain only where there is a common interest that reflects the nation as a whole, and that means that society must to some degree transcend all particular interests. It is for this reason that Hegel says that true ethical life does not and cannot exist without the state, without the strictly political realm.

Hegel's concept of the state's political apparatus is vague and something of an anticlimax after so many preliminaries. But for my purposes, there are several essential elements that must be outlined. As I have shown, Hegel understands the state as a distinctive and sovereign unity. "[T]he state is an individual, unique and exclusive."[4] That is, each state has its own identity, its own will, its own personality. Hegel's notion of *Sittlichkeit* reflects the fact that a nation's ethical life is tied up with issues of culture, history, religion, and so forth. The relevant fact here is that this uniqueness helps to determine the form that the nation's government must take. "If the 'people' is represented . . . as an inwardly developed, genuinely organic, totality, then sovereignty is there as the personality of the whole, and this personality is there, in the real existence adequate to its concept."[5] If the state possesses a unique ethical identity, it must be represented concretely through a similarly unique representative. *Sittlichkeit* thus necessitates an individual leader; therefore, Hegel affirms a monarchic form of government.[6]

But if Hegel affirms a monarchy, it is a constitutional monarchy. The monarch executes governmental acts, but it is pro forma only. Hegel argues that if laws and procedures are firmly in place, "what has been reserved to the sole decision of the monarch ought to be considered as slight with respect to what is substantial."[7] The monarch "has only to say 'yes' and dot the 'I'"; the bureaucracy, "the universal class" of civil servants, is where the real business of making and executing laws takes place.[8]

The bureaucracy is the institutionalization of a *universal* set of interests; it is oriented by the needs of the state as the state—unified, undivided, and wholly rational. As a universal class, the bureaucracy is the means by which the executive's demands are institutionalized and activated. It is thus also the main mechanism by which ethical unity is achieved—the means by which self-interest is further directed and contained. In other words, if the Corporation functions as a kind of surrogate family in the realm of civil society, the bureaucracy creates the feeling of patriotism, which lends a feeling of solidarity to the nation as a whole.

Civil servants are selected from throughout the society, based on their intellectual and moral aptitude, for this express purpose: they are to "explicitly take up the standpoint of the state from the start and devote themselves to the universal end."[9] Hegel does not maintain that bureaucrats have no self-interest; he rather believes that their self-interest can be trained and directed to disassociate itself from any particular group or class, and instead find satisfaction in fulfilling the interests of the state.

> What the service of the state really requires is that men shall forgo the selfish and capricious satisfaction of their subjective ends; by this very sacrifice, they acquire the right to find their satisfaction in, but only in, the dutiful discharge of their public functions. In this fact, so far as public business is concerned, there lies the link between universal and particular interests which constitutes both the concept of the state and its inner stability.[10]

To this degree, they—like the monarch—represent the unity of the state in their own individuality, and model the rational harmony of the particular and the universal. To be sure, the realm of freedom and self-interest, i.e., the very impetus for civil society, does not disappear. The moments of particularity are preserved in Hegel's ethical life, but they are oriented away from that particularity, and toward the common good. They are likewise—and what amounts to the same thing— oriented away from the pragmatic and self-interested reasoning associated with the understanding, and toward the objective, the universal, and the reasonable.

Because they have achieved full rationality and full universality, the members of the bureaucracy oversee the affairs of state and serve as the final court of appeal. But there is more to the legislative aspect of Hegel's state. The final part of Hegel's schema is the two estates. The first class, the agricultural class, represents those individuals whose identities are tied to, even submerged within, the land and its rhythmic patterns. The natural immediacy associated with this class thus echoes the undifferentiated unity of the family. The business or industrial class, by contrast, reflects the particularity and instrumental rationality of civil society.

These estates represent a degree of unity that is similar to that of the Corporation: here, too, the members of each estate remain tied to a form of particularity; yet the will of the individual is oriented around, to some degree even subsumed within, a collective good. Each estate is thus defined by a common but class-constricted interest. Its ethos and raison d'être are particular. The estate's role is therefore more advisory than legislative. They do not make decisions but mediate, give voice to, the interests and concerns of the people to the executive officers and the monarch. At the same time, each estate is constrained to concern itself with laws and policies that affect all members of the society. Indeed, promotion of the nation's common good is the duty of every member of the legislature. Therefore, they are likewise constrained to present their arguments and objectives in such terms. The ensuing debate between classes thus helps to focus the populace on, and educate them about, a common good that transcends particularity.[11] It is for this reason that these two estates are part of the legislature: for they are part of "the power to determine and establish the universal."[12]

I must reiterate: Hegel is no democrat. The real business of governing, Hegel believes, cannot be left to the tender mercies of the capricious, undisciplined, and ill-informed mob. He appears genuinely to hold that a bureaucrat can come from any class, even the hoi polloi.

But once accepted into that fraternity, he enters a new aristocracy of the wise and rational. They alone have the ability to discern, and the courage to act upon, the nation's best interest. As I have noted, this conception is both foreign and offensive to American sensibilities. I have no wish to defend it. However, in light of my purposes here, it is worth defending him against the likely impression that the state can, effectively, do whatever it wants.

Hegel insists that he is offering an analytical description of the terms under which human freedom is actualized. And to this end, Hegel regards the state as indispensable. "Since the state is mind objectified, *it is only* as one of its members that the individual himself has objectivity, genuine individuality, and an ethical life."[13] But the rather obvious point is that the state cannot achieve this end, cannot function as part of this actualized freedom, unless it behaves justly toward its citizenry. The unity that Hegel seeks is not forced; on the one hand, the state's institutions are judged according to "their capacity to further and sustain our mutual desire for freedom,"[14] and, for their part, individual citizens should wish to "pass over *of their own accord* into the interest of the universal."[15] As a result, the strength and legitimacy of the state center on "the unity of its own universal end and aim with the particular interest of individuals."[16] In the state, the modern problematic is solved, because it represents the "union of right and duty."[17] Hegel was not a fool; he was wary of state institutions. Yet he rejected the liberal belief that the state is inherently and incorrigibly dangerous. What's more, he thought that the American system of checks and balances made national unity an impossibility. But while he might have underestimated the state's innate oppressive tendencies, he affirmed the idea that the state must conform to the strictures of justice and must at once conform to and actualize the society's traditions, religious beliefs, mores, and the like. For Hegel, too, the state exists to serve the commonweal.

Let me reiterate that the point here is not to disavow the tradition of American liberalism. (Indeed, one could argue based on the last paragraph that Hegel would not advocate such a change either.) In the next section, I spell out my notion of how the state and civil society should interrelate within American political culture. But for now, I simply wish to show that even though Hegel saw civil society as essential to the task of building a restored sense of moral cohesion, he knew it was not sufficient to that task. Civil society is inherently pluralistic and particularistic; its role in advancing ethical life is inherently limited, and it can work toward the achievement of moral unity only if it is directed and limited by a universal set of interests and moral norms. For Hegel, a moral society required a concern for the common good, and that concern finds its fullest and most essential expression in and through political institutions.[18]

Tocqueville and the Prerequisites for Civil Society

Because Tocqueville's concept of civil society more closely informs the American concept, and because what one might call the hierarchical dimensions of his thought are less well known than those of Hegel, it is worth laying out the Tocquevillian argument in more detail. In this section, I want to show that while Tocqueville's analysis is obviously far more tied to the specifically democratic features of American political culture, he nevertheless shares Hegel's concerns about undirected civil society, and he likewise outlines elements within American society that are both authoritative and universal in their outlook. For Tocqueville, too, unadorned, undirected civil society is at worst dangerous and, at best, inadequate to the task.

As I have shown, Tocqueville maintained that the proliferation and normal operation of associations within American society accounted for the success of the American experiment. Recall that within his concept of associations, Tocqueville wants to draw a distinction between civil and political associations, a distinction that centers on the objectives of the association in question. Political associations develop in order to "attack existing laws and to formulate, by anticipation, laws which should take the place of the present ones."[19] The shared objectives associated with civil associations, whatever they might be, are not focused around the law. Hence, political associations include local government, political parties, and the political activities of interest groups, while civic associations include churches, charities, and groups organized around various nonpolitical avocations and interests. Political associations are subject to far less scrutiny. I will say much more about this in the next section. But I merely want to note here that while Tocqueville thinks this distinction is very important, it is not cause for him to ignore one or the other. Tocqueville sees political associations as an essential part of American civil society. Indeed, as I have noted, he sees them as schools at which citizens might learn a whole host of democratic habits and dispositions. They are thus yet another essential explanation for the success of American democracy.

Yet Tocqueville is clear that political associations, for all their advantages, are potentially very dangerous to the social order. To be sure, Tocqueville concluded that the political operation of American civil society was almost universally benign. "Political associations in the United States," he said, "are . . . peaceful in their objects and legal in the means used; and when they say that they only wish to prevail legally, in general they are telling the truth."[20] Nevertheless, Tocqueville was quite aware that such was not always and everywhere the case. And his explanation for how American society avoided these dangers is very instructive for the question at hand.

Tocqueville acknowledged what everyone in nineteenth-century France already knew—French culture still bore deep wounds from the centralized, all-consuming monarchy of the Old Regime, and, later, from the Jacobins' systematic efforts to either wipe out or wholly reconfigure the most basic features of French social life. Born of this patrimony, the political associations in Tocqueville's France were combative, militaristic, and single-minded, even ruthless, in the pursuit of their objectives. Not only was the operation of such groups not felicitous, it was positively destructive of the body politic. Indeed, the unsavory characteristics of these political associations were so apparent to Tocqueville's audience that it accounts in large measure for his vigorous defense of American civic institutions.

Along with this legacy of absolutism, Tocqueville also believed that the difference between French and American political associations resulted from the extent of political suffrage; in France, political associations could at least claim that they represented the disenfranchised, the unheard majority. But most importantly, Tocqueville believed American political associations had positive effects because in America, "differences of view are only matters of nuance."[21] The arguments that appeared so pivotal to the American body politic were couched within an underlying agreement that made these disagreements, in reality, matters of subtle distinction. Indeed, the latter actually served to strengthen the former.

Tocqueville took it as a general rule that "[f]or society to exist and, even more, for society to prosper, it is essential that all the minds of the citizens should always be rallied and held together by some leading ideas."[22] What's more, he regarded the mores ("the sum of ideas that shape mental habits")[23] operative in America to be particularly helpful in sustaining American society. But more to the point, the unity born of this underlying set of ideas also had the favorable effect of diminishing the formation of militant and militaristic groups. In the face of decisive agreement on basic political questions, such groups knew they had no chance of making an impact. Instead, American political culture fostered the development of groups that actively yet independently promoted political and cultural unity. Tocqueville thus maintained that the political associations within American civil society functioned well and served the body politic because they operated within the context of a shared set of mores, values, and beliefs. The rampant association building that so characterized American society was able both to secure pluralism and to foster the ethos of American citizenship because there was already basic agreement about the features of that ethos. Thus, Tocqueville, too, recognized that civil society is not enough to create a sense of civic virtue. Mores and a sense of social unity are sustained by civil society, but they are not produced there alone. In order for civil society to do its job, something is needed to set the parameters for its free expression.

One finds parallels to this argument throughout Tocqueville's book. As we have seen, Tocqueville scours American society for any institution that might moderate the negative effects of equality of conditions. To that end, he celebrates the jury system as a means for reminding citizens of their status as rulers. It also has the indirect effect of instilling concern for others. It is an important institutional device that helps preserve democracy. Tocqueville famously notes that

> [j]uries invest each citizen with a sort of magisterial office; they make all men feel that they have duties toward society and that they take a share in its government. By making men pay attention to things other than their own affairs, they combat that individual selfishness which is like rust in society.[24]

So far so good. But for Tocqueville, these felicitous by-products are not solely the result of democratic deliberation with fellow jurors. Rather, jury service provides a valuable pedagogical device only if it takes place in a court run by a quality judge and quality lawyers. For Tocqueville, these professions represent (and ought to represent) "the best-educated and most-enlightened members of the upper classes."[25] Thus, they help to serve as yet another functional equivalent for the aristocracy. Lawyers and judges are members of society who are better educated, and who hold a higher status, than the rest of the population.

(Tocqueville even says that, as a result, they "conceive a great distaste for the behavior of the multitude and secretly scorn the government of the people.")[26] By their actions in and out of the courtroom, lawyers represent to the people—that is, the jurors—the standards of the broader society. Most importantly, they manifest certain essential democratic virtues: they exhibit a conservative reverence for the law and for democratic institutions, they show how one subverts personal interest to the demands of justice ("directing the blind passions of the litigants toward the objective"),[27] and how one maintains civility within the confines of argumentation and competition.

Notice how similar Tocqueville's lawyer and judge are to Hegel's bureaucrat. Tocqueville insists that lawyers, like everyone else, are driven by self-interest. Even so, Tocqueville's lawyer is, like the bureaucrat, aware of the demands of universal reason, similarly willing to act according to its dictates, and similarly able to tie self-interest to the objective interests of the state. In the courtroom, these qualities are made manifest, and the jury is thereby instructed. "It is upon the qualities of such men," Zetterbaum writes, "that Tocqueville relies in his belief that the jury system will form the judgement of the people and instill in them an awareness of the requirements of justice."[28] Thus, the officers of the court are to the jury as mores are to civil society. They guide the jury's functioning and set a universal standard of values and behavior, which the latter is constrained to uphold. Tocqueville surely does regard jury service, as he does political associations, as "a free school," but the judge and lawyers, at least as much as one's fellow jurors, are the teachers.

Tocqueville notes that in America, a lawyer "is somewhat like the Egyptian priests, being, as they were, the only interpreter of an occult science."[29] This statement calls to mind another example of how Tocqueville shows that civil society is not enough, and how its actions must be guided and directed if it is to help undergird a well-ordered polity. I have noted that Tocqueville regards religion as a bulwark for a civic moral consensus. Religion in America to a significant degree conforms its demands to the new realities of democratic society. But by so doing, it lends its support to an overarching set of moral claims, and develops into an essential social actor. Religion, then, moderates the materialism and self-interest that can destroy a democracy, and nurtures a concern for the common good. In effect, it places moral limits on the vast possibilities loosed by political freedom. Again, for

Tocqueville, the importance of religion is not primarily that it serves as another opportunity for face-to-face interaction, but rather that it lends a sacred air to the mores of democratic society.

This review is essential because we must be clear that while all religions serve this role to one degree or another, for Tocqueville, Catholicism is the most ideal religious form for fulfilling this purpose. That is, Tocqueville judges the Christian denomination that (he acknowledges) conforms the least to democratic practices to be the best suited for preserving American democracy. Why? The answer is the same one I have outlined before. Tocqueville thinks democracy works best if it operates within the confines of an undisputed and authoritative set of moral precepts. The arguments that are part and parcel of American democratic life are benign and help to foster a well-ordered polity only if there are certain ideas agreed to by everyone that possess a status to which everyone defers. Democracy needs a social force that inspires "discipline" and the Catholic Church, Tocqueville believes, is uniquely suited to doing so.

Here again, the desire to limit the expression of freedom within the institutions of civil society rests on a concrete person: in this case, in the priest. The priest, Tocqueville argues, has a different status, a different authority. "For Catholics religious society is composed of two elements: priest and people. The priest is raised above the faithful; all below him are equal."[30]

Now in the first place, the priest's higher status is important because it reinforces a sense of equality among the laity. Whatever else separates American Catholic laypeople—economic status, politics, ethnicity, etc.—all are united by the fact that they are not priests. Thus, they all share the same status within the faith. Perhaps more importantly, however, Tocqueville believes that Catholicism is better because it is more rigid. All must "subscribe to the same details of belief . . . follow the same observances . . . [and] the same austerities."[31] And Catholicism is more rigid, Tocqueville implies, because of the strict separation of the priest and the laity. It is the priest who determines the scope of any internal debate, who pronounces from the pulpit the view of the church on moral questions of the day. Within the Catholic Church, then, the priest is the functional equivalent of the judge.

American Catholic priests have divided the world of the mind into two parts; in one are revealed dogmas to which they submit without discussion; political truth finds its place in the

other half, which they think God has left to man's free investi-
gation. Thus American Catholics are both the most obedient
of the faithful and the most independent citizens."[32]

Tocqueville never says that priests profess anything different from,
let alone at odds with, the statements of other American clergy. Indeed,
his discussion ends with a long quotation from a priest that clearly
illustrates that, in Tocqueville's view, the average American priest accepts and affirms the civil religion just as much as, if not more than,
any other Sunday preacher does. The difference is not the content of
such pronouncements; the difference is the standing of Catholic priests
compared to other ministers. When a priest submits to something without discussion, there was no question what the response of the laity
would be: they were to act likewise. Thus, for Tocqueville, Catholicism
is better because it brings its rigidity to the American civil religion,
cordoning off a set of moral precepts as sacrosanct and unquestioned.
As a result, Catholicism leaves American civil religion all the more
secure, and all the more able to identify and constrain unacceptable
human behavior. Faced with the constant dangers associated with the
equality of conditions, Catholicism is a powerful and beneficent social
force. And all of that benefit, Tocqueville argues, is made possible,
made active, by the distinction between the priest and the laity. This
distinction in status thus serves to reinforce the limits that ensure the
proper functioning of American civil society, and that is why Tocqueville prefers it over any other form of religious organization.

Finally, there is the matter of what Tocqueville says about the law.
Civil society advocates are quick to note Tocqueville's belief that mores
were more important than the law in maintaining a well-ordered democratic society. And while I have shown that other institutions are likewise indispensable, it is undeniable that, for Tocqueville, political and
civil associations are the central means by which these mores are cultivated and preserved. It is thus well established that Tocqueville held
a healthy, active civil society as vital to a healthy democratic society;
indeed, in Tocqueville's mind it may well be more important than any
other single social factor. But contrary to many contemporary advocates, Tocqueville saw that the law, that is, the political order, was also
essential to this task. Like Hegel, then, Tocqueville argued that the state
had a significant role to play in cultivating the mores that sustain democratic society.

I have noted that most of Tocqueville's analysis is predictive. He does not tell democrats how to extricate themselves should they find themselves under the possession of a benign despot. He is concerned that they know how to prevent such an event in the first place. But in one relevant passage, Tocqueville offers an important prescription. He begins by describing the alienated condition of the citizenry in some unnamed European countries. He says that in these countries, the inhabitant feels "like some sort of farm laborer indifferent to the fate of the place where he dwells." Tocqueville says that this indifference leads him to deny any responsibility for the unmet problems around him. "[H]e thinks that all those things have nothing to do with him at all, but belong to a powerful stranger called the government."[33] In these countries, public spirit has died, and citizens have become mere tenants before a powerful but distrusted landlord. In all of this, there is an uncomfortable ring of familiarity. Too many Americans recognize their attitudes and those of their neighbors in Tocqueville's description.

What, then, does Tocqueville prescribe? He begins by acknowledging that "[n]o laws can bring back life to fading beliefs." A nation cannot legislate itself back to good health. But Tocqueville goes on to show that while the law cannot achieve such a goal on its own, neither is it anything less than indispensable to that objective. Tocqueville thus goes on immediately to insist that "laws can make men care for the fate of their countries. It depends on the laws to awaken and direct that vague instinct of patriotism which never leaves the human heart, and by linking it to everyday thoughts, passions, and habits, to make it a conscious and durable sentiment."[34] Tocqueville's conclusion, then, is this: for any leader contemplating an enervated, thoughtless, and disconnected citizenry, laws alone will not solve the situation. But Tocqueville is quite clear that government and laws are also essential to that end.

The above passage on laws is in a chapter of *Democracy in America* subtitled "The Political Effects of Administrative Decentralization." This context is significant, for central to Tocqueville's meaning of the very word "laws" is the way American government orders itself. In other words, part of the reason laws in the United States instill patriotism is that, in contrast to many European nations, governmental administration is decentralized. The government is not a powerful stranger; it is accessible and accountable to each citizen's needs. One can go down to the county seat, or even the state capital, and see law being made and carried out. All of this fits naturally with what we have already noted about Tocqueville's desire to uncover democratic solutions to democratic problems. If a nation wants to overcome the problems of equality, it must allow its citizenry the responsibilities of self-government. Here again, we might well say that this constitutes the more significant aspect of what Tocqueville means, but it is not all of what he means.

Tocqueville argues that many political thinkers fail to distinguish between two important forms of centralization: governmental and administrative. If the power for directing "the enactment of general laws" is concentrated in the same place, that constitutes governmental centralization. If the same concentration exists for "other interests of special concern to certain parts of the nation, such, for instance, as local enterprises," this constitutes what Tocqueville calls administrative centralization.[35] Regarding the latter, Tocqueville celebrates the fact that America is radically decentralized. Citizens are left able to determine and look after their own best interests, and patriotism, civic-mindedness, and an appreciation of government all develop out of this state of affairs. But in terms of governmental centralization, Tocqueville believes America rivals any other nation. "In no country in the world are the pronouncements of the law more categorical than in America."[36] Tocqueville does not offer specifics about how governmental centralization functions in America, but his basic point is this: most often, and particularly regarding the matters that affect them most closely, people are left to judge for themselves. But on general matters, matters that reflect the fundamental need for social order and social unity, the law pronounces universal prescriptions for behavior.[37] The structure of American law is relevant and works so well at preserving democracy for both reasons.

This dual dimension serves as a remarkable and rather precise demonstration of the Catholic principle of subsidiarity (again, the notion that, whenever possible, decisions should be left to the individuals affected).[38] I have shown that Tocqueville effectively and repeatedly affirms this principle. The idea that government must be decentralized, and that society must accept the inevitable loss in governmental efficiency, so that citizens are able to exercise political control over their lives is wholly consistent with this principle. But it is self-evident that, as far as the Catholic Church is concerned, there is more that must be said. Popes advocating the principle of subsidiarity clearly did not believe that *all* decisions should be left to the will of the populace. For

Roman Catholics, some decisions, indeed, those most decisive in their importance, should be removed from independent choice and be decided by a higher authority. Decisive matters about the faith are left to the papacy (including the magisterium and other appropriate bodies). In the realm of politics, a similar principle applies. In *Quadragesimo Anno*, Pius XI acknowledges that there are tasks that should be left to the state: "directing, watching, stimulating, restraining, as circumstances suggest and necessity demands."[39] My point, then, is that Tocqueville is saying something very similar. For him, the genius of American politics is that it has also lived up to both sides of this dichotomy. Freedom operates, civil associations thrive, and democracy flourishes, all within the confines of a few general laws.

Now as both advocates and critics of the Catholic Church are quick to note, the church is not a democracy. There is, of course, a strong disparity between a political organization that is most closely identified with the monarchy, and one in which the people rule. Tocqueville knows this, too. And yet he is quite convinced that the removal of some central issues from democratic contestation is essential for democratic health. This dilemma again points to the importance, for Tocqueville, of lawyers and judges. Because of their inherent respect for governmental institutions, for the founding documents, and for precedence, they stand as a class apart; they instinctively stand against the people's ardency for change. Because America affords a unique power to judges and lawyers, they are able to exercise these innate tendencies, thereby raising the standing of general laws, and thereby controlling democracy's worst proclivities. For Tocqueville, "[t]he extension of judicial power over the political field should be correlative to the extension of elected power. If these two elements do not progress together, the state will end in anarchy or servitude."[40] The judiciary and the bar operate as America's aristocracy, inculcating a conservative respect for the general principles under which the republic operates.

Thus, both aspects of American law—both the administrative decentralization and the governmental centralization—combine to develop "the vague instinct of patriotism" into "a conscious and durable sentiment."[41] Patriotism unites all citizens with a common goal, a common affection for their nation, and a common identity as its citizens. It offers a reason for action that transcends base self-interest, and provides a ground for presuming the goodwill of the stranger. What's more, if this patriotism is allied with a nation's civil religion, Tocqueville be-

lieves this sentiment limits and directs the natural expression of democratic civil society.

None of this is meant to deny what has been said before. Tocqueville
is quite clear and quite adamant that the state is dangerous, and that the
citizenry must be constantly on guard to check its centralizing instincts.
What's more, the state is never sufficient to achieve the goal of patriotism. You cannot compel someone to practice self-government.

> A government, by itself, is equally incapable of refreshing the
> circulation of feelings and ideas among a great people, as it is
> of controlling every industrial undertaking. Once it leaves the
> sphere of politics to launch out on this new track, it will, even
> without intending this, exercise an intolerable tyranny. For a
> government can only dictate precise rules. It imposes the senti-
> ments and ideas which it favors, and it is never easy to tell the
> difference between its advice and its commands. . . . It is there-
> fore necessary that it should not act *alone*.[42]

We have seen that associations are of critical, even primary, importance for performing this task. But the notion that therefore the state
is irrelevant to the objective of establishing a well-ordered democracy
is equally foolhardy. Throughout *Democracy in America*, the institutions
of civil society operate well because they operate within and under an
acknowledged authority that sets limits to acceptable expression. Civil
society is not enough.

As with Hegel, we are not required to accept any specific elements
within Tocqueville's solution. But we must acknowledge that, for
Tocqueville too, civil society is necessary but not sufficient to the task
of building a more moral, more civically engaged social order. For both
Tocqueville and Hegel, something more is required. In order to achieve
a well-ordered polity, Tocqueville and Hegel agree, three additional
elements are needed: first, a universal agreement about values, norms,
objectives, etc.; second, an interest or concern that rises above self- or
group-interest and attends to the common good; third, a mechanism or
series of mechanisms whereby that universal agreement and universal
perspective are both created and rendered operative. Finally, Hegel
and Tocqueville agree that the single most effective mechanism for
inculcating this universal agreement is politics: that is, the ongoing
moral conversation among and within political institutions. If one of
these three elements is missing, society (any society) will be unable to

achieve a sufficient degree of moral and civic unity. In particular, they maintain that without these additional elements, the normal operation of the institutions of civil society cannot be expected to work effectively toward building a more moral, more civic-minded society. It is ironic and, more to the point, problematic that both the Hegelian and Tocquevillian legacies inform a movement that appears to have lost sight of this basic reality. If the goal of that movement is indeed the one I have articulated, then civil society advocates must address this glaring inconsistency.

Chapter Nine

The Contemporary Concept and the Question of Sufficiency

In the last chapter, I argued that the progenitors of the two intellectual traditions that inform the contemporary concept, Tocqueville and Hegel, maintain that the institutions of civil society are not sufficient to the task of building a moral social order. Again, they claim that three additional elements are needed: first, a universal agreement about values, norms, objectives, etc.; second, an interest or concern that rises above self- or group-interest and attends to the common social good; third, a mechanism or series of mechanisms whereby that universal agreement and universal concern are both created and rendered operative. These additional elements ostensibly obtain universally, regardless of the operative circumstances.

Yet I have also argued that there are distinctive elements to the American concept of civil society. In two fundamental ways, these features ostensibly allow the civil society movement to acknowledge the force of these arguments, while maintaining the sufficiency of the civic-cultural realm. Interestingly, these strategies are also associated with the more contemporary manifestations of the Tocquevillian and Hegelian legacies. In this chapter, therefore, I want to consider the issue of sufficiency with respect to the concept of civil society operative in America today.

The first argument centers on the neo-Tocquevillian concept of social capital. Civil society advocates argue that certain essential institutions within American civil society lead to the development of trust among participants. They further claim that this trust ultimately permeates throughout the entire society. Universal social norms are produced and sustained through institutions that facilitate face-to-face interaction. Thus, the social capital argument claims that civic virtue is built, as it were, from the ground up; the universal does indeed emerge from and through the particular. On the Hegelian side, the experience of Solidarity shows, in a similar way, that civil society itself can create the very elements that Hegel and Tocqueville believe to be external to civil society. Solidarity proves, in other words, that pluralistic institutions *can* achieve national unity. In Poland, the revitalization of local institutions did indeed lead to what Timothy Garton Ash has called a civic crusade for moral renewal. We have a similar, if less dire, set of problems, and there is no reason to presume that Solidarity's success cannot be duplicated here.

I will argue, to the contrary, that in the contemporary American context, both of these arguments fail to show either the sufficiency of civil society or the irrelevancy of the political realm. An analysis of the contemporary American concept of civil society thus confirms the theoretical analysis outlined in the preceding chapter. That is, it confirms the necessity of politics.

Sufficiency and Social Capital

The Fungibility of Social Capital

A short review is necessary. I have argued that the desire for moral and civic renewal that grounds the contemporary debate is tied to the concept of social capital. This concept is at the core of the public concept of civil society. Social capital maintains that trust among persons, the expectation that you can rely on and predict the behavior of the other, is built up through face-to-face interactions. As it is produced, it then permeates through the broader social fabric. Trust among individuals fosters trust among strangers and trust of social institutions. If the institutions in which these initial interpersonal interactions take place are compromised or depleted, the argument goes, the larger social fabric inevitably decays, and, at a certain point, this decay starts to manifest itself in serious social problems. In sum, then, civil society advocates maintain that our sorry social condition results from a depletion of social capital. And if we are to rectify this condition, they argue, we must restore those institutions that are most able to create social capital.

I noted in chapter 4 that the civil society movement's understanding of, and interest in, the concept of social capital stems primarily from the work of Robert Putnam. Putnam's article "Bowling Alone" concludes, "High on America's agenda should be the question of how to reverse these adverse trends in social connectedness, *thus restoring civic engagement and civic trust.*"[1] Putnam maintains that the state as well as large political associations can have an active role in encouraging social capital formation. Yet he also contends that the production of social capital is primarily, if not exclusively, limited to unstructured face-to-face interactions. He notes that "[f]rom the point of view of social connectedness, the Environmental Defense Fund and a bowling league are not in the same category." Thus, Putnam maintains that a more moral and civic culture is constructed primarily through face-to-face, and usually informal, association. Civic trust is born of interpersonal trust.[2]

This causal relationship accounts for Putnam's focus on informal civic associations: choral groups and soccer clubs in Italy, PTAs and the Kiwanis in the United States. In the public debate, this same understanding accounts for the fact that the family, church, and neighborhood are seen as the most significant institutions for civil society advocates. These institutions—stable, more affective, less contentious, and effectively separate from politics and the state—are judged most likely to produce informal and fairly intimate forms of social interaction and thus social capital. On the other hand, the civil society movement likewise distrusts and denigrates those social institutions that are seen to be the most hostile to this task: especially the state, the market, and political partisanship. To be sure, civil society advocates acknowledge that the state can help to establish the conditions under which more efficacious institutions can emerge. But this is to say little more than that the state can help most by getting out of the way. Beyond this, the state and its actions are understood to be largely detrimental to the task at hand.

Now I have argued that civil society has both a normative and an analytical dimension, and that the former conditions the latter: civil society is what you want it to do. The differences between Putnam and the civil society movement reflect this distinction. Thus, the featured institutions differ because their understanding of social capital differs. Following James Coleman, Putnam presents trust as the rational expectation that the other will perform as desired. It reveals a fundamental association with game theory. In the public debate, trust is a fundamentally moral concept, based on the belief that the person in question is a decent, fair, and just person. This subtle difference centers on Putnam's fundamental desire for what he calls civic engagedness on the one hand and the civil society movement's equal if not primary concern for a kind of moral renewal. Yet for all this, the basic similarity holds. In both instances, the interpersonal trust that is produced through what we might call social capital institutions is judged the most likely means for producing, or, more accurately, reproducing, the universal trust that comes from a generalized set of moral beliefs.

It is uncontroversial to argue that every society needs social capital, and hence needs the institutions that inculcate it. Yet it is quite another thing to understand these social capital institutions as being the sufficient means by which a more civic culture can be restored. In a review of Putnam's work on Italy, Margaret Levi argues that the latter claim is far from established.

> The major issue for Putnam is how social trust, that is, trust among those lacking intimate knowledge of each other, develops and is maintained in a society. The answer that Putnam provides is only partially satisfying. It may be correct but is incomplete. . . . To determine whether there is a connection between such memberships [i.e., soccer clubs and bowling leagues] and generalized trust requires a more precise concept of trust than Putnam offers.[3]

More recently, Jean Cohen has presented a similar set of concerns.

> Why does the willingness to act together for mutual benefit in a small group like a choral society translate into willingness to act for the common good or to become politically engaged at all? Indeed, *is the interpersonal trust generated in face-to-face interactions even the same thing as "generalized trust"?*[4]

Cohen, too, complains that this relationship has not been established.

It is essential to note that the issue here is one of sufficiency. Neither Levi nor Cohen (nor I) disputes the idea that "trust lubricates cooperation." Rather, the point for my purposes is that civil society advocates follow Putnam in equating the restoration of social capital, and hence, the institutions most able to produce it, with the restoration of a more moral, more civic social order. But these concerns illustrate that while social capital is surely a good thing, and even a necessary thing for a well-ordered society, it is not clear that it is sufficient: social capital does not necessarily get you to universal trust, or to the universal moral and civic norms that undergird that trust. There is, to be sure, an intuitive association between informal, personal forms of trust and more generalized, abstract forms. Indeed, it is at best unlikely that such generalized forms of trust and cooperation could be produced at all without the prior presence of more informal forms. But the necessity of social capital is not an argument for its sufficiency. In order to get from A to B, it seems likely that something more is required.

It is no doubt apparent that this argument (or really, at this point, this concern) recalls the broad features of the arguments of Tocqueville and Hegel outlined in the last chapter. The complaint that the concept of social capital does not demonstrate how interpersonal trust translates into universal trust echoes Tocqueville and Hegel's claim that a moral society requires more than the institutions of civil society, on their own, can achieve. Trust that obtains between strangers, and between citizens and social institutions, depends on a concomitant and nearly universal agreement on norms and values. Thus, the goal of trust and the goal of moral unity are one and the same. And for both Tocqueville and Hegel on the one hand and Levi and Cohen on the other, civil society is a necessary but not sufficient means to that end.

The American Public Moral Consensus

To this point, I have left the argument against sufficiency undeveloped. I have done so because there is a more sophisticated version of the social capital argument that attempts to accommodate the concerns outlined above. And it is here that the issue must be engaged. This version acknowledges that the trust that develops among individuals does not automatically develop into a nationwide set of expectations regarding behavior, values, and the like. But it goes on to note that civil society advocates are not concerned about social capital as an abstraction; they are concerned with how it does or does not function here in America. And in this context, this development, this upward movement, does indeed take place: face-to-face interaction does indeed create the mechanisms by which universal, nationwide social trust is created. Why? Because we Americans already have the universal moral consensus that Tocqueville and Hegel demand. We already have a strong, universal, and authoritative set of beliefs and values that define us as a people. This consensus is indeed vague and inarticulate, but the operation of civil society provides the opportunity whereby it can be put into action. The social capital–producing institutions thus give these norms and values form and content even as these norms constrain and direct the operation of civil society. In effect, then, the American public moral consensus completes the circle; the more that is needed is already here. The concerns of Levi and Cohen, along with the theoretical arguments of Tocqueville and Hegel, are answered.

Before addressing this claim in more detail, I want to say a little about the notion of a public moral consensus and the specific features of the American public moral consensus.[5] Recall that for Hegel, the goal of ethical life is specific to each society. That is, each nation is a unique ethical community; each has its own identity, or, in typically Hegelian language, spirit. Z. A. Pelzcynski summarizes the point. In *Philosophy of Right,* Hegel argues that ethical life is achieved when citizens "share certain ethical ideals and are united by a generally accepted system of social morality prescribing their duties, roles or functions in society."[6] Recall also that Tocqueville uses mores as a similarly overarching concept. Mores are a set of common values, beliefs, and expectations; they at once transcend and ground politics, for they constitute the "mental habits" that shape the whole of social life. Given that the question occupying this work is the relationship between civil society and the desire to build a moral yet modern and democratic society, the commonality between Tocqueville and Hegel on this point is striking.[7]

The basic notion that a society both requires and is constituted by a public moral consensus is hardly peculiar to Tocqueville and Hegel. Indeed, it is a common refrain throughout Western political theory. Given America's uniquely pluralistic history, the issue of establishing and maintaining a public moral consensus has been particularly important. To be sure, there is a chronic, and often heated, debate about the content and import of that consensus.[8] Yet almost all agree with Tocqueville that something like the mores he observed still remain. That is, there is still an operative set of norms, values, and expectations that achieve widespread if not quite universal affirmation and constitute or help to constitute a uniquely American identity.

These mores find their core expression in the nation's founding documents: the Declaration of Independence, the Preamble to the Constitution, and the like. As Tocqueville noted, it also reflects the nation's unique tradition of civil religion. These elements have shifted and been reinterpreted throughout our nation's history. But for my purposes, it is sufficient to focus on the contemporary context. That is, what are the norms, values, and beliefs to which all or almost all present-day Americans assent, and what is their status within the broader society? An answer to those questions provides ground from which to address the matter of civil society and its sufficiency.

The Gallup Organization, along with the Post-modernity Project at the University of Virginia, recently completed a comprehensive survey that seeks to understand the current state of American political and public culture. This study, *The State of Disunion: 1996 Survey of American Political Culture,* written by James Davison Hunter and Carl Bowman, frequently echoes the civil society movement itself. For both are driven by widespread concern about the condition of the American body politic. The study notes that

> [e]very day's news presents us with disheartening signs that America is fragmenting; that tensions over social issues, like abortion, school prayer, gay rights, and the like, are undermining the cohesion of our union, that Americans have lost the capacity to speak a common language that would enable us to deal with our problems.[9]

Hunter and Bowman's data show that these concerns are well founded. Americans are cynical and pessimistic about the present and future condition of their society and culture. The report notes that "[a] full 50 percent of respondents . . . admitted to the view that the US is actually in decline."[10] Americans are especially cynical about the condition of their government. An amazingly high 81 percent "agree with the stinging indictment that 'political events these days seem more like theater or entertainment than like something to be taken seriously.' "[11] Americans display a similar if not quite so universal dissatisfaction with a host of social institutions, including the economy (56 percent), public schools (54 percent), and the family (60 percent). These data confirm many of the findings noted in chapter 1. Whether or not civil society advocates have the right answers, it seems clear that their concerns are well founded.

Yet despite these deeply troubling levels of public dissatisfaction, *The State of Disunion* nevertheless confirms the continued resiliency of a robust and nearly universal set of values and beliefs. These results are directly relevant to the questions that occupy this work. It is therefore important to lay out their findings in some detail.

Noting that the nation's identity is transmitted to coming generations through education, the survey asked respondents whether they felt it important to teach certain beliefs to school-age children. The results are remarkable. Consider these findings:

- 94 percent of Americans "agree that it is important to teach children that 'America's contribution is one of expanding freedom for more and more people' ";
- 92 percent agree that "children should be taught that 'our founders limited the power of government, so government would not intrude too much into the lives of its citizens' ";

- 95 percent agree that "America is the great melting pot";[12]
- 96 percent agree that "[w]ith hard work and perseverance, anyone can succeed in America";
- 95 percent agree that "democracy is only as strong as the virtue of its citizens."[13]

Hunter and Bowman acknowledge that these findings do not contradict concerns about the enormous controversy regarding many educational issues. Nevertheless, they do reveal that despite this contention, many elements of the American public moral consensus continue to enjoy robust and practically unanimous support, support that holds uniform across race, ethnic, religious, and class lines.

The survey also reveals what the authors call "principled support of democracy as a system of government"; 80 percent expressed strong support for our system of government. A similar percentage expressed their belief in political participation; 81 percent said that "they plan[ned] to vote in the 1996 election."[14] Relatedly, the survey found "a fairly high degree of civic-mindedness." It reports that "just under nine out of ten respondents had positive to very positive feelings toward the terms 'community' and 'civic responsibility.'" Nine out of ten also said that they considered the following to be "very important or absolutely essential obligations":

- "treating all people equally regardless of race or ethnic background";
- "reporting a crime that one has witnessed";
- "taking action to help if [one hears] someone screaming or see[s] [someone] being attacked";
- "being civil to others with whom [one might] disagree."[15]

Finally, there is strong support for America's strong tradition of civil religion. Eighty-seven percent of Americans agree that children should be taught that "our nation was founded on Biblical principles" and that from its beginnings America "has had a destiny to teach other nations."[16] It needs be said that in contrast to the points noted above, support here is not quite so ubiquitous. Within this large majority, there is rather dramatic disparity; as religious orthodoxy decreases and education levels rise, levels of affirmation decrease. For example, only 56 percent of so-called social elites believe children should be taught that the country was founded on biblical principles; the number among evangelical Protestants, on the other hand, is 94 percent. Nevertheless,

Americans have always demonstrated a unique commitment to religious faith, and to the civil dimension of that faith, and this survey does nothing to contradict that.

Beyond the dramatic levels of support for these values, beliefs, and virtues, it is also important to note that these results are strikingly similar to the political principles outlined and implied by the Declaration of Independence and the Constitution: i.e., rule of law, democratic government, equality, individual freedom, justice, and a concern for the common welfare. There is also an affirmation that individual freedom brings with it a concomitant demand for self-reliance and personal accountability. This ideal has an economic dimension of course, but it is also behind the near universal commitment to civic participation. While racial and ethnic tensions seem more intractable than ever, Americans are united in their support of the ideal of tolerance and the idea that we find strength through diversity. Finally, for many, American identity continues to include a sense of divine charge, guidance, and judgment. In every instance, then, this generation of Americans holds to the same ideals that have perennially attested to the American identity. Indeed, if one were to look at these results alone, one might likely conclude that America is a stable, well-ordered country in which the public moral consensus is readily transmitted to new generations.[17]

But, of course, the feelings of discontent and worries for the future, as noted above, indicate that there is much more to the story. Hunter and Bowman's findings thus reveal an odd and dramatic disconnect. The authors conclude that "a basic idealism about America and a commitment to work toward the realization of this ideal in public and political life undeniably exist. Even if it is somewhat romantic—even fanciful—in character, the idealism remains strong."[18] Despite the fact that Americans are indeed pessimistic, cynical, and disconnected, they are at least equally united in their affirmation of "the same general idealism in their understanding of America's past and they also, on the whole, hold to the same civic and political obligations and commitment to the political system."[19] How can both of these facts simultaneously be true? Why do we Americans feel so strongly positive about our ideals and so strongly negative about those ideals in practice? For Hunter and Bowman,

[t]here is a counterpoint to what appears to be America's rather blithe consensus of values, ideals, and political commitments.

> In order to make sense of this counterpoint, it is useful to think of American political culture in terms of two distinct dynamics: the ideal and the substantive. The *ideal* of political culture is defined by its mythic vitality—the narratives that constitute its collective memories, the standards by which it measures its relative goodness, its place in the cosmos—its perceived grandeur. The *substance* of political culture is defined, by contrast, by the actual operation of the political system, and more specifically, the effect of the political regime on the people who live within its boundaries.[20]

Thus, the authors of this study argue that while the norms that constitute the American public moral consensus are real and constitutive of our identity as Americans, indeed as real as they have ever been, they have become merely abstract ideals. What makes our generation different is that American citizens now feel that there is a strong and pervasive disconnect between those ideals and their application (or, rather, misapplication) in the concrete, everyday world of American politics. Moreover, the disconnect is not limited to the other guy or to the political leader. Clear differences are also manifested between what Americans say they do (vote, volunteer, etc.), and what Americans *really* do. Similarly, near universal support for civic ideals like tolerance, fair housing, and racial equality does not explain the intransigence of racial and ethnic discrimination. In all these instances, affirmation of a common moral consensus reveals, once again, that talk is cheap. But more to the point, it also shows that Americans live in tension, even, at times, outright conflict, with their own ideals. As numbers expressing faith in central social institutions continue to decline, as voter turnout continues to fall, the tension rises, and that rise likely accounts for much of our contemporary cynicism and disquiet.

It is difficult to imagine that such a state of tension could long sustain itself. We are thus left to wonder how long our ideals can maintain themselves as mere abstractions, and what might happen to our nation were the consensus to collapse altogether. For civil society advocates, as I will show, this disconnect confirms their anxieties and helps to confirm their basic strategy.

So how does a society reestablish the connection between ideals and flesh-and-blood institutions? Hunter and Bowman note that their study supports a very Tocquevillian point: "[A]s one moves to the local community, the sentiment of disaffection begins to change appreciably." For government and a host of other social institutions, "legitimacy increases as that institution moves closer to home."[21] Americans are thus significantly more likely to feel that their local institutions are doing what they are supposed to be doing. They also note that "the more physically distant a region is from the seat of national power, the more distrustful are its inhabitants."[22] The implication of the data is clear: the problem is structural; it relates to the distance (actual and perceived) between individuals and the institutions in question. And, apparently, the way to solve this problem, the way to eliminate the disaffection, is to bridge that distance. That is, move control to local, more accessible levels. When institutions operate at a manageable, face-to-face level, cynicism declines and affirmation rises. If this is true, then the prescription follows readily. In short, Hunter and Bowman's study supports Tocqueville's statements of long ago. "Every citizen of the United States may be said to transfer the concern inspired in him by his little republic into his love of the common motherland."[23] More to the point, the data confirm the contemporary claim that the revitalization of America centers on the revitalization of American civil society.[24]

Here, then, is the far more powerful version of the social capital argument. Civil society needs a set of beliefs to rein it in, to make sure its free and natural operation works to support moral and civic virtue; and that consensus needs civil society to give it content, to make it operative, actualized, and concrete. That means that civil society, the institutions that build interpersonal trust through face-to-face contact, is not sufficient to rebuild a moral society. But the data show that it does not have to be. Civil society merely has to be restored to operative levels so that the abstract set of American ideals can once again be concretized, and thereby rendered operative, and so that the reciprocal relationship between civil society and public moral consensus can be restored. All of this confirms many of the arguments that are closest to the hearts of civil society advocates. For within this dynamic, social capital institutions reveal their indispensable social role.

In families, children begin to learn what it means to treat everyone equally and with fairness. Modeling their parents, children also learn self-reliance, respect for law, property, and authority, and respect for others. Neighborhoods, if they are operating effectively, confirm and strengthen this emerging ethos. They are the environments in which children learn subtle but fairly "thick" sets of social cues and expectations. In short, they help children further acquire the moral foundation upon which democratic life depends. For adults, neighborhoods give us the opportunity to watch each other's kids, to borrow and return lawn equipment, to take a turn organizing the annual block party. Through such apparently mundane and small-time acts is interpersonal trust constructed. Neighborhoods also offer the chance to learn that working together as equals is an effective way to achieve common objectives—hence, one also learns tolerance, moderation, and civility. Finally, many of the same things can be said of churches. First, churches almost invariably strengthen the set of shared values that characterize a neighborhood, because in a church the moral consensus is explicit, very thick, and strongly supported. In social science language, the opportunity costs for disregarding church teachings are often very high indeed. Second, churches afford similar opportunities for social interaction, for building a sense of reciprocity and a sense of common responsibility for the whole.[25]

By fostering face-to-face interactions, these social capital institutions provide the context in which the American public moral consensus is activated and actualized; it is here that the meat is put on the bone. The values of freedom and justice, majority rule, equal rights, and the rule of law, and the virtues of self-reliance and a concern for the common good—all of these are advanced and given content in the institutions of family, church, and neighborhood. What's more, one could extend this argument to any institution of civil society that operates at a face-to-face level. Though they figure less centrally in the contemporary American concept of civil society, one could presume that local civic and political associations would have a similar, and similarly felicitous, effect on the American public moral consensus.

I have no desire to contradict this analysis. Indeed, I believe this argument ably confirms the necessity of the social capital–building institutions within American civil society. However, at the risk of repeating myself, the question is not one of necessity but one of sufficiency. Assume that this argument is wholly correct; does it therefore allow one to assume that no other institutions are necessary for concretizing the American consensus? In particular, does this argument legitimate the decision among civil society advocates to ignore and disparage government and politics? I will argue that the answer to these questions is no.

The American Dilemma

In 1944, Gunnar Myrdal published his seminal work, *An American Dilemma*. Of course, the dilemma to which the title referred was racism, the segregated, often oppressive, and often antagonistic relationship between blacks and whites. In his book, Myrdal argued that for all its longevity and malevolence, racist treatment of African Americans would eventually die out. Why? Myrdal believed that racism would slowly but inexorably decline because it stood in irresolvable conflict with what he called "the American creed." Myrdal meant by this something very similar to the public moral consensus I have outlined. That is, Myrdal was referring to a set of moral propositions that define the American identity. Central among these propositions for Myrdal was the notion of equality—especially equality of opportunity. Because these values were universally assented to, and because they conflicted so directly with the treatment of African Americans in American society, Myrdal argued that the American creed provided civil rights advocates with a ready and formidable weapon. In effect, they were better, or at least more consistent, Americans, and therefore history was on their side.[26]

Many have noted that the civil rights movement revealed the prescience of Myrdal's analysis. But for my purposes, it is worth recalling the point. In a commencement speech at Lincoln University, Martin Luther King Jr. referenced and reinforced Myrdal's work, noting that "America is essentially a dream"; that is, America is defined by its ideals. He then goes on to identify that dream with the central words of the Declaration of Independence. King contends that "very seldom if ever in the history of the world has a sociopolitical document expressed in such profoundly eloquent and unequivocal language the dignity and worth of human personality. The American dream reminds us that every man is heir to the legacy of worthiness."[27]

King was masterful in invoking white Americans' own words against them. During the civil rights struggle, America possessed an active and robust moral consensus, and King and other civil rights activists argued in terms of that consensus to make their case. This strategy, this very Myrdalian demand for consistency, must be regarded as at least one reason for the successes of that movement. Yet none would dispute that the American dilemma remains. As I noted, a series of disturbing recent events, and the widely disparate reactions evoked by them among blacks and whites, does indeed lend credence to the notion that we are and remain, in the words of the title of a book by Ellis Cose, a nation of strangers.[28] Indeed, criticism of our contemporary culture by civil society advocates and others have led many to conclude that in at least one respect, things have gotten worse. For in the thirty years since King's death, many representatives of African Americans and others have abandoned his strategy of appealing to the moral truths that continue to define us all as Americans. In other words, the growth of identity politics; the pursuit of group identity and group goals without concern for the goals and identity of the nation as a whole; the belief that such universal goals are at best merely impossible and at worst a cynical mechanism for exploitation and oppression—all of this continues to undermine and unravel the American body politic.

The issue might be specific, but the point is general. In chapter 1, I showed that civil society advocates see contemporary concerns about partisanship and identity politics as part of a more fundamental social phenomenon—namely, the souring of social relations, the fraying of the social fabric, and the collapse of common values. The problem of a moral and civic decline is thus tied to a decline in moral and civic unity. And if that is true, then the problem of race—and, more broadly, the problem of partisanship and identity politics—is inseparable from the problem of civil and moral renewal. The question of sufficiency is therefore joined precisely here: in short, can the social capital institutions of civil society achieve the mending of this frayed social fabric?

Civil Society and the Disuniting of America

With this question in place, I am ready to return to the analysis of Levi, Cohen, and others. For the issue of whether interpersonal trust translates into trust on a national, society-wide level is most significant, most relevant, when it concerns the issue of interreligious, interethnic, and interracial relations. And when we consider the question of generalized trust with that issue in mind, the viability of the social capital argument becomes impossible to sustain.

Consider, first, that any connection between relations among persons on the one hand and relations among groups on the other is often tenuous, at best. In any of a disturbing host of contemporary examples of the worst kinds of ethnic civil strife, citizens routinely recount their friendship and trust with individual members of the opposite camps. Thus, Israelis trust their children with Palestinian nannies, Bosnian Muslims lived and worked alongside Bosnian Christians, Hutus lived next door to Tutsis, all in ostensible and long-standing harmony. Yet these relationships were not enough to foster universal feelings of transethnic trust. Indeed, in all three cases, they have not even been enough to prevent paroxysms of hatred and violence. Trust of the single other did not alter one's ability to abstract, objectify, and thereby continue to despise the other as a group. Relatedly, consider the hackneyed response of the bigot: "Don't get me wrong, some of my best friends are. . . ." It is surely likely that, at least in some instances, this statement is true. Yet this fact fails rankly to mitigate significantly a series of sweeping, objectively false, and socially disastrous judgments about an entire group of individuals.

In each one of these examples, then, Cohen's worries are strongly reinforced. "The argument that repeated interaction games within small-scale face-to-face groups of strategic calculators can generate universal norms of law-abidingness or reciprocity is unconvincing."[29] There is no reason to assume that the production of social capital will foster some form of generalized, nationwide trust. Cohen goes on to note that while capital, i.e., money, is fungible, social capital is not. "Capital accumulated in one context can of course be invested in another place. . . . Interpersonal trust, on the other hand, is by definition specific and contextual."[30] Thus, the unauthorized assumption behind the concept of social capital stems from the inapt use of the term "capital." And if that term is stretched to focus less on productive efficiency and more on restoring a broader sense of community, the problematic nature of that assumption becomes all the more apparent.

With respect to the issue at hand, then, the point is that affective, informal, long-term, and face-to-face forms of interaction between individual members of differing racial and ethnic groups do not necessarily result in the amelioration of tensions between those groups, or even between those individuals and different representatives from the other groups. There is, therefore, no reason to assume that the day-to-day operation of the institutions of American civil society will help ameliorate deteriorating relations among racial and ethnic groups or that it will help to restore a feeling of common obligation and common purpose.

"Thickness" and the Problem of Homogeneity

But there is much more to be said. For we must consider the actual operation of American civil society as it relates to questions of racial, ethnic, and religious interaction. The fact is that most social capital institutions in America operate within a thick set of moral and cultural presuppositions. And more often than not, such thickness means that they are constituted around one cultural subgroup. In a free society, individuals select the groups to which they belong, and when they are afforded that choice, most Americans prefer to associate with others who share the same set of cultural expectations. We are, in Tocqueville's words, inclined to "establish . . . little private societies held together by similar conditions, habits, and mores."[31] To be sure, the sources of these similarities are themselves diverse. As I will note, some forms of identity cross lines of class, ethnicity, and race. Nevertheless, the fact remains that human community is a hard thing, and the social ease that comes from knowing that members share a set of common expectations, norms, and values is grease for the wheels. We may decry the fact, but it is simply the case that families, churches, and neighborhoods, like all forms of civil society in America, are more likely to be constituted *by* racial, ethnic, and religious identity than they are to offer opportunities for interaction *across* such identities.

What is more, there is, to say the least, compelling evidence that institutions like families, churches, and neighborhoods work best, that is, operate in a way that most effectively furthers the objectives of civil society advocates, when they are so oriented—that is, when they possess a constricted, even exclusive identity, and when they are ethnically, racially, or culturally homogeneous. If that is true, then the goal of a restored universal ethic recedes even further, and the claim that social capital institutions are commensurate to the goal of civic and moral renewal is rendered all the more problematic.

In chapter 1, I referenced a recent and celebrated study about the effectiveness of neighborhoods in Chicago. The study concluded that "there are lower rates of violence in urban neighborhoods with a strong sense of community and values."[32] The conclusions of this study are likely music to the ears of the civil society advocate. If you want a better-ordered society, you start with better-ordered neighborhoods. And well-ordered neighborhoods are not a product of police patrols, zoning changes, or other forms of governmental interference; rather they are the product of interpersonal trust—trust built up through informal face-to-face interaction.[33]

But those same advocates are less likely to notice that the study's conclusion also returns us to David Popenoe's uneasy call for the enforcement of "community moral standards" and the protection of "homogeneous neighborhoods." For, all things being equal, if neighborhoods are stronger when there is a sense of common values and objectives, then it simply follows that neighborhoods that are ethnically homogeneous would be better able to create that common sense. Ethnicity implies and indeed cannot be understood apart from a distinctive culture, and culture invariably involves a set of values, norms, beliefs, and expectations. For those ethnic groups that are identified by, or closely associated with a common *religious* heritage (Italians, Mexicans, Jews, Sikhs, etc.), one could reasonably presume that the vitality of those community moral standards would be all the stronger.

To be sure, neither Popenoe nor the Sampson, Raudenbush, and Earls study[34] want to maintain that such cohesion is possible only in ethnically or religiously homogeneous neighborhoods. As I noted previously, Popenoe says that he is referring to "family-focused enclaves of people who share similar values and have a similar lifestyle." Similarly, the Sampson study noted that Chicago's Hyde Park (a high-income, well-educated, mixed-race area around the University of Chicago known for used book stores and liberal politics) is presented as one example of a successful neighborhood.[35] Yet it is equally important to note that the Sampson study showed that in neighborhoods with relatively high levels of violence, "the population was unstable and racially and ethnically mixed."[36] Thus, the study supports the presumption that (again, all things being equal) neighborhoods in which a shared moral consensus is less likely to obtain, and where whatever moral consensus does obtain is likely to be thinner, will be at a comparative disadvantage in preserving the peace. The disadvantage neighborhoods like these have in cultivating trust and solidarity is surely all that much greater.

It is also worth noting that the issues at stake here should not be associated merely with white ethnic groups. Indeed, racial, ethnic, or religious cohesion can be an extremely effective means for overcoming obstacles of income, education, and prejudice. Glenn Loury has written that "just about every effective strategy of which I am aware that is being carried out in poor black communities to combat the scourges of violence, low academic achievement, and family instability builds positively on . . . ethnic consciousness."[37] Just as important, the successful assimilation of virtually every ethnic group into American society began with a similar sense of common purpose, identity, and obligation. And those strategies are no less operative in contemporary American society.

If this is all true, the civil society argument appears to hold, and to hold universally. Growing up in a fairly cohesive, even insular, cultural environment is a singularly effective means by which an individual might develop into a whole, healthy, and morally grounded adult; it is thus an indispensable foundation for creating a healthy society. And there is, to say the least, reason to believe that ethnic, cultural, or religious homogeneity is a singularly effective means for bringing that about. But if this is so, then how is it that the development of this distinctive, even exclusive, moral identity ameliorates the racial and ethnic tension in this nation?

The operations of churches raise many of the same questions. Indeed, if anything, the issue of homogeneity is perhaps even more stark with regards to religious institutions. For while congregations are less likely than a generation past to represent one predominant ethnic group, they remain among America's most racially segregated institutions. It is worth quoting Loury again: "Racially mixed congregations are so rare that they make front-page news."[38] More often than not, religious forms of civil society operate in the context of some form of cultural, ethnic, and racial homogeneity. What's more, even when integration does exist within a congregation, it is often limited to the church rolls. That is, even among congregations whose members represent more than one ethnic or racial group (in large urban Roman Catholic parishes, for example) church leaders often struggle mightily to transcend those divides in worship and social activities. In other words, in those very activities that ostensibly produce social capital, de facto segregation remains. Finally, it also must be said that churches that strive to achieve real integration sometimes find that their religious identity thins out as a result. In one study of a forthrightly integrated church in Chicago, the researchers noted that "[m]ore than one member we talked to stated that they were 'not very religious.' One staff minister suggested that beyond a general belief in Christianity, there was probably little faith agreement among members."[39] The quest for integration often requires the winnowing down of one's cultural commitments, and that, in turn, sometimes leads to a decline in religious commitment.

There are, of course, exceptions. In the Chicago area, I have talked to several evangelical Christian churches that work hard to build genuine integration. Similarly, the Promise Keepers, an important (if perhaps waning) expression of contemporary religious civil society, are expressly committed to racial reconciliation. But while these associations do not restrict themselves to some form of racial or ethnic homogeneity, they operate according to a transracial conception that is parochial in another way. Evangelical Christianity is premised on the belief that Christian commitments are distinctive and separate Christians off from the rest of society; Christians are called to be in the world, but not of it. Thus, the very features that enable these religious communities to overcome the comfort of cultural homogeneity rests on a strong and unique set of beliefs that is similarly exclusive. If I am a Muslim or a Jew, for example, I may applaud the moral ethos of evangelical Christianity, but it is highly unlikely that I would be able to share in its claims. In any case, these examples are and remain exceptions, despite the fact that most religions (and perhaps especially Christianity) have strong internal strictures against segregation. I believe one is therefore constrained to conclude that there is, in Nancy Ammerman's words, "a natural particularity of congregations," an innate insularity that lends itself to thickness and thus to homogeneity, and is overcome only with difficulty if it is overcome at all.[40]

What of other forms of civil society?[41] The interactions that take place in the context of a youth soccer league or PTA meeting might be less affective and less thick than those that take place in churches, families, or neighborhoods, but their normal operation certainly produces its own form of social capital. Just as certainly, however, these associations are often neighborhood institutions, conforming to neighborhood boundaries. Thus, many (if not most) do not significantly increase the opportunity for building social capital across ethnic and racial lines.[42] On the other hand, some forms of civil association do indeed transcend such boundaries. Some of these organizations are dedicated to building interracial, interethnic, and interreligious institutions of civil society. One is reluctant to say anything that might appear to disparage such efforts, but it is a fact that many of these organizations are artificial and many remain that way. The Human Relations Foundation of Chicago developed the idea of holding dinners in which members of various ethnic and racial groups had a chance to interact in a casual face-to-face setting. The foundation rightly celebrates the fact that in April of 1994, 920 people took part in these dinners. But even the federation acknowledges that it is "struggling with how to create discussions that move beyond the artificial, since many participants never interact outside of dinners."[43] Given that social capital is a product of informal interactions that take place over a long period of time, one must question the transformational power of these efforts.

My point, then, is that if one is eager to tout social capital institutions as the primary means by which our society can reconstruct a moral and civic culture, then one must confront the problem of parochialism. In contrast to the hopes of civil society advocates, the sense of common purpose and consensus that emerges from social capital institutions is particularistic. Indeed, it is quite possible that the better an institution is at building social capital, the more particularistic, the more homogeneous, it is. Social capital is a good thing, even a necessary thing. Its production certainly helps one to develop a strong sense of identity, values, and virtues, and all of this would appear to be prerequisite to furthering a universal, transracial harmony. But why should one assume that it is a sufficient means for addressing one of the central problems that motivates the civil society movement?

Civil Society: Good and Bad

Finally, anyone hoping to save this argument must also attend to a glaring if often unacknowledged problem: many of the very cultural conditions that civil society advocates decry, and in particular the problem of an unraveling social fabric, are themselves manifested and exacerbated by examples of civil society. As many have mentioned, Timothy McVeigh frequently went bowling with friends. Can one but assume that this association fostered a great deal of interpersonal trust and solidarity between him and his cohorts, even as it nurtured his most vile antisocial instincts? The Michigan Militia, the Nation of Islam, skinheads: these are all forms of civil society. So, too, are a host of political associations that practice a more or less ardent form of identity politics. But just as certainly, these examples do not foster a more unified, more moral society. There are a growing number of gated neighborhood associations that ably reflect the call for a "new localism" but are organized around a barely hidden segregationist agenda. There are ever more Christian groups who have judged the culture at large so corrupt as to require their opting out. They live, play, educate their young—separately. In all these instances, the dynamic contemporary expression of civil society not only does not alleviate our growing discord and dissension, it furthers them.

It is routine for civil society advocates to acknowledge these "bad" or counterproductive examples of civil society. According to the goals of the movement, there are, all would admit, bad churches, bad neighborhoods, and bad families. Further, they admit that a growth in these kinds of institutions would not be a good thing for society. But they make little effort to account for such institutions: to explain why they are bad, and how it is that a restoration of civil society will not automatically or even predominantly result in the further proliferation of such examples. The civil society movement is largely convinced that more civil society means more trust, more solidarity, and ultimately moral and civic unity. But without such an account, that belief is romantic and unpersuasive.

Nancy Rosenblum's prodigious work, *Membership and Morals*, argues that distinguishing between good and bad forms of civil society is a hopeless enterprise. She maintains that the moral uses of pluralism are myriad, and cannot be constrained or steered according to the needs of the greater society. Nervous political theorists conjure up the idea that society needs the institutions of civil society to nurture and cultivate democratic virtues, and that when they do not, they should be compelled to do so. Rosenblum, in terms to which I assent, calls this belief a "liberal expectancy"; and she argues that it is both psychologically unsophisticated and politically illiberal. It is politically illiberal because civil society is a take-it-or-leave-it proposition. There are, to be sure, weeds along with the flowers, but anything beyond the most minimal and principled efforts at cultivation will mean the death of the whole garden. It is psychologically unsophisticated because distinguishing between good and bad forms of civil society is not so simple. Even the most noxious weeds are not without their felicitous effects. Even the militias and religious cults, for example, can "serve the purpose of containment" and they can act as "safety valves" for individuals who would otherwise probably not have them.[44]

There is much with which I agree in Rosenblum's argument. Indeed, the belief in "liberal expectancy," or something very similar, is precisely what I am taking issue with here. I also generally accept her well-argued point that even bad forms of civil society are not always all bad. But while perhaps it would be more accurate to say that there are better and worse forms of civil society, the point remains that some forms of civil society are noxious (Rosenblum certainly does not dispute this) and their operation largely undermines the efforts to reconstruct a more moral order; other forms of civic society abet those efforts. For a society concerned that it is losing its sense of the civic, this cannot be a trivial distinction. And therefore, neither is the effort to offer the best account for it.

For his part, Putnam has tried to explain the difference. Drawing on his experience with the Mafia in Italy, he notes that bad forms of civil society often maintain a hierarchical organizational form. Putnam argues that this form severely undermines the ability of these groups to produce social capital; bad civil society is thus often associated with undemocratic groups.[45] But if social capital means what Putnam says it means, namely, the development of interpersonal trust and solidarity, then the claim that these institutions are less effective does not stand up. Indeed, it is just as possible that the authority structures within institutions like these—the Mafia, street gangs, or the Catholic Church—foster a *higher* degree of group commitment. In any event, it is clear enough that the distinction does not solve the problem. Assume for a moment that we limit the question to the social capital institutions of neighborhood, church, and family. Surely one can posit family or neighborhood interactions that meet every external criterion that Putnam and others would want to maintain, yet inculcate a very similar set of antisocial norms.

I contend that here, too, the better account is found in Hegel and Tocqueville. For the question of why some examples of civil society are good and some are bad is related to the question of unity and particularity. And the answer is determined not by the internal structure of the organization but by its principles: that is, whether or not the institution in question operates within and thereby affirms the American public moral consensus. From the standpoint of social capital production, institutions of civil society can be as thick and as homogeneous as they choose to be, provided that their thickness is not in conflict with the broad, capacious, but very fundamental terms of what it means, morally, to be an American. If a given institution operates contrary to that consensus, then it is, on balance, a counterproductive form of civil society.[46]

Indeed, if civil society advocates are correct, this is precisely what American neighborhoods used to do—namely, operate within the framework of the American public moral consensus. It is a historical fact that in our nation's past, almost all American neighborhoods reflected just this sort of thickness, just this sort of ethnic and religious homogeneity. In Robert Ezra Park's famous words, these "natural" neighborhoods constituted a "mosaic of little social worlds which touch but do not interpenetrate."[47] These neighborhoods were noted for ethnic homogeneity. Strong lines of demarcation separated these neighborhoods, and they were often crossed only with impunity. What is more, churches and other forms of civil society (PTAs, fraternal associations, etc.) likely reinforced this strong ethnic and cultural heritage. To be sure, that consensus was a racially constricted conception, even a racist one. But it is also the case that American neighborhoods in previous generations were less prone to many of the unhappy circumstances contemporary Americans decry.[48] Every one of the neighborhoods Alan Ehrenhalt describes (in the Chicago of the 1950s) displayed what he calls in the subtitle to his book "the forgotten virtues of community."

It is because of this reasoning that the civil society movement wants to restore these vibrant, more communal neighborhoods. Now while there is no basis to conclude a causal relationship (the reasons for changing neighborhood life are numerous and complex), I am willing to concede the idea that in generations past, most neighborhoods and churches were, strictly speaking, good forms of civil society: that is, they affirmed and thereby inculcated a universal moral consensus despite the fact that they were segregated.[49] But if the degree of segregation has not changed significantly, then how is it that these institutions were, in generations past, able to inculcate a shared moral consensus despite strong exclusivity?[50]

The most significant difference between our generation and those past is not found in the racial makeup of American civil society. Rather, the difference is that in those generations past, there was, to use Hunter and Bowman's terms, no significant disconnect between the ideals of the American public moral consensus and their substance. Ehrenhalt also recounts the fact that in the social world of the 1950s, there was deep and widespread respect for authority and for public institutions. Thus, local, state, and federal government, the press, public and parochial schools, the corporate world, the military, and a strong sense of civil religion all provided a common fabric, as it were, within which ethnically homogeneous neighborhoods functioned. In our generation, on the other hand, the institutions that concretize and actualize the American public moral consensus—in particular, the Congress, the presidency, and the press—have all lost significant respect. As a result, the underlying agreement no longer has the power that it once did to direct and constrain the day-to-day operation of American civil society. In generations past, civil society and the American public moral consensus operated in partnership: supporting each other in a balance of plurality and consensus. It is apparent to all that both sides of that partnership have decayed greatly. But if that is so, then the restoration of one half of the partnership will not be sufficient to ensure a revitalized American society.

This hypothesis offers a better account of the argument between Putnam and his critics. For it allows that the question of whether or not American civil society is in trouble does not turn on mere numbers, or even on questions of vitality. Rather, the difference between social capital institutions in our generation and those of generations past centers on their relationship with the broader American public moral consensus. Recall Cohen's argument about the fungibility of social capital. If this account is correct—if, in generations past, the institutions of American civil society operated within the parameters of the broader moral consensus—then social capital was more fungible than it is now. Indeed, one might say that social capital used to be a harder form of currency—in the 1940s and 1950s, one could expect that the trust and solidarity produced within groups was exchangeable for a national form of trust and solidarity. In the contemporary context, America may well produce just as much social capital, but the currency appears to be growing ever more soft—viable, exchangeable, only within the group's ostensible borders, bringing ever less value in exchange for a national currency.

Of course, this account begs the question: what accounts for the collapse of social capital? More specifically, why is it that Americans have lost faith in their social institutions? This is a critical issue, which I will take up in chapter 11. But for now, my conclusion is more specific: I am content to show that the strategy of attending to the health of American civil society as a means of restoring the moral fabric of American society is inherently inadequate. Indeed, the very "thickness" that makes social capital institutions so powerful, so felicitous in terms of building a moral, stable, and secure individual, as well as solidarity and trust between individuals, makes them inherently unable, on their own, to ensure the maintenance of a transethnic, transcultural, transracial moral agreement. The task of restoring our moral and civic well-being will require that we attend to both sides of that partnership. And that means that we must attend to those social institutions that are universal in their purview and domain.

There are surely other examples that help to demonstrate the insufficiency of social capital institutions. Social problems associated with the environment and the economy often transcend local domains, and thus they cannot be adequately dealt with within the confines of social capital institutions. Indeed, here too local or class-based solidarity may gravitate against responsible and even viable solutions, let alone solutions that build solidarity and trust across boundaries. I do not want to speculate further on these matters. For I offer these specific conclusions about the fungibility of social capital only to make a general and rather Hegelian point. Ultimately, the issue of thickness and homogeneity reveals the problem that is elemental to the civil society movement. Even at its most universal, civil society is, and in some sense must always remain, particular. And particular institutions cannot give adequate content to principles that are universal. If trust is to transcend neighborhood and congregational lines, it requires a commitment to a specific conception of fairness and justice that is practically universal and that surely transcends the insular ethos of any one homogeneous community. Civil society can reinforce such a conception, but it cannot build or restore one. A fortiori, it cannot do so single-handedly. The American public moral consensus requires more than the social capital institutions of civil society to give it form and content: moral renewal requires institutions that articulate the American consensus in universal, i.e., national, ways.

A restored, operative, public moral consensus would effectively set limits on American civil society by outlining and actualizing a universal and hence very thin set of goals and beliefs within which every such institution should operate. That is, whatever else such institutions seek to achieve, they ought to affirm democracy, justice, equality, fairness, tolerance, and the like. So constituted, a public moral consensus condemns and thus undermines racist or otherwise discriminatory forms of social capital, and increases the likelihood that social capital institutions will operate in a manner that advances moral and civic renewal. It also outlines one hopeful strategy for addressing the realities of American society and, perhaps, the exigencies of social capital institutions, while simultaneously attending to larger objectives regarding the American dilemma. In the next three chapters, I turn to the institutions that express this universal dimension: the institutions of politics. But first, I want to address another aspect of the argument for sufficiency.

The Experience of Solidarity

The notion that the revival of certain essential social institutions advances a more moral society is central to the contemporary concept. But there is more to the contemporary concept than the exchangeability of social capital. As I have argued, the civil society movement calls for a reconsideration of the relationship between religion and the American public order. Advocates therefore claim that civil religion affords universality in a way that preserves the inconsequence of government. In addition, one could argue that the movement's animosity toward the state itself provides the unity whereby the problem of sufficiency can be solved. In both instances, these alternative strategies recall the experience of the Solidarity movement. A comparison is therefore in order.

American civil society advocates, like their Polish counterparts, want to restore civic and moral unity through the institutions of civil society. And the experience in Poland, so the argument goes, shows that it can be done: pluralistic institutions, able to disencumber themselves from the long reach of the state, can build a unified, powerful social movement. This unity was made possible by the enmity Poles felt toward the state on the one hand and the strong and unifying connection between religion and culture in Poland on the other. We have a similar, if less dire, set of problems, a similar connection between religion and culture, and a similar distaste for the state. Therefore, there is no reason to presume that their success cannot be duplicated here.

I will argue that the analogy breaks down. In neither instance does the experience of Solidarity support the argument for sufficiency. Nor, I will argue, does it make sense to pursue either strategy. I will begin with an argument about the state and then turn to the issue of American civil religion.

Social Unity and Animosity toward the State

As I showed in chapter 6, the use of the term "civil society" predates the Solidarity movement. But as the very progenitors of that movement understood, the objectives of social revolution could not be achieved through pluralistic institutions alone, or at least not in the sense in which that term is applied in liberal-democratic societies. Of course, there have been cohesive and organized social movements throughout American history, many of which have altered the most basic features of American life, but there is nothing in our national experience that approaches the scale of Solidarity. The idea that American civil society might achieve a movement of this scale is unlikely at best, and deeply misapprehends the elemental nature of democratic government.

The reason centers on the fact that Solidarity was organized and unified by its members' common enemy, the state. Whatever the differences among the various elements within Solidarity, all of these paled into insignificance next to their feelings toward the state. The Communist government was regarded as an outside oppressor, the instrument of a foreign power. What is more, the state possessed all the tools of oppression. The police, the courts, the army, the media—all of these mechanisms of social control were in the hands of the enemy. Therefore, any lack of unity would have meant certain defeat.

Thus, to the extent that Solidarity succeeded, it did so precisely because it was not a movement of civil society at all. While Solidarity was surely independent of the state, it was not in any meaningful sense a collection of pluralistic and independent groups and associations. Solidarity was able to stand against the state because it was a massive social movement orchestrated under the rubric of one extremely cohesive, well-organized, and well-nigh monolithic organization. Indeed, Solidarity is the story of one trade union representing one group of workers in one shipyard growing to represent ultimately the entire nation. As I have noted, the fact that Solidarity quickly disintegrated into a disparate collection of competing groups and interests reveals just how important the state was in effecting a movement of startling unity and national proportions.

The American movement surely echoes a feeling of distaste, if not outright animosity, toward the state. As I have shown, advocates routinely regard the state as, to say the least, one of the agents responsible for the sorry condition of American civil society. Further, the movement is characterized by the belief that if American society is to recover, the state is almost irrelevant to that exercise. Yet while the American movement echoes the feeling that the state is the enemy, it cannot sustain it.

In the first place, American civil society requires the state. In a liberal-democratic society, civil society refers to a collection of otherwise unconnected groups and associations, formed through the free association of individuals with common interests and objectives. This conception is possible only in a society in which certain rights, most relevantly the rights of association and assembly, are preserved. And that preservation is the responsibility of the state. Thus, civil society cannot achieve anything, indeed, it cannot exist at all, if the state does not preserve the political liberties that make it possible. Far from being irrelevant to the goals of the civil society movement, the state is one of its few indispensable prerequisites. On the other hand, if the state does indeed fulfill this responsibility, it is unlikely that civil society will ever be anything but a collection of otherwise disconnected groups and associations. In other words, the very fact that the Polish state thwarted free expression and free association explains the univocal nature of Polish civil society. If rights are preserved, no such cohesion can be expected. In radical contrast to Polish society, the state is indispensable to the objectives of the civil society movement, and that very fact likewise undermines the possibility of a unified social movement.

Most fundamental, however, is the difference between the Polish and American states. Whatever the compromises, in the latter instance, the people still rule. Militia members may revile, and most Americans may well regret, the tragic and reprehensible events at Waco and Ruby Ridge, but to offer rhetorical comparisons between the federal government and the Polish state under Communism is an abuse of language and an ardent disregard for the facts. For all the rhetoric, the American state is not the enemy. Indeed, in any state, the condition of the government, for good or ill, is the responsibility of the sovereign. To be sure, the phrase "government by the people" may well overstate the matter. The people's sovereignty is often attenuated and always indirect.[51] But never does it lie elsewhere. And because it does not, to damn the state is to damn ourselves.[52] If the state is operating in a manner inconsistent with the will of the people, it is their prerogative, and their duty, to change it. It is therefore imperative to conclude that any perceived crisis regarding the state is, in fact, better understood as a crisis of citizenship. The analogy thus breaks down, and, as a result, so too does the claim that civil society alone is able to achieve civic and moral renewal.

Solidarity and Civil Religion

Despite sometimes disturbing manifestations of animosity, civil society advocates would almost certainly acknowledge that the actions of the state do not warrant rebellion, nor do those advocates hold out any hope for unifying the disparate, nay, cacophonous expressions of American civil society. But there is far more contention surrounding the issue of religion. Here, too, the experience of Solidarity is ostensibly instructive. For Poles were able to achieve the unachievable because, the argument goes, their culture was undergirded by a shared foundation of religious belief. This gave a sense of meaning and purpose to their struggle, and that made unity and revolution possible. While our comparable sense of religious unity is moribund, beaten back by a virulent secularist attack, it, too, has a long and storied history. The two Great Awakenings, the abolitionist movement, Prohibition, the civil rights struggle—all of these national events are inconceivable without the impetus and driving force of religiously motivated citizens drawing on the religious roots of the American consensus. Properly restored, American civil religion offers the means by which moral renewal can take place wholly within the cultural realm. As Tocqueville saw, while churches may be parochial, religion need not be. Indeed, civil religion is universal. Religion—that is, the religious institutions that make up such a large and meaningful part of American civil society—can once again foster a cultural and moral common denominator.

This argument references the discussion outlined above, for it is self-evident that religious institutions are more than mechanisms for building social capital. Religious associations do indeed build social capital: fellowship hours, Bible study, and the like. But they are, more fundamentally, houses of worship—places where people unite around a shared understanding of the way the world is and of how human life ought to be led. It is a common refrain among civil society advocates that the moral and civic decline of American society results from a decline in American civil religion. To bring back the former, therefore, requires a revitalization, in one form or another, of the latter. I want to argue, to the contrary, that prospects for such revitalization are wholly dubious.

Among historians and sociologists of religion, the argument about the past and present condition of American civil religion is hotly debated. For my purposes, it is enough to acknowledge simply that whatever it was in the past, it is not what it used to be. The former days of McGuffey's readers and Sunday school parades, of public admonitions against greed, drunkenness, and other forms of sinfulness, all of this appears long gone.[53] Religion is also dramatically less associated with the fields of education, social work, and health care than it once was. Whatever has happened to individual levels of religious commitment, the public role and status of religion had declined precipitously, and with it, the prospects for a renewed civil religion.

A sharp and recent rise in religious pluralism has likewise compromised the likelihood of a new religious consensus. Immigration during the last thirty years or so rivals that in any period in our nation's history as far as entry of new religious groups is concerned. In the 1950s, Will Herberg's *Protestant Catholic Jew* outlined the terms of the civil religion consensus. At the end of the 1990s, Muslims nearly outnumber Jews, and there is significant dissension within Catholic and Protestant communities. The numbers of self-declared secularists and agnostics continue to grow, as do Buddhists and others for whom the notion of a deity, if it exists at all, does not conform to the Heavenly Father portrayed in Western traditions. These are the daunting social terms within which a new civil religion would have to be constructed, and I am not aware of the civil religion advocate who can show that he or she is prepared to do so. Finally, one should note that Americans appear unwilling to afford them the opportunity. In *One Nation After All* Alan Wolfe concludes that "there is not much support out there in middle-class America . . . for the notion that religion can play an official and didactic role in guiding public morality."[54]

The more salient issue, of course, is whether civil society advocates and others should try to bring it back. In a previous work, I have a lot to say about the issue of whether religious claims should be explicitly included within the American moral consensus.[55] I will not rehash that debate here. But as I have shown, both Hegel and Tocqueville argue for something very similar to those calling for a restored American civil religion, and therefore, it is legitimate and indeed necessary to frame an answer in these terms.

Again, for Tocqueville, the success of the American polity rests on its ability to inculcate a moral consensus despite the incipient condition of American pluralism. As I noted, Tocqueville is struck that for all the alleged differences between denominations, "all preach the same morality in the name of God."[56] The civil religion makes a common denominator out of all religions, and thus all religious citizens are able to connect their religious faith with their affirmation of the civic order. Many within the public debate argue that something like this common denominator remains a sine qua non for a well-ordered society. They therefore advocate a restoration, and perhaps a reformulation, of American civil religion.

But surely this is not as simple a matter as many advocates of this position make it out to be. I am inclined to believe that even in Tocqueville's time, the idea that there was some kind of underlying unanimity among religious adherents was at best overstated. But regardless, the social features of our own time make any question of restoration deeply problematic. I have shown that for Tocqueville, the viability of American civil religion depended on unique features of American family life. Specifically, American civil religion is preserved and transmitted by women, for "it is women who shape mores."[57] But Tocqueville is equally clear that such an ability requires that American women be excluded from the worldly world of commerce and self-interest. Instead, they are conditioned, by a variety of cultural forces, to focus their efforts and interests wholly on hearth, home, and raising the children. Civil religion in America is possible because of a radical sexual division of labor that leaves women at home. Here at the end of the twentieth century, almost all would agree that this understanding of the role of women is, at best, morally problematic; speaking merely pragmatically, it also appears to be gone forever. Yet Tocqueville is quite convinced that you can't have one without the other.[58] Therefore, if advocates want to restore civil religion in this very different climate, and, in particular, if they appeal to Tocqueville to justify and explicate this objective, then it is their burden to say how such a thing would be possible and legitimate.

The other issue is Hegelian. Hegel, too, supported the idea of a civil religion. In words that are dramatically similar to Tocqueville, he argues that "religion is an integrating factor in the state, implanting a sense of unity in the depths of men's minds."[59] Indeed, Hegel was so convinced of the value of religious belief that he went on to say that "the state should even require all its citizens to belong to a church."[60] Now the right to free exercise would appear to preclude this option in the American context, but here again, things are not so simple. Hegel's strictures illustrate the very American point that the line between cultural and legal proscription regarding matters of civil religion is fuzzy at best. In our nation's history, that line has often been crossed. McGuffey's readers, for example, surely served to inculcate a strong sense of American civil religion. Yet its celebration of the Protestant roots of the American experiment fostered a feeling among Catholics and others that their Americanness was being disparaged. The Catholic parochial school movement is the result of this assessment.

Here, too, the Solidarity experience is instructive. Adam Michnik has noted that one of the chief reasons for Solidarity's success is that the nation was united around one religious belief system—a systematic, unifying, and oppositional belief system. Yet in the aftermath of Solidarity's success, this critical benefit has became a source of concern. Even before the post-Solidarity era, Michnik worried about the "Iranization" of Poland: a culture that is tied to a specific faith can easily lead to the more or less overt, more or less onerous, oppression of religious dissenters.[61] To be sure, I believe that many of the fears of the left regarding religious expression and language are overstated. Nevertheless, many Americans professing religious views outline a conception of American public policy that resonates exactly with Michnik's fears. Bills seeking to restore school prayer, for example, illustrate the insurmountable difficulties associated with maintaining a strong religious consensus in the culture and not having that consensus spill over into political unfairness.[62] Again, I have said more about this elsewhere; I outline these issues merely to show that the questions associated with a vibrant civil religion are formidable and by no means trivial. I, for one, would have to be convinced that American civil religion could be restored to the level necessary for it to be operative without relegating all nonbelievers to a form of second-class citizenship.

Now the argument against civil religion is an argument against religion as a universal. But nothing in that argument should be construed as an argument against religion or religious revival in the particular. Religious communities are almost invariably effective producers of social capital. They also instill a concern for virtue and service that no secular ethos can hope to match. Religion is by definition deeper and more powerful. Anyone concerned about the condition of the American polity must come to terms with the fact. As John DiIulio rightly insists, "When you look at the gutbucket stuff, the everyday, in-your-face working with troubled kids in these neighborhoods across the country . . . almost all of it is being done by people who are churched."[63] But the very power of the churches comes from their thickness, from the specific nature of the unifying claims. Thus, as with neighborhoods, the same features that make religions necessary (or at least felicitous) render then insufficient. Religion cannot concretize and actualize the American public moral consensus in a way that is incumbent upon and accessible to all.

Among those seeking to advance the religion-culture solution, the rebuttal is always to turn to the Promise Keepers. Indeed, in light of the concerns outlined above about race relations, Promise Keepers are particularly important, for one of the association's seven tenets is the healing of racial divisions. Thus, civil society advocates might well counter that here is an institution that builds social capital but that also transcends racial and ethnic boundaries. This might well be so. But there are also reasons for doubt. In general terms, the larger an association gets, the more likely it is that it will transcend racial and ethnic boundaries, but the less likely it is to foster social capital. This is Putnam's point about the Environmental Defense Fund. Even for an organization like Promise Keepers, the ability of stadium-sized rallies to generate social capital (that is, feelings of trust and solidarity) must be regarded an open question. The length of the association, for one thing, is nothing like that between church members or neighbors. Indeed, the absence of such features may help to account for the fact that the phenomenal growth of this group appears to have ebbed.[64]

But let us stipulate that Promise Keepers is an example of a large association that builds trust and feelings of solidarity among members and thus among races and ethnicities. Even if one grants the point, the argument continues to hold. Promise Keepers is able to transcend ethnic and racial divides because it is premised on a robust form of evangelical Christianity; it is a "Bible-centered" ministry. As a result, the consensus it engenders is thick. It may therefore be more likely to cause genuine and valuable change in the behavior of men, but for that very reason, the consensus it engenders is limited to those who share that specific set of religious claims. An American society that fosters organizations like Promise Keepers will be better able to address the American dilemma than one that does not, but it cannot foster a universal moral consensus.[65] Religion, even religious revival, is one thing; the revival of an American civil religion is something else again. The presumptive success of Promise Keepers, even on matters of racial reconciliation, does nothing to compromise that point.

Conclusion

After this survey, we are left with a rather startling conclusion: the civil society movement in America centers on a claim that is at odds with its own wellsprings. Civil society advocates want civic and moral renewal. Yet this review shows that civil society as it is currently understood—that is, as institutions that interact only minimally with the state and serve primarily to inculcate social capital—cannot achieve that goal. Civil society operates at a parochial level—a level that, as Hegel argued, does not and cannot move to a level of universality. Thus, the very features that make civil society necessary also make it insufficient. The intimate, face-to-face, and ethically thick features of social capital institutions also make them parochial, bound to an ethnically, culturally, or metaphysically discrete set of values, beliefs, and expectations. With regard to religion, there is thus an interesting and important note of commonality here. For the idea that all specific forms of religion will lend support to the maintenance of a national civil religion is of a piece with the idea that all forms of civil society will lend support to a unified and unifying moral consensus. Both claims are premised on the romantic and unsupported belief that particularity leads to unity. And both claims are rendered necessary by an unreasonable animus toward politics and the state.

As individuals move out of social capital–building institutions, they almost invariably move beyond the interpersonal trust that these institutions create. But they also move into a dimension that activates the public moral consensus in way that social capital institutions cannot.

The goals of the civil society movement therefore require that advocates attend to all the social mechanisms by which the American public moral consensus is inculcated and concretized. In order to do so, they must first acknowledge that social capital is a necessary but not sufficient aspect of moral and social renewal. Second, they must accept that the primary mechanism by and through which this national public consensus is inculcated is politics.

Part Four

The Necessity of Politics

Medium Party Political Associations

The civil society movement has abandoned politics for at least two reasons. First, advocates of the movement judge that governmental actions, and the actions of large political organizations, are at best irrelevant to, and, at worst, inimical to, the production of social capital. Big government kills social capital institutions. Second, and relatedly, civil society advocates argue that they have been driven to reject politics because of the sorry condition, and unhappy performance, of this arena. Contemporary politics is all too often characterized by gridlock, petty partisan bickering, and the unseemly influence of money. When legislation finally is passed, it often fails to ameliorate and, in many cases, only exacerbates our society's most serious problems. In the face of both these reasons, it only makes sense to look elsewhere for solutions.

To some degree, at least, I am willing to grant these judgments. Interpersonal trust and feelings of solidarity do appear to be created largely through face-to-face institutions. And the expansion of the welfare state over the course of this century does appear to have undermined some of these very institutions. But in at least two instances, the resulting rejection of politics throws the baby out with the bathwater. In the first place, the distaste civil society advocates feel for extreme partisanship and identity politics has caused them to reject the possibility of what I will call "medium party politics." In the second, the perceived failure of welfare state liberalism has caused them to reject the possibility of government—that is, the possibility, indeed, the inevitability, of expressing shared and considered moral judgments in and through political institutions and public policy.[1]

In this chapter, I address the status and function of political associations. To be sure, few (if any) individuals associated with the civil society debate in America would dispute that such associations are one aspect of civil society. But a similarly small number attend to the specific role these institutions play in American life, let alone the role they play in advancing the movement's own goals. There are a number of reasons for this, but a few basic distinctions follow from what has already been said. The civil society movement distrusts and disparages the state. It is judged largely irrelevant to the goals of the movement. But clearly, political associations do not see the state as irrelevant at all. Indeed, they see politics as the most important, if not the sole, arena in which to pursue and actually achieve their objectives. More fundamentally, for reasons I will outline, political associations are less effective at producing social capital. Civil society advocates are therefore prone to ignore such institutions in favor of family, neighborhood, and churches.

Following Tocqueville, I will argue that political associations are indeed different from civic associations, let alone the social capital institutions of family, neighborhood, and church. But while these differences help to account for the lack of attention paid to them by civil society advocates, they also account for their relevance to this discussion. In this chapter, then, I want to move up the ladder of abstraction. That is, I want to move away from institutions that are primarily face to face, and move out to consider larger, more organized, and less affective organizations. In Putnam's language, I want to move from the bowling league to the Environmental Defense Fund.

Political Associations

On several occasions, I have mentioned Tocqueville's distinction between civil and political associations, a distinction that centers on whether the association in question has an explicit political agenda. Now it bears repeating that this distinction is by no means always precise. Churches and civic associations often concern themselves with political issues, just as political associations often function as opportunities for making friends and interacting socially. Verba, Schlozman, and Brady rightly conclude that "the unclear distinction between political and non-political activity is a fact of life in American politics."[2] Yet while the middle may be fuzzy, significant differences remain. By definition, political associations seek to influence public policy; they are formed either to alter some perceived deficiency or excess in existing law or to defend an ongoing interest within the political process. They have agendas that they seek to advance over and against those who support any competing agenda, and politics is the medium in which the promotion of those goals is secured.

The point, then, is that because of this basic orientation, all political associations are partisan, and are constituted by partisans: that is, in the words of the *Oxford English Dictionary*, they are made up of individuals who meet the following definition: "One who takes part or sides with another; an adherent or supporter of a party, person, or cause; a devoted or zealous supporter; often in unfavorable sense: One who supports his party 'through thick and thin'; a blind prejudice, unreasoning or fanatical adherent."[3] I have also shown that the civil society movement is characterized by a strong distaste for partisan politics, at least as it is often currently displayed, and an equally strong desire to quell the bickering and find some more productive common ground. In Don Eberly's words, the civil society movement maintains that "our public discourse has become thin cover for power brokers who make their livelihood by producing clout for factions."[4]

Thus, partisanship both defines political associations and helps to account for the lack of attention paid to these associations by the civil society movement. Now, as I have noted, the reason for civil society advocates' distaste is not partisanship per se, but rather the perceived emergence of a partisanship that knows no bounds, a partisanship that routinely sacrifices the state of political discourse, the virtues of civility and moderation, and even the collective good of the nation, for the sake of some particular interest. It must surely be acknowledged that many political associations exemplify these "unfavorable" elements of partisanship. But I want to insist that such condemnation does not legitimate a rejection of partisanship per se, nor does it obviate the necessary and distinctive role political associations play regarding the development of the American political consensus.

There is another relevant aspect of the distinction between political and civic associations. I have noted that every political association is defined and constituted by a particular political goal. In general, the group's ability to effect this goal is directly related to political power—to matters of money, influence, and numbers. In comparison to civic associations, then, this orienting quest for power means that political associations tend to be bigger, more organized, and more focused. The kinds of interactions that take place in such organizations are, accordingly, less intimate, less affective, than those normally associated with neighbors, parishioners, and families. Putnam maintains that broadly speaking, the ties between members of political associations (especially large ones) "are to common symbols, common leaders, and perhaps common ideals, but not to one another."[5] Thus, we can assume that political associations are generally less effective in producing the trust and feelings of solidarity that emerge from social capital institutions. We can likewise assume that this very fact helps to account for civil society advocates' indifference.[6] Yet it is important to be clear here, for while this comparative ineffectiveness holds for all political associations, not all political associations are the same.

Politics is always a game of numbers. In order to play this game, interested parties must strive to build coalitions with other interested parties. And in order to do that, they must find common ground and be prepared to forgo diverting and polarizing issues and to compromise on others. Political problems almost always transcend the boundaries of one neighborhood, especially the so-called "cognitive" neighborhood of a few blocks. Political organizations are therefore more likely to bring together individuals of various ethnic and racial groups. Just so, despite their shared interest in one issue, members are likely to differ on a number of substantive moral questions. They are brought together by their common objective only, and they must pursue that objective despite their significant differences and disagreements. Thus, political associations almost invariably manifest features that distinguish them from social capital institutions.

What is more, these general tendencies are rendered ever more operative by the size of the political venue. When the political body in question is local, the numbers necessary for effective action are relatively small. A single pressure group or a small coalition can often have a dramatic impact. Often, this constituency is united by a fairly thick set of moral beliefs. During the civil rights movement, in city after city, the political work grew out of, and was sustained by, the black churches. The shared belief system gave members the strength to endure the protracted and profound difficulties associated with that struggle.

More recently, the Industrial Areas Foundation in Texas and elsewhere has achieved amazing reforms in local public schools, and has helped to restore public services to poor neighborhoods. Here, too, the movement comes out of the grass roots, and organization and mobilization take place primarily in churches. Many times, the groups have reflected the ethnic and racial homogeneity of the neighborhoods involved. But not always. The racial and ethnic makeup of public high schools is often diverse, and therefore, so too must be the group that addresses its problems. But even when IAF organizations organize across racial and ethnic lines, their shared Christian commitment undergirds their coalition and makes it possible to articulate a strong ethical consensus.[7]

In both cases, then, local political associations draw from the thick features associated with the institutions of social capital: families, neighborhoods, and especially churches are their foundation. What is more, insofar as they are similarly constituted, they achieve similar effects: the benefits associated with the parochial world of social capital institutions are distributed through any accompanying political association. By bringing people together, either in people's homes or in churches, local political associations often produce social capital: feelings of trust and even solidarity among individuals.[8] In other words, the smaller the political body, the more likely the corresponding political associations would inculcate something like social capital.[9]

Now many of the processes identified above are virtually identical for larger political venues. But as the scene expands, so, too, must the political association. It is rare in American politics that a political association connected to any one constituency can single-handedly decide the fate of pending legislation. (The AARP and, in previous generations, the AFL-CIO, serve as counterexamples.) As a result, the effort to build coalitions inevitably extends beyond natural partners to include anyone who shares, or anyone whom you can convince to share, your position. In order to practice larger-scale politics, the need to bracket divisive issues, to find common ground, and to compromise requires that these thick and local political associations have to be willing to "thin out" their expression of the ethical norms and values that define and motivate them.

This dynamic is almost always operative in national politics, but it also applies when the local coalition proves insufficient to achieve its goals. For example, when the civil rights movement was unable to effectuate meaningful local change on its own, King and other leaders would move out into the national forums, arguing their case in order to bring the weight of national opinion, and the power of national institutions (the Supreme Court, the National Guard, etc.), to bear on their struggle. Similarly, when the Texas IAF found itself unable to get local politicians to address the problem of poor children who had walk past a derelict house on their way to school, they invited local television crews to document the problem, thereby making a moral claim to the community at large.[10]

Both of these examples imply that the move from smaller to larger political venues (or from private to public venues) is undertaken by the politically disadvantaged, a point articulated some forty years ago in E. E. Schattschneider's book, *The Semisovereign People*. In his words, "[I]t is the weak, not the strong, who appeal to public authority for relief. It is the weak who want to socialize conflict, i.e., to involve more and more people in the conflict until the balance of forces is changed."[11] For Schattschneider, politics is the management—in his words, the socialization—of conflict. In both cases outlined above, the desire to broaden the conflict, to enlist the support of public opinion and public institutions, was clearly born of the awareness that the goals could not be achieved without making such a move.

But Schattschneider's analysis also supports the broader argument I wish to make. In the first place, he argues that the move to a broader public is a strategic concession: the weaker party knows that its claims will thereby have a better chance of prevailing. But it also knows that its claims will inevitably be attenuated by such a move. The broader public's interest in the conflict is "sufficiently remote" that it is neither the same nor as strong as their own. In Schattschneider's terms, the appeal to the broader public moves a group from "pressure politics" to "party politics," and the claims of the group are moderated in the process.

Finally, Schattschneider contends that the nature of coalition politics in America makes this move almost inevitable. In terms of his analysis (or perhaps, a Schattschneiderian reading of Madison), the pluralistic nature of American politics means that in any conflict, some party thereto will inevitably feel the need to appeal to a broader public. This fact, along with the inexhaustible quest for numbers and dollars, renders coalition politics inescapable. The need for power, the need for numbers, requires that groups join forces with other, more or less like-minded, groups.

Thus, politics is about conflict, and conflict tends to expand from the private to the public, and then on to ever larger publics. To be sure, this development is not without loss. Again, smaller political organizations are usually very good at developing social capital. And while face-to-face interaction may be part of building even the largest political coalitions, increased size usually means increased bureaucracy, and an ever greater split between an organization's leadership and the rank and file.[12] But I want to argue that the production of social capital is not the only relevant function or even the most important function that these national political associations play. Rather, their most important impact centers on their role in articulating the terms of the American public moral consensus.

Tocqueville and the Concept of
Medium Party Political Associations

All political associations want to change or at least influence the making of law. In most every case, they judge that the nation's public policy manifests (or risks manifesting) some deficiency or excess. They therefore enter the political arena in order to make their case for change. But along with his distinction between civic and political associations, Tocqueville also distinguishes between great and small party politics. And this distinction is particularly relevant to the case I want to make. Here is Tocqueville's summary:

> What I call great political parties are those more attached to principles than to consequences, to generalities rather than to particular cases, to ideas rather than to personalities. Such parties generally have nobler features, more generous passions, more real convictions and a bolder and more open look than others. . . . On the other hand, small parties are generally without political faith. And they are not elevated and sustained by lofty purposes, the selfishness of their character is openly displayed in all their actions. They glow with a factitious zeal; their language is violent, but their progress is timid and uncertain.[13]

All political associations, according to Tocqueville, are motivated to some degree by their members' common self-interest. Yet the question of justice or fairness is also almost invariably involved in the claims they make. Tocqueville's distinction thus centers on the way self-interest is understood, on the depth with which those moral claims are held, and the manner in which they are presented.

It is interesting to see how Tocqueville applies this distinction to the American context. For all his rather apparent distaste for small parties, Tocqueville believed that America's success and stability were directly connected to the fact that small parties had come to completely dominate the political scene. Small party politics allows American society to creep along, contesting greatly over minor and self-interested matters (Tocqueville calls them "wretched trifles") but leaving untouched the most basic features of government and society. It may make for less noble, or even ignoble, politics, but it makes for a stable society. Great party politics, on the other hand, is always disruptive and dangerous. At its most extreme, great party politics is revolutionary politics; damning the torpedoes, it strives to overthrow and reestablish the social order. By practicing small party politics, therefore, America has maintained itself as a well-ordered society, and avoided the cataclysms that Europe had been subject to.[14]

Tocqueville is correct to argue that truly revolutionary politics has been, for the most part, blessedly absent from American history. (The Civil War and to a lesser degree the civil rights movement stand as stark, if anachronistic, counterexamples.) But it is also true that our political history is marked by a succession of more or less controlled upheavals in which the peaceful transfer of power has taken on many of the features of great party politics. The elections of Jackson in 1829, Roosevelt in 1932, and Reagan in 1980 signaled dramatic if not revolutionary changes in the American body politic.[15] The congressional elections of 1994 fall into this category as well. The revolutionary rhetoric of the freshman Republicans, the ideological fervor of Speaker Newt Gingrich, Dick Armey, and other House leaders, and the constant attention to the "angry white male" all evoked a contest more closely attuned than usual to great party politics.

Great or at least greater party politics also features in the historical role of political associations in American society. Tocqueville himself mentions both the abolitionists and the temperance movement[16] as important social actors during the mid–nineteenth century. Thereafter, the suffrage movement, Prohibition, the civil rights era, the antiwar movement, and, more recently, the nuclear freeze movement all were characterized by associations that directly and explicitly sought to affect the public policy decisions of our nation. Certainly few would judge all of these movements as correct in their advocacy or that the results were felicitous for our nation or its history. But what is essential to note is that all of these associations were primarily motivated by a strong moral imperative. These movements and others were made up of fierce partisans. There was nothing factitious about their feelings, nothing timid or uncertain about their actions, nothing small about their politics.

For all their zeal, however, it is also essential to notice that in each case, one might say that there is also a limit to their "greatness." The politics practiced by these movements was not great (or at least, not wholly great), in other words, because the participants had no intention of rejecting or bringing down the established terms of the political and social order; rather, they were driven to reject and reform only one significant subset of that established order: the political status of women, the proliferation of alcoholic beverages, etc. Just as importantly, those claims were formulated in terms of the prevailing ethos.[17] These associations argued their case within the very terms of the American public moral consensus. Indeed, they argued that their objectives were required by anyone who affirmed the terms of the American moral consensus. Many of these arguments stand among the greatest political statements in our nation's history. Consider Frederick Douglass's Fourth of July oratory, the Seneca Falls Declaration, and King's "I have a dream" speech. To be sure, such claims were not always formulated in terms of our nation's founding documents. The abolitionist and temperance movements frequently appealed to the nation's civil religion rather than to the Constitution to make their case. But in every instance, the basic argument was quite similar: "We Americans profess to believe x. Indeed, that belief is, by all accounts, a significant part of what constitutes us as a people. Well, if you, my fellow citizens, really do believe that, then you are constrained to support my claim."

Thus, my point is that if America does not often suffer from great party politics, it often experiences what one might call medium party politics: that is, politics that is not so great as to be revolutionary, but is nevertheless far too ideological to be small. Medium party politics is ideological, too, but its ideology is grounded in, and hence limited by, the abstract contents of the American public moral consensus. Medium party political associations, then, argue in terms of the American consensus, and maintain that some aspect of public policy is rendered unacceptable or necessary by that consensus.[18]

This notion, as well, is commensurate with Schattschneider's analysis. The socialization of conflict means that sooner or later the weaker group will turn to a broader public. And almost always, that turn involves an appeal to the public moral consensus, or what Schattschneider calls "universal ideals in the culture,"

> universal ideals concerning equality, consistency, equal protection of the laws, justice, liberty, freedom of movement, freedom of speech and association and civil rights [that] tend to socialize conflict. These concepts tend to make conflict contagious; they invite outside intervention in conflict and form the basis of appeals to public authority for redress of private grievances.[19]

Thus, the move from pressure politics to party politics means moving from self-interest to a common public interest. Schattschneider recalls the famous remark of Charles Wilson (Eisenhower's secretary of defense, formerly of General Motors), "What is good for General Motors is good for the nation."

> Presumably, Mr. Wilson attempted to explain the special interest of General Motors in terms of the common interest because that was the only way he could talk to people who do not belong to the General Motors organization. *Within* the General Motors organization discussions might be carried on in terms of naked self-interest, but a *public discussion must be carried on in public terms*.[20]

The relevance of this kind of claim, of course, centers on the effect it has on the American public moral consensus. For by making this kind of a claim, the political association in question asks all affected parties to evaluate its arguments according to their own understanding of the American consensus. Thus, as it expands, politics not only becomes thinner and more moderate, it becomes ever more likely to require that political claims be expressed in terms of the moral beliefs we all share as Americans.[21] And that expression is indispensable to the construction of a national moral consensus. In the words of Grant McConnell, "many of the values Americans hold in highest esteem can only be realized through large constituencies, some indeed only by a genuinely national constituency."[22]

To the degree that their action and rhetoric are effective, medium party political associations create a public political dialogue through which the American public moral consensus is given form and content. The ensuing debate takes place in the press, through contributions, through countervailing political action, and, as I will show in the next two chapters, through legislative debate.[23] When these sorts of political associations practice this kind of politics, they drive and manifest an ongoing public moral debate, in and through which the American public moral consensus is explicated and concretized.

To the degree, then, that the action or rhetoric of any political association can be understood within the terms of medium party politics, it plays a decisive and constructive role in constituting the American public moral consensus, and thus in building a more moral society. This is a social benefit that social capital institutions cannot provide.

For medium party politics involves claims that appeal, at least implicitly, to all Americans. They are universal claims that speak to the moral beliefs and values that define us as Americans.[24] The proper functioning of organizations making such claims is therefore constitutive of our nation's moral thriving.

Medium Party Politics: Two Examples

Two associations, in particular, seem to me to exemplify the role of medium party politics in the contemporary political environment: the Concord Coalition and Common Cause. In order to illustrate the point further, I therefore want to focus on these institutions to show what medium party politics is and how it works.

The Concord Coalition

The Concord Coalition is an independent, nonpartisan organization devoted to reducing America's federal debt. In part, it makes this case through pragmatic appeals regarding the consequences of large-scale deficit financing—consequences to living standards, interest rates, global competitiveness, and the like. But Concord Coalition members admit that the negative effects of the debt on the present-day economy are dwarfed by its effects on coming generations of Americans. For that reason, their primary argument is not pragmatic at all; it is civic and moral. Central to their case is the claim of generational fairness and duty. At the end of their mission statement, the founders make a stark distinction between this generation and the immediately preceding one.

> Our parents built for us the greatest country on earth. They lived up to the cherished responsibility of keeping a nation alive and thriving. When they said they loved America, it meant more than just words. . . . That is the legacy they left to their children. That must be the legacy we leave to ours. If, as an American citizen, there is any lingering doubt in your mind, gaze carefully into the faces of your children, or your grandchildren, and ask yourself a single question: What will be their future? Will it be better or worse than yours?[25]

This, then, is their argument: previous generations have understood that it is the responsibility of each generation of Americans to preserve a heritage of freedom and prosperity for its posterity. This responsibility is properly understood as part of what it means to be an American; it is an expression of patriotism. Insofar as our inability to control our nation's debt undermines this ability, the current generation has failed to live up to its civic duty. Therefore, if we really love our country, if we really affirm an American creed, we are constrained to address and alter this state of affairs.

The Concord Coalition has been one of the central agents in producing a sea change in Washington. Politicians now feel compelled (or at least more compelled) to address forthrightly the hard budgetary questions associated with entitlements, automatic cost of living adjustments, and the like. To be sure, not everyone agrees with the Concord Coalition's economics or with its modus operandi.[26] But such specific arguments should not obscure the more basic point. The significance of the Concord Coalition is not limited to whether or not its economics is correct (though I must say that I am convinced that it is). Rather, its significance lies in the fact that this kind of moral argumentation is presented by Americans to Americans. Claims about generational responsibility are, to say the least, uncommon in contemporary American politics. But it is fair to say that the basic features of democratic government make such arguments particularly necessary. William Galston, among others, has noted that democracy is predisposed to almost pathological shortsightedness.

> The greatest vices of popular governments are the propensity to gratify short-term desires at the expense of long-term interests and the inability to act on unpleasant truths about what must be done. To check these vices, liberal citizens must be moderate in their demands and self-disciplined enough to accept painful measures when they are necessary. From this standpoint, the willingness of liberal citizens to demand no more public services than their country can afford and to pay for all the benefits they demand is not just a technical economic issue but a moral issue as well.[27]

The Concord Coalition makes just this sort of moral claim. Indeed, it professes a notion of generational obligation that is more at home in the tradition of European conservatism than it is in American political thought. Thus, what I said in chapter 1 about the civil society movement could be said for the Concord Coalition as well. For there is more than a little Burke in the above statement. Again, I judge that the concerns expressed by the Concord Coalition are justified. Therefore, I judge it a laudable enterprise. But even more important is the way the Concord Coalition strives to connect these sorts of generational obligations with the extant terms of the American moral consensus. By so doing, it concretizes and vivifies that consensus in new, unusual, and important ways. That effort must, to my mind, be regarded as a rather extraordinary public service.

Common Cause

Common Cause was founded in 1970 as a "non-partisan citizens lobby"; that is, it sought to employ the same techniques used by PACs and other interest groups, but operate in the interest of the broader public. From its very beginning, Common Cause was built on the recognition that politics was indispensable to the building a nationwide moral consensus. In 1972, founder John Gardner wrote, "[P]olitics and government are the instruments through which we achieve our shared purposes, if we achieve them at all."[28] What's more, he also recognized that a revitalization of the American identity can take place only through the actions of citizens organized around specific political issues:

> That is why Common Cause . . . is concentrating on tangible, specific battles. As we discover that we can win specific battles, we will regain our sense of the future. We will build our shared vision out of a common set of practicalities—jobs, health, housing, and workable political institutions. It is the only way to create a moral framework for a skeptical generation. We must create political, economic, and social institutions that make possible a realization of moral values—in other words, institution-building with a moral purpose.[29]

This raison d'être continues. In 1996, Common Cause launched Project Independence in order to further the organization's long-standing interest in campaign finance reform. In support of the McCain-Feingold Bill, it collected signatures to the following petition:

> We, the undersigned, in order to reclaim our democracy, demand that Congress declare independence from the influence of special-interest money by passing effective bipartisan campaign finance reform. . . . Reclaiming our democracy be-

gins with our citizens. Campaign finance reform is a down payment on reclaiming our democracy. . . . The American people want a government they can be proud of, a government that is open and honest and free from special-interest domination.[30]

This project concluded with the presentation of one million signatures right before a crucial vote on the McCain-Feingold Bill. This is, to be sure, a sizable number, but it was well short of the goal of 1,776,000. The organization as much as admitted defeat for this round. And though Common Cause also promised that the battle was not over, many used the occasion to question the group's effectiveness. But again, the question of political effectiveness cannot be limited to the concrete question of legislation. Because of Common Cause, the argument for and against campaign finance reform centers on questions about our fundamental understandings of, and objectives for, our democratic government. By stressing the civic issues involved, Common Cause has helped to create a public political dialogue through which the American public moral consensus is given form and content. Its actions thus exemplify medium party politics.

Now it is important to reiterate that both the Concord Coalition and Common Cause are part of American civil society. Their organizational work centers in local chapters and volunteer workers. That means that they both afford some opportunities for personal interaction, and thus for the inculcation of democratic habits and dispositions and for the production of social capital. Yet at the same time, I argue that their effect on American civic culture is not limited, indeed, does not even center, on this production. Both organizations practice medium party politics because both maintain that the government has failed in some significant way, and that its failure has a distinct moral or civic dimension. These organizations argue in terms that recall King and Myrdal: i.e., if you really believe the terms of the American consensus, then you are constrained to believe this as well. By making their cases in these terms, they help to remind us all of our shared beliefs and values, and further, they help us concretize and specify the terms of those beliefs; they give content to our American creed in a way that social capital institutions cannot. Associations that practice medium party politics are thus the mediating institution par excellence. For they allow a subset of society to express its fairly specific, but indisputably moral judgment about the condition of polity to the nation as a whole. They bring the particular up to the level of the universal.

Medium Party Politics and Partisanship

The objection will surely rise that these examples, whatever their value, are not representative of American political associations. Indeed, for many civil society advocates, these associations are nothing short of anomalous. Most relevantly, Common Cause and the Concord Coalition scrupulously strive to be nonpartisan: they cultivate support from both Democrats and Republicans. The Concord Coalition was founded by former senators from both parties, and Common Cause strives for balanced representation on its governing board. Yet most political associations in this country are self-interested and strongly partisan, even combative. Their actions and rhetoric appear to foster not a more robust moral consensus, but its further breakdown. To focus on the Concord Coalition and similar organizations is therefore to offer a skewed view of American politics and to fail to even address the reasons for the distaste so many Americans feel toward politics and political associations. Proper consideration of the role of political associations must therefore come to terms with the realities of partisanship in American politics.

It is true that political associations in America commonly manifest a style and presentation that differ significantly from the two outlined above. It is also true that at least some of the reasons for this state of affairs are endemic to American politics. Any political association that wants to enter the fray at the national level must acknowledge and attempt to operate within two inexorable facts. First, the competition for the attention of the American public is intense. There are thousands of associations currently operating in Washington, D.C. And while many of these are content to lobby behind the scenes (taking their case directly to legislators and the like), many more seek to bring their case directly to the American people, joining a seemingly never-ending appeal for their time, money, and commitment to a given cause.

The difficulties associated with this competition are compounded by the second fact: most Americans are not particularly interested in politics. In their study of civic voluntarism, Verba, Schlozman, and Brady conclude that "beyond the domains of work and the family, which are the main concerns of most people, politics takes a secondary place to church and to other voluntary activities. Although Americans remain comparatively active in politics, the bulk of voluntary participation in this country takes place outside of politics."[31]

Now if Americans are continually bombarded by appeals for time and money, and if most Americans are already fairly uninterested in politics, then what is a political association to do? The only way, or at any rate, apparently the most successful way, to get people interested—that is, to raise one's organization and its case above the cacophonous fray—is to raise the stakes, and the only way to raise the stakes is to raise the rhetoric. As Rhys Williams argues, "war rhetoric"—the propensity to see an issue in stark terms, to outline a condition of rank injustice, and to identify the good guys and the bad guys—is particularly suited for breaking through a fairly self-absorbed citizenry and spurring them to action.[32]

As I noted in chapter 1, all Americans are familiar with this kind of strategy. In recent years, the National Rifle Association rather notoriously appealed to its members for contributions to combat "the jackbooted thugs" operating in the FBI and other federal agencies. The Christian Coalition and Focus on the Family routinely condemn the American Civil Liberties Union and People for the American Way as "militantly anti-Christian"; the latter respond by calling the former "militantly intolerant." The parties to the abortion debate confront each other with even more vituperative attacks. This is the kind of rhetoric that Americans have come to associate with political associations and with which many have grown weary.

But it is a fair question whether there are any viable alternatives. Political associations need power to effect their goals, and power is related to money, time, and numbers. Associations that employ this kind of rhetoric are far more likely to get media attention, to receive donations, and to marshal volunteers.[33] Just so, political associations that eschew the demand to paint the opponent as an enemy are less likely to be powerful. They are likely to achieve less, and therefore it is less likely that anyone has even heard of them. To be sure, the Concord Coalition and Common Cause are successful despite the fact that they are officially nonpartisan. But their very uniqueness stems from the fact that they are able to generate the same warlike passion, and the same partisan spirit regarding the mission and the enemy, without limiting the battle to one side of the aisle or another.[34] Such an achievement is inherently unusual. American politics almost constrains political associations to be very partisan, both in their rhetoric and their orientation. And the more explicitly partisan an organization becomes, the less likely it will resemble the Concord Coalition or Common Cause.

These more partisan associations are also surely part of American civil society, and they are surely national. More importantly, they also make claims about the American public moral consensus. Therefore, these organizations are not great in the sense of being revolutionary. The very names of these organizations (People for the American Way, or the Concerned Women for America, for example) often explicitly reflect the fact that members see themselves as honoring the terms of the public moral consensus. What is more, Verba, Schlozman, and Brady discovered that individuals who were politically active thought of themselves as acting for the common good.[35] To be sure, this claim is not always genuine. It is easy to overstate the likelihood of sheer duplicity; nevertheless, Kenneth Karst is right to note that "[i]n American history . . . the expressed concern for values has often provided the excuse—as well as the emotional fuel—for hostile action aimed at preserving interests that are mainly economic."[36] But regardless of the sincerity with which these claims are presented, the more fundamental issue is that while these organizations may be medium with regard to the content of their claims, their strong partisanship and ideological, warlike rhetoric moves them closer to great party politics.[37] Their appeals may very well be outlined in terms of the American public moral consensus, but in contrast to the claims of the Concord Coalition and Common Cause they are not made to all Americans. Rather, they address a large subset of Americans who ostensibly understand and appreciate the true contents and meaning of that consensus better than their opponents do. Thus, the very conditions of American society work against medium party politics, for they constrain political associations to operate in a manner closer to great party politics—i.e., they are more likely to be ideological, partisan, and unbending.

As I have shown, Tocqueville fully believes that great party politics is dangerous; indeed, he celebrates its absence in American society.[38] Thus, the problem that civil society advocates and others bring to light is that this more common political association practices a more dangerous form of medium party politics. By skirting closer to great party politics, these associations undermine standards of fair dealing and civility: the possibility of dialogue, compromise, and the ability to accept unfavorable or ameliorated outcomes all decline as a result of their actions. Even more importantly, these political associations undermine the process by which the American public moral consensus is rendered explicit and concrete. And thus, whatever their attitude toward that consensus, their actions serve to weaken it.

The tension that is surfeit throughout our contemporary political life, talk of "culture wars," of a body politic that is riven by an entrenched conflict over values and beliefs—all this seems to belie any easy confidence in an American creed. Perhaps we do all agree on a set of abstract goods, but these are just empty words. When the question turns to what those claims actually mean, and how they should be implemented in our political structure, the quest for agreement goes out the window, and we are left with distrust, gridlock, animosity, and meanspiritedness. What is more, the debate shows that ideological politics often only serves to reveal the abject lack of consensus on a particular issue. If the American public moral consensus is constitutive of American identity—that is, any American's identity—then such a list must be extremely limited. As a result, competing claims often cannot be adequately adjudicated within the terms of this universal consensus. And so the resulting debate may not resolve anything; it may only reveal and exacerbate underlying tensions and distrust. If all this is true, then how does it make sense to tout the unifying role of political organizations when their actions and warlike rhetoric undermine the body politic?

Medium All the Way Down

The first point is that, to some degree, the value of a claim holds regardless of the vitriol that accompanies it. A claim about the relationship between some public policy initiative and the American public moral consensus asks or demands that Americans evaluate that claim. And the subsequent debate helps to give the consensus content regardless of how that claim is presented. The abortion debate, for example, has often been characterized as rancorous and personal. For the stakes on both sides are perceived to be very high. Yet for all the rancor, it is not at all self-evident that this debate has been a net loss for the moral condition of our nation. On the contrary, it has focused our attention on our understanding of rights (most relevantly: privacy, self-determination, and life) and the inevitable conflicts often contained therein.[39] As the debate continues over the years, as it surely will, it is quite likely that here and elsewhere consensus on at least some of the associated issues will be forged. It is also worth noting that regardless of how people act and talk within political associations, Verba, Schloz-man, and Brady have discovered that their very involvement is associated with higher than average levels of tolerance. Association does not prove causality, but it is quite possible that political activity moderates even when the political rhetoric does not.[40]

The more fundamental response is to turn the most virulent claims about the content and true meaning of the American public moral consensus back on themselves. For surely standards of public discourse are also part of that consensus. If politics are to be medium in their practice—that is, if claims are made in terms of a common creed—then they must also be made in a way that acknowledges our commonalty. Thus, to make a claim about the content of the American public moral consensus is, at the same time, to hold oneself to a politics of civility, a politics in which a belief in and desire for the common good orients and constrains rancor and contention. Civility thus does not mean rejecting partisanship; it does not mean being nice or tabling divisive issues. The ardor of many association members properly reflects the fact that the moral stakes associated with a given political issue are often extremely high. But it does mean that precisely on those matters on which there is the most disagreement, political associations are also constrained to accept their opponents as fellow citizens and as persons of good will. Their claims are, putatively at least, grounded in the affirmation of a common set of American ideals, and those ideals stipulate such an acceptance. Indeed, those ideals make such an acceptance at once necessary, legitimate, and real. Charles Colson surely has strongly held views regarding the content of the American public moral consensus. That makes his observations on this point particularly relevant.

> The real danger is not just bigotry toward one group of Americans but rather a larger question that concerns us all: it is whether this inflammatory rhetoric will so polarize us as to cripple our capacity for what the moral philosopher Hannah Arendt describes as "democratic conversation." Politicians and journalists alike need to remember: Responsible rational discourse, not name-calling, is the key to maintaining the moral consensus on which free societies depend.[41]

Without responsible rational discourse, partisan politics does indeed risk undermining the American public moral consensus. But to the very degree that it does, it cannot be properly understood to stem from, nor to reflect, that consensus. Indeed, if some form of political expression does not live up to the standards Colson articulates, then that would constitute grounds for disregarding the sincerity, and thus the worthiness, of the claim itself.[42]

Any political association thus faces this dilemma: it must appeal to a common moral consensus as a basis for its claims, yet it must strive simultaneously to stir people to action. If one makes appeal only to the most platitudinous renderings of what it means to be an American, the claim is likely to fall on deaf ears and fail to excite any interest or effect. If, on the other hand, one accepts the claim that a standard of dialogue is part of the American public moral consensus, then one implicitly affirms the fact that a style of measured, fair, even-handed argumentation is itself part of the American public moral consensus. And to ignore this fact is equally to jeopardize one's position. Many may judge that the condition of the body politic has rendered this kind of jeopardy obsolete. But recall the vehement (and costly!) outcry against the NRA for its "jackbooted thugs" remark. The organizational change of the Moral Majority to the Christian Coalition likewise reflects the broader public's demand for balance, fairness, and accountability. Americans may be less willing to reject an association's claim based on the incivility with which it is presented, but the basic dynamic remains.

Finally, it is essential to note that the question about ideological politics does not gainsay what has come before, because the dangers exist on both sides. As Tocqueville well knew, to reject the very possibility of medium party politics is to risk a politics that is factitious and selfish, crass and morally vapid. It is also to risk leaving the terms of the American moral consensus abstract, empty, and utterly unable to direct or focus the moral activity of American civil society. Engaging in medium party politics means striving to be both passionate and cool, ideological, yet grounded in an ideology that unites all of us—friend and foe alike—in a common, and uniquely American, enterprise. Medium party politics requires an uneasy yet deeply principled balance between an ideological fervor that undermines the body politic and a petty struggle in which hostile identity groups engage in war by other means. It cannot be otherwise.

Those concerned about the moral and civic condition of the American polity, and especially those concerned about the unhappy effects of partisan political associations, would do well to remember two things. First, it is reasonable to presume that the prospects for achieving this kind of balance rise significantly if they and others like them were to cease their abdication of politics and join in the debate. Second, it is necessary to recall that the question of how politics gives form to our shared moral judgments only begins with political associations: the problematic actions of these ideological, partisan groups thus reinforce the need of politics and the state, for once the issue moves to politics and government, the institutions there serve to moderate the discussion still further, and move it yet closer to the middle. Thus, the very partisanship that civil society advocates often abhor only reinforces the need for robust, morally cognizant, and national governmental institutions. In the next chapter, I turn to an analysis of these institutions.

Chapter Eleven

Government and the Construction of the Moral Society

Political associations, whether they practice medium party politics or not, whether they operate on a national scale like the Concord Coalition, or whether they reflect the local, even neighborhood concerns of an Industrial Areas Foundation group, are surely part of American civil society. Whatever contemporary advocates make of the role and importance of such institutions, there is little disagreement that they fit the analytical definition of the term. Yet, for my purposes, the relevance of these political associations stems from the fact that they have a different, or at least additional, social function. The indispensability of civil society is not limited to the benefits associated with interpersonal interaction—that is, it is not limited to increasing trust and solidarity among participants. Rather, as the institutions of civil society extend beyond what I have called social capital institutions to larger, more organized political associations, they often make universal claims about the content of the American public moral consensus. These claims start a debate by and through which we Americans come to define more precisely the values for which we stand, the values that define us.

Yet while that process, that debate, almost invariably begins with political associations, it does not end there. The debate eventually moves out of the exclusive realm of civil society and into the processes associated with the making and administration of law. It is here that we Americans articulate and institutionalize our shared moral judgment. Thus, the relevance of political associations is also related to the fact that they point to and acknowledge the state's role as moral pedagogue. I argued in the previous chapter that the civil society movement had thrown the baby out with the bathwater: it had let its distaste for political partisanship allow it to discount the proper and necessary moral function of political associations. In this chapter, I argue something very similar about the necessary role of government.

This decade, even more than the one before it, is characterized by the belief that government, particularly the federal government, has gotten too big and overstepped its limited role: there are, it is argued, too many programs, too many regulations, and too much taxation. The growth of the welfare state—institutionalized, long-term entitlement programs often derisively referred to as the Nanny State—has been similarly repudiated. The civil society movement clearly echoes this broad position, and, as before, there are good reasons for it. The case is often facile in its presentation, but the growth of federal agencies and programs does appear to have led to a decline in the autonomous, unregulated work of American civic institutions. Americans have therefore come to the conclusion that the political appeals commonly associated with these entitlement programs, e.g., the notion of an American family, or the idea of a national community (appeals that, it is fair to say, are more commonly associated with the Democratic Party), are romantic, oxymoronic, and even dangerous.

Yet whatever the worth of this or similar conclusions, they do not legitimate the wholesale rejection of politics and government. I have argued that a more or less universal agreement on a set of moral propositions is a sine qua non for a moral society. American society is surely so constituted, but the agreement is abstract and indeterminate. Construction of a more moral and civic society therefore depends on mechanisms by which that moral consensus is given concreteness and content. I argue that despite the general agreement regarding issues of governmental downsizing and the like, the rejection of the welfare state in no way prescribes or legitimates the rejection of politics and government. For politics and government are the principal and indispensable means by which such concreteness and content are achieved.

In this chapter, then, I continue to move up the level of abstraction, and, ultimately, to move out of the realm of civil society entirely. The previous chapter employed a Tocquevillian category to outline the normative function of political associations. In this chapter, I employ a Hegelian notion of government as moral pedagogue. I show that the actions of political associations inform institutional political rhetoric and debate, which, in turn, leads to the passage of laws. These laws, and the institutions that administer and enforce them, inevitably reflect the institutionalization of a moral judgment. Thus, politics and government are the means by which the moral argument is rendered into a moral judgment and then reflected back down to the American people. This unique action is surely important in its own right. But just as important is the role this action plays with regard to the institutions of civil society. By establishing and implementing policy, government sets the minimal yet universal terms within which civil society ought to function. It is thus the primary means by which the felicitous operation of civil society is established and fostered. For all its worth, the civil society solution is insufficient; it reveals and underscores the necessity of politics.

Why Civil Society Rejects the State

The most commonly articulated problems with government and law are that big government is inefficient and wasteful at best, harmful to individuals' lives and democratic processes at worst. Such sentiments have been appreciable at least since the presidency of Ronald Reagan. But in recent years, they have come to predominate within Congress and society at large. Passage of welfare reform legislation, for example, was driven by precisely these attitudes. I have also noted that the civil society movement reflects these beliefs as well. The federal government, it is argued, is inherently ill suited to deal with social problems. It cannot make meaningful distinctions among people and circumstances; it can only outline blanket criteria that often take on a life and a bureaucratic constituency all their own.[1]

This apparent sea change in public opinion has its own independent justifications, but it was likely exacerbated by the end of the Cold War. In the second half of the twentieth century, the federal government expanded in order to combat a strong and determined adversary. At varying intervals, and sometimes all at once, the American state was occupied with fighting, containing, and preventing a protracted and expensive war. That task is behind us, and therefore so, too, is the rationale for a big, centralized, federal government. But there is more to the contemporary context. For the more basic question is this: why should we Americans believe that government, and particularly the federal government, can help to construct and sustain a moral society? Even if one were ready to accept my claim that the American public moral consensus requires a mechanism by which its contents are rendered concrete and specific, it is another question entirely whether the state can perform this role well enough to abrogate the search for alternatives. Many Americans have come to believe that their government institutions, and the people who run them, are, at best, inept; at worst, they constitute a positive barrier to achieving a more moral, more civic society.[2] While Americans still affirm a rather robust set of American ideals and values, they have largely lost respect for the individuals and institutions through which those ideals and values are given content. Thus, the very disconnect that proves the inadequacy of American civil society and the need for universal, national institutions would appear also to prove that government is not the answer, that we most look elsewhere to meet that need.

For civil society advocates, these two issues are related. That is, the reason people have grown disconnected with and disrespectful of government, politics, and politicians stems from the very fact that the state has grown massively in the past generation. It has lost its connection with people's lives, it has spawned a new and more vigorous form of rent seeking (making a problem and constituency permanent in order to do the same to one's employment prospects), and, as a result, it is under democratic control in name only. Cut back on government, return decisions to the people, and to institutions that are closer to the people, and the disconnect will diminish. Once again, the civil society solution appears to close the circle. Even if the disconnect renders the civil society solution insufficient, the only way to address the disconnect is by means of civil society.

The Importance of National Political Institutions

There is no denying that government has expanded dramatically in the twentieth century. In 1929, the share of the gross national product devoted to government spending stood at 8.5 percent. In 1990, it was 39 percent. Even in the last generation, since 1960, federal expenditures have increased fifteenfold. As well, this vast expansion no doubt accounts for similar increases in collateral groups and institutions. As federal programs, employees, clients, and expenditures have grown, so, too, have the number and activity of public and private interest associations, political action committees, and media coverage. Finally, while the number of representatives in Congress has not changed, the national population has increased, and therefore the number of individuals represented by a given representative has grown dramatically as well, thereby continuing to eviscerate the relative importance of each one of us.

It is highly doubtful that such a dramatic change would leave citizens' opinion of their government unaffected. To the contrary, it is eminently plausible that there is a correlation between the increase in federal government and the increase in people's dissatisfaction. And if this is true, then the idea that one would turn to that same federal government as a means of fostering a renewed moral consensus becomes a deeply problematic notion. Indeed, the contemporary antigovernment animus, and the belief that government's discredit stems from its growth, has lead to a call for governmental *devolution:* that is, moving power from the federal to the state and local levels.

As before, this argument has its salient beginnings in the Reagan era. The reasons for supporting devolution are diverse, of course, but they most often relate to issues of experimentation, efficiency, and the underlying notion that a government that is literally closer is more responsive and less alienating than government that is larger and farther away. For the civil society debate, this last reason is the most relevant. Civil society advocates are, generally, far less unhappy with the operation of government on a local scale. As I noted, they are inclined to believe that a government that is closer is more accountable, and is more likely to involve citizens (either as individuals, or united in groups) engaging in a face-to-face dialogue with each other and with their elected leaders. These face-to-face interactions create social capital and are therefore able to effectuate a more moral and civic order in a way that the operation of government on a federal level simply cannot. While I do not dispute the importance of local, face-to-face politics, I nevertheless argue almost the very opposite of this claim.

While state experiments in welfare and education reform offer intriguing and often promising results, I am not persuaded that the devolution of political power and decision making from the federal to the state level will automatically result in more responsive government. In the first place, the vast majority of federal programs are implemented and the vast majority of federal dollars are allocated indirectly, through state and local governments and then on to businesses and not-for-profit agencies. In other words, much of the authority associated with these federal programs is already in local hands. What is more, state governments are, at best, only marginally less inefficient than the federal government.[3] Thus, even on its own terms, the case for devolution is not as solid as advocates would make it out to be.

But regardless, the issue ought to turn on more than merely the issues of experimentation and efficiency. Rather, for the purposes of this study, the heart of the matter is whether and how governmental institutions serve to concretize and specify the terms of the nation's public moral consensus. It follows from all that has been said that returning politics to a more face-to-face level may well increase the possibility of a politics that builds social capital and that fosters civic engagement and civic competency. The actions of the Texas IAF, for example, illustrate that the opportunity for hands-on democracy offers direct and indirect benefits for the polity at large. This possibility certainly lends support to the devolution argument, and nothing in this chapter is meant to deny that support. Just the same, I stress that there are no guarantees. These forms of government are often seen by constituents as only marginally less accessible and less arcane than the federal government. Thus, an ostensible increase in the opportunity for face-to-face interaction may remain nothing more than that.

More important, however, is the Hegelian response. For if the operative concern is the moral condition of the American polity, and if the American public moral consensus is largely constitutive of American identity, then the necessity of a political mechanism in which all Americans have a say, and to which all Americans are accountable, ought to be self-evident. For those concerned with constructing a moral politics and a moral society, the argument for devolution cannot gainsay the continued necessity of national political debate and of national political institutions.

The necessity of national political institutions also follows from what has been said about political associations. I noted in chapter 10 that there are endemic features of the American political scene that encourage political associations to outline the issue in stark terms, identify a political enemy, and employ a militant form of rhetoric. But again, this is only where the process begins. Political associations, by definition, seek to influence the making of laws, and they do so by employing political institutions. As they do so, the same endemic features of American politics encourage not militancy, but moderation, compromise, and the pursuit of comparatively minor change. Consider the well-known problems associated with the move from presidential primaries to the party conventions: the very same appeals that allow a candidate to garner the support of a few ardent (and, with luck, well-heeled) supporters in the primaries render it extremely difficult for the candidate to win nomination (examples abound: Pat Robertson, Pat Buchanan, Jesse Jackson, Phil Gramm). The goal of winning the general election further compromises militant rhetoric (Barry Goldwater is likely the most apt example here). At each stage, then, the need to fashion appeals commensurate with what I have called medium party politics increases dramatically.

This same transition takes place in the legislative process and in congressional and senatorial elections as well. Rhys Williams summarizes the point this way:

> American political institutions cannot, and are not intended to, represent all the opinions of all Americans. They are designed to marginalize uncompromising minorities. By forcing public positions into the center, and by forcing compromise in the formulation of policy, the institutions of American politics have diffused and defused the passion necessary for war.[4]

There are exceptions of course, but the larger the political venue, the more the two-party system gravitates against political leaders who spurn medium party politics. For this reason, as well, I would argue that the national government remains essential.

But along with misapprehending the necessity of national political institutions, the devolution argument also misunderstands the reasons for their compromised condition. Against many devolution advocates, I insist that the argument that big government means bad government is an insufficient explanation for the disconnect Americans feel. A more sophisticated explanation does not necessarily make government any more viable, but it does more adequately outline the terms within which viability must be established and maintained.

The first point is that Americans' dissatisfaction transcends government. The media, the family, public and higher education, big business—all of these social institutions have experienced a similar loss of confidence over the past generation. And the idea that the expansion of the federal government or even some putative universal growth is responsible for this nearly ubiquitous decline is far-fetched at best. It is far more likely that much of the decline associated with any authoritative social institution stems from a decline in the very concept of authority. Counterculture movements of the sixties and the growth of postmodernism—inside and outside the academy—have all created a climate in which claims of standing and authority are automatically suspect. Thus, our discontent with government stems from the fact that we have gotten so good at seeing through rhetoric that we are disinclined to do anything else.[5]

But it is also worth noting that the condition of American government and American society during this same era gave citizens good reasons for developing these very skills. Thus, the reason for the rise in suspicion stems from the fact that there was much that the public should have been suspicious about. The most precipitous decline in public confidence in government (and, indeed most social institutions) took place between the years 1968 and 1974: i.e., the years corresponding to the nation's unprecedented cultural upheaval, its worst race riots, the ever-more apparent morass of Vietnam, and the resignation of a scandal-ridden president.[6] In other words, most people who came to the opinion that government was both corrupt and ineffective did so when they were presented with overwhelming evidence of ineffectiveness and corruption.

Thus, a more sophisticated explanation for the disconnect of which Hunter and Bowman speak certainly includes the growth of government, but it also acknowledges the effects of an ever more widespread hermeneutic of suspicion, and of a era of dramatic governmental failure. But even if this bigger explanation is more satisfactory, how does it change the basic response? How does it make the appeal to government any more viable?

One must begin by acknowledging that these circumstances do indeed make the possibility of furthering moral renewal through national politics far more difficult. While our problems are quite similar to those that have occupied thinkers throughout the modern era, our ability to respond to those issues has been significantly undermined. We are right to be circumspect in our efforts, and to measure our expectations accordingly.

But I also believe that we cannot responsibly declare that the game is lost. In the first place, while corruption may be endemic to government, government is not incorrigible. The American state is and remains democratic. Changes in the popular will do indeed result in policy changes—even when such changes compromise the goals of key interest groups (big business, labor, the elderly, even Congress itself). Changes in environmental laws, automobile safety regulations, and the states' newfound intolerance of drunk driving—these and a host of recent policy initiatives have no other plausible explanation. What is more, if the current operation and performance of government and governmental institutions are judged unacceptable—insufficiently responsive, insufficiently democratic, or what have you—there are surely policy avenues that might alter that assessment. That is, there are policy avenues that might render government more accountable and more democratic. In chapter 12, I commend campaign finance reform as one important vehicle by which we might try to restore a sense of democratic equity and governmental integrity. But the specifics of that debate are not needed here. I merely want to make the uncontroversial point that the law affects, and thus can affect positively, the civic condition of our polity.

But perhaps this reform or others are beside the point; perhaps democracy itself is obsolete. Perhaps the discredit now commonly associated with the concept of authority and the very plausibility of universal truth renders moot the possibility of constructing a shared moral identity. As John Courtney Murray wrote a generation ago,

> We are aware that we not only hold different views but have become different kinds of men as we have lived our several histories. Our styles of thought and of interior life are as discrepant as our histories. The more deeply they are experienced and the more fully they are measured, the more do the differences among us appear to be almost unbridgeable.[7]

I am deeply sympathetic to this problem; indeed, I believe that if our differences do indeed go all the way down, then democracy as anything more than a pragmatic struggle for power becomes impossible. But the evidence is clear that our differences do not, or at least do not yet, go all the way down. Whatever the effects of postmodernism, the working out of Enlightenment logic, or what have you, the fact remains that the ideals and values that constitute the American public moral consensus remain strong and nearly universal. What is more, those ideals are held to be universally true; they are not seen as handy fictions or as ideals that are true merely for us. It is surely the case that abstract agreement is easier than agreeing on questions of application, but as Murray also argued, an agreement on principles at least makes meaningful disagreement about policy possible in the first place.

Thus, while today's circumstances are far more difficult than those that occupied Murray, let alone Tocqueville and Hegel, I can see no reason to conclude that those changes have rendered obsolete the possibility of coming to meaningful moral judgment through politics and governmental institutions. More to the point, I am unable to conjure an adequate alternative. The fact that the task is more difficult does not mean we are justified in abandoning an indispensable and still viable tool. In order to illustrate how that tool might yet again function, I want to outline the Hegelian dimensions of the American federal government.

The Hegelian Backdrop

Since Hegel sets the backdrop for this discussion, it is appropriate to begin with him. In chapter 8, I showed that Hegel's description of the state centers on three unified but distinct features: the monarchy, the legislature, and, operating within both of these, the universal class or the bureaucracy. Hegel argues that because each nation has its own distinct identity, that identity must be incarnated in and through one individual. In Hegel's schema, this is the king. But as I noted, the king's role is primarily ceremonial. While the king signs the law, and, in his very person, embodies the law, the bureaucrats are the king's executive agent; it is principally they who prescribe, codify, and enforce the law. The final part of Hegel's political apparatus is the two estates. These estates strive to articulate the universal, even as they represent a class-constricted interest (the agricultural and the industrial classes, respectively). While they are associated with the legislative role of government, their role is more advisory than active. They do not make decisions but mediate—give voice to—the interests and concerns of the people to the executive officers and the monarch.

Again, Hegel argued that the central purpose of the state is to construct ethical unity within the modern context. My immediate task, therefore, is to consider the relevance of this central purpose, and the relevance thereto of these three governmental functions, in the American context. For my purposes, I want to present a Hegelian reading of the actions of three comparable institutions within the national government: namely, the rhetoric of the presidency,[8] the drafting of laws in the Congress, and the implementation of those laws through governmental institutions.

The Presidency as Seen through Hegelian Eyes

To state the obvious, there are significant and conspicuous differences between the elected president and Hegel's hereditary sovereign. Perhaps the most relevant point is that Hegel's sovereign is almost entirely ceremonial. His actions are far more in keeping with the president's role in parliamentary systems than they are with the rough-and-tumble world of American presidential politics. But because the American president is an individual, and because his (to this point, a sufficient pronoun) is the only office that is elected by the entire nation, he nevertheless takes on a very Hegelian role within the American body politic. For like Hegel's monarch, the president concretizes the individuality of the American people within his person, and reflects that individuality back to the American people. What is more, the president presides over a number of ceremonial occasions within American civic life. On these occasions, the president's words and actions can be understood as America speaking to itself. And therefore, they have a profound influence on the concretization of the American public moral consensus.

The relevance of presidential rhetoric for the question occupying this chapter is brought home with startling clarity by Wayne Fields's recent work on presidential rhetoric, *Union of Words*. Fields does not reference Hegel in the book, but in many ways, the parallels are striking. First, Fields argues that much of the importance of the presidency attaches to the simple fact that he is an individual. "If Congress embodies the many which Americans so zealously champion on the one hand, then the president embodies the *one* that the many must also, corporately, affirm—either as a reality or as an aspiration."[9] Second, Fields connects this embodiment and its relevance not to the nuts and bolts of crafting and passing legislation, but to the far more ceremonial task of presidential rhetoric. For Fields, the stages associated with a presidential campaign and with the life of an administration are marked, more often than not, by a speech. And on these occasions, the president speaks for all Americans; indeed, for better or worse, he speaks *as* America.

> Thus the rhetorical presidency has emerged with the specific challenge of helping Americans maintain a delicate balance between our instinctive move toward the many and our desire to become one. Our chief executives are called not to overwhelm either with the other but to interpret national life in ways that affirm both with the loss of neither. Ironically, they manage this through personalizing the government whose impersonality we fear, by giving a sense of the particular to the general.[10]

Finally, it is worth noting how this function relates to the relationship between political associations and political institutions. Fields argues that vitriolic rhetoric associated with talk radio and the like "seeks not to persuade but only to excite already entrenched opinion. It plays to believers while deliberately antagonizing those of differing views."[11] Presidential rhetoric, on the other hand, cannot adopt such militant expression, for it has an entirely antithetic set of objectives and constraints. The burden of the president's speech is to confine itself to the terms of medium party politics: it is "to keep a constituency in community even when it cannot be kept in agreement, and by its own example to witness to our capacity, when consensus is impossible, to disagree rationally and respectfully."[12]

Fields wants to claim that affirming and articulating the moral consensus that unites and identifies all Americans is the perennial task of the presidency. The inaugural address, for example, is always used to mark the end of partisan bitterness and the evocation of common themes and aspirations. But this is not the whole of it. The inaugural address seeks to draw out and thereby concretize the relevance of those themes to the contemporary context. "These first words announce the beginning of a new regime and provide a foundation upon which the incoming executive can build, a perception of the idiosyncrasy of his own time contained in some larger vision of America and its purpose."[13] Lincoln's inaugurals, of course, manifestly demonstrate this principle. But Fields argues that while the second inaugural is indeed "astonishing," it is also "paradigmatic"; no speech matches and few even come close to Lincoln's magisterial achievement, yet the same drive for a renewed commitment to wholeness within the specific circumstances of the time resonates in virtually every inaugural address.[14]

Fields sees the same basic purpose in every major event of the rhetorical presidency. Regarding the annual state of the union address, Fields concludes that

> [f]or all their differences in temperament and abilities and for their widely contrasting views of what their country could contain, they have been of remarkably similar moods as to the nature of their elected duty. The job is always, as Washington foresaw, the difficult business of building affection, affection for one another and for the Union itself.[15]

In special, nonscheduled speeches as well (declarations of war, dedications, commemorations, and the like), "[t]he task of interpretation, of bringing the present into line with the past, lies behind all presidential eloquence. In representing a union that transcends the moment, they seek to demonstrate a consistency of purpose and will in America's history."[16] Thus, Fields shows that the president returns to the "past" because the past is the source of the American self-understanding. It is constituted by an ongoing sense of purpose and will—by a set of beliefs about what is important and valuable, about what ought to be striven for and what ought to be preserved. As America's chosen representative, the president faces the task of connecting that past, that identity, to the specific challenges of the contemporary era. He must, through his words more than his actions, read America's past through the present, thereby rendering the American consensus once again concrete and meaningful.

Congress: Establishing the Universal

As with the executive, the differences between Congress and the merely advisory role of Hegel's estates are all too apparent. Indeed, one can view Hegel's legislature more as a mechanism for mediating the interests of the people *to* the state than part of the state itself.[17] Again, Hegel is no democrat, and he would likely view with disgust the contentious arm-twisting and logrolling that characterize the normal activities of Congress. Yet the makeup of the legislative body does not contradict the more fundamental Hegelian point: public policy is properly understood as society's effort to develop, maintain, and express its considered judgment about a common set of shared civic and moral values, and to outline the demands such values properly make on us citizens—both as individuals and as members of groups. The legislature, in Hegel's language, determines and establishes the universal. And, as Hegel well understood, that means its enterprise is a fundamentally moral one.

The making of laws necessarily involves the evaluation of different and competing conceptions of future conditions for society. Should we widen this road? Build a new sewer system? Raise or lower taxes? All of these seemingly pedestrian political subjects involve an implicit value choice. Indeed, it is difficult to find any legislation, or, just as importantly, any decision not to legislate, that does not involve the consideration of competing values. Any political question devolves to a question of what we want and how much we want it in comparison to other things we want. Politics, in David Easton's famous definition, is "the authoritative allocation of values."[18] To be sure, not all values have moral content—i.e., the question of whether someone prefers chocolate or vanilla ice cream does not involve a moral judgment. But any conceivable conception of the political good involves questions of deciding among and distributing scarce resources, and therefore involves questions of just distribution and fair dealings. Political questions are thus constituted by, and in turn give content to, a shared conception of the good. The idea that morality should be removed from political discourse (or, in more common parlance, the idea that you can't legislate morality) could not be more false.[19] Whatever else they are, political questions are inexorably moral questions.

The making of laws thus constitutes the authoritative answers to these moral questions. That is not to say that government is the only or even the supreme authority, nor is it to say that there are not other social and cultural institutions the reach and import of which are equally universal.[20] It is only to say that our national government is the only *common moral* authority; it is the only moral authority that makes equal and more or less coercive claims on all citizens.[21] In the words of Philip Heymann, "only through government expressive action can an entire society define its public attitudes, beliefs, and philosophies."[22] If the content and understanding of the American public moral consensus are constitutive of American identity—constitutive, that is, of what unites us as Americans—that is a singularly important role. For anyone concerned about the moral condition of American society, the operative question, then, is not whether political discourse and political decisions ought to reflect moral values, for inevitably they will. The questions are which values it should it reflect, and how those values should be reflected. Glenn Loury summarizes the point well: "[T]he key point to recognize is that the state cannot escape the necessity to communicate some moral message by the actions it takes, even if only by default."[23] Laws orient these actions, and the Congress drafts and passes laws. Therefore, the role of the latter is indispensable to furthering the moral condition of the republic.

To be sure, making laws (like making sausage) isn't pretty. Debate is contentious, sometimes vituperatively so, bargaining and gamesmanship sometimes swamp even the veneer of public service, and partisanship characterizes every step along the way. But while all this is indisputable, it is not sufficiently descriptive. While the institution is driven by the particular interests of a legislator's constituency and by his or her own self-interest (and is often abetted in this regard by the committee and seniority systems), it is also designed to allow, enable, and even constrain legislators to attend as well to the interests to the nation as a whole. In his book, *The Mild Voice of Reason,* Joseph M. Bessette outlines a series of constitutional devices that were explicitly designed with this end in mind. The presidential veto, the length of terms, the small size of the legislative bodies, the indirect election of the Senate and the size of congressional districts, Bessette argues, were all designed to promote attention to and concern for the common good. He concludes that

> [a]lthough it was not the framers' plan or expectation that de-
> liberations in the new government would ignore the interest
> of their parts, their intention and hope was that service in the
> national House of Representatives and Senate would broaden
> the perspective of legislators by showing them how the well-
> being of their district or state was inextricably bound to the
> well-being of the nation.[24]

Here, then, is another connection with the Hegelian state: for both
institutions are characterized by the fact that each representative is concerned with a set of particular interests even as he or she is obliged
to consider and articulate the interests of the commonweal. The most
fundamental features of Congress at least encourage a synthetic combination of group interest and commonalty that has a distinctively Hegelian ring.[25] Bessette goes on to maintain that those features operate
more frequently and more successfully than we often allow.[26] I agree;
and in the next chapter, I will outline one occasion in which legislative
debate appealed directly to the terms of the American public moral
consensus, and thereby improved the moral condition of the American
polity.

The Bureaucracy as Mediating Institution

Finally, we return to Hegel's conception of the bureaucracy. Hegel argues that "the conduct and culture of officials is the sphere where the
laws and the government's decisions come into contact with individuals and are actually made good."[27] Thus, because they have developed
an ethos of professional and rational public service, Hegel's civil servants are the most essential feature of the state. They actualize, enforce,
and even embody the state as a moral unity.

To say the least, few in America would conjure up a similar description when asked to define *bureaucrat*. Americans are far more likely to
recount the myriad examples of bureaucratic abuse, waste, corruption,
and intransigence revealed since the Watergate era. Indeed, few terms
are more likely to evoke such spontaneous, widespread, and virulent
distaste.[28] Politicians know this, of course, and therefore they reflect
this attitude as well. Congressional hearings on the IRS in 1997 and
the Clinton administration's National Performance Review in 1993 are
only the latest of a seemingly perennial effort by politicians to expose
and reign in the excesses of the bureaucratic state.[29] Finally, this attitude
is pervasive in the academic literature. There are some stalwart defend-

ers,[30] but for the vast majority, "the rise of the bureaucratic state" is a persistent, unyielding problem.[31] For my part, I am inclined to think that Americans too easily disparage both the notion and the reality of civil service within national governmental agencies. But I do not dispute (indeed, I do not see *how* one could dispute) the sorry record of abuse, intransigence, and incompetence. But my point here is more general. Yet again, I want to argue that on a more general level, there are fundamental, substantive connections between Hegel's conception and the American equivalent.

The term *mediating institution* normally refers to both the status and function of civil society as operating between the state and the individual. But as is often the case, this meaning has been lost (or at least obscured) within the contemporary American debate. For just as the public debate focuses on institutions that build social capital—that is, intimate, informal institutions—it thereby focuses on institutions where the issue of what is being mediated and how is never successfully addressed.

I have argued that social capital institutions do indeed mediate between the individual and the American public moral consensus. When these institutions are operating as they should—loving families, vibrant churches, friendly, peaceful neighborhoods—they provide opportunities whereby we Americans learn and are reminded of the moral requirements of being an American. We learn to trust each other, and to treat each other with fairness and respect, and we learn how to strike a balance between self-reliance and a concern for the common good. But I also showed that the very nature of social capital institutions make their concretization of the American moral consensus inadequate. Political associations, particularly when they are practicing medium party politics, make universal claims about the content of the American public moral consensus—claims that are incumbent upon all Americans. Thus, political associations are the means by which the particular is brought up to the level of the universal. They therefore mediate the concerns of the particular group to the nation as a whole.

But just as the process does not stop there, neither does the concept of mediation. The state, too, has its mediating institutions, and it is primarily through them that the state's role as a moral educator is advanced. State institutions are the mechanisms by which the entire polity imposes its moral judgments, and thereby reflects those judgments back onto the people themselves. Thus, while American civil society mediates upward to the state, the state's mediating institutions, in effect, mediate the nation's shared moral judgment back to itself, back to the citizenry. They express the thin, universal judgment to which all are accountable, and within which all must operate.

For most people, this mediation is most often represented in the person of a governmental bureaucrat. The IRS agent, the OSHA inspector, the TANF (formerly AFDC) caseworker—in each of these instances and hundreds of others, the bureaucrat is responsible for implementing or enforcing the law of the land.[32] For this very reason, Hegel's conception is fundamentally apt: the civil servants associated with the federal government, and the institutions within and through which they work, act as mediating institutions. They represent the state to the people with whom they interact. Do these representatives always comport themselves with a Hegelian aura of professionalism and detachment? Of course not. But however professional and disinterested they are or are not, whether they serve the commonweal or not, these bureaucrats represent the state in their action and in their persons, educating the broader public, for better or worse, through their enforcement of the nation's laws.

Conclusion

To be sure, the enactment of laws, and the enforcement and implementation of those laws by bureaucrats, not only enables, it often constrains the affected parties to evaluate whether their considered moral judgment is being properly expressed. Political associations routinely answer this question in the negative, and mobilize themselves in response to that evaluation.[33] But that is just to say that the mediating institutions of civil society and governmental institutions constitute an ongoing dialogue about the moral condition of the polity. In effect, government articulates the public consensus through its laws and institutions, and medium party political institutions tell the state when it is failing in that task.[34] A free and well-ordered democratic society requires that each half of this moral dialogue be operative and engaged.

In every instance, then, I am thus arguing for the relevance, the applicability, of Hegelian categories. While the presidency, the Congress, and the bureaucracy are decidedly (and in some cases, thankfully) different from Hegel's system, there are fundamental and significant points of similarity as well. But Hegel's point, and my objective, is to show how it is that the operation of these institutions promotes a national moral identity. In the last chapter, therefore, I outline both the history and the possibility of the state as moral pedagogue.

Chapter Twelve

The American State as a Moral Actor

My argument against the sufficiency of social capital institutions has centered on the problem of a fraying social fabric. In particular, I have been concerned with the question of racial, ethnic, and religious division. For that reason, it is worth relating this Hegelian analysis to the actions of the federal government. In this chapter, I outline one especially important example from our recent past. Specifically, I focus on the Voting Rights Act of 1965. I show that while the achievements of the civil rights era began in the realm of civil society, they are not attributable solely to those institutions, or to the production of social capital. Rather, the last years of the civil rights era serve to remind us Americans of the pedagogical role politics and government inevitably play in our society. I conclude by suggesting several contemporary issues that might afford us a similar opportunity.

The Voting Rights Act of 1965: A Hegelian Analysis

The role of the national government in the last years of the civil rights era centers on the leadership of the Johnson presidency. Of course, Johnson's administration had its tragic beginnings in the very midst of the civil rights movement; some attention to the issues of segregation and systematic discrimination was therefore inevitable. But Johnson clearly felt the matter deeply, and he believed that his own experience as a southerner gave him a unique opportunity and responsibility to address the problem. Evoking the mantle of his predecessor (whether more than history warranted is a question I leave to others), the Civil Rights Bill of 1964 was Johnson's first major legislative initiative. And when he was elected to a term of his own, the theme of racial justice only increased in intensity. In his inaugural address of 1965, Johnson again spoke directly to the issue of race, and to the suspicion and distrust born of exclusivity. "Justice," Johnson said, "requires us to remember . . . that when any citizen denies his fellow, saying, 'His color is not mine,' or 'His beliefs are strange and different,' in that moment he betrays America."[1] The Voting Rights Act of 1965 presented Johnson another important opportunity to make this case, and his special message before Congress on March 15, 1965, is particularly relevant to the point at issue here.

Johnson begins by setting the problem in terms that recall Gunnar Myrdal. "There is no Negro problem," Johnson began. "There is no Southern problem. There is no Northern problem. There is only an American problem. . . . This is one Nation . . . in which no section has fully honored the promise of equality."[2] After presenting a long litany of abuses against "the most basic right of all: the right to choose your own leaders,"[3] Johnson argued for the "Americanness of the civil rights movement." He therefore presented the Voting Rights Act as a means for supporting the movement's goals. After acknowledging the failure of previous statutes, Johnson's bill called for strong federal intervention against the Jim Crow policies of the South. Against the inevitable charges that the statute amounted to an unconstitutional expansion of federal power, Johnson took the case to a yet higher plane of argumentation; he rejected any claim against strong federal enforcement as, in Fields's words, "a repudiation of fundamental American values." Johnson's speech thus repeats a basic and, for my purposes, highly relevant theme. Johnson avers that America's racist treatment of African Americans contradicted the American public moral consensus, and thereby contradicted and undermined American society and American identity.

To be sure, the claim that the terms of the American public moral consensus required support for civil rights legislation only reiterated a refrain continually voiced by King and other leaders of the civil rights movement. But because the words were uttered by the president, in the halls of Congress, and with respect to a newly introduced piece of legislation, the terms of the debate changed. With this speech, the moral claims of the civil rights movement were turned around: no longer was a segment of society pointing up to government; rather, the shared judgment of America began to point down at itself. Thereafter, civil society could no longer legitimately operate in ways that openly defied these judgments, because these judgments were now understood to be constitutive of American identity. This distinction, and its importance, was evidently not lost on King himself. He reportedly wept as he watched Johnson's speech.[4]

Most Americans will concede that Johnson was not Lincoln. Fields notes that even within this very speech Johnson's eloquence and best instincts for leadership conflated with some of the worst impulses of his own ego.[5] Thus, the speech merely echoed the combination of motivations that marked Johnson's entire civil rights policy.

> Johnson's decision . . . to press forward with a voting rights statute reflected a combination of factors: the inability of previous civil rights laws to crack white resistance to black voting, a changing climate of public opinion outside the Deep South, the heroism exhibited by many civil rights activists, Johnson's concern with his place in history as well as his genuine desire to guarantee black voting rights, and calculations of Democratic advantage at a point when white southern support for the Democratic national ticket was eroding.[6]

It is commonplace to argue that political decisions typically involve the adjudication of such varied factors. One must therefore acknowledge that whatever the profundity and difficulties associated with this fundamental presidential task, profiles in political courage—that is, the willingness to lead based on a moral imperative even at the risk of one's own political career—are and have always been few and far between. Hegel himself notes that the state "stands on earth and so in the sphere of caprice, chance and error, and bad behavior may disfigure it in many respects." Yet while Hegel is smart enough to acknowledge the seamier side of politics, he claims that this is only a side—it is not the whole story. Hegel insists, to the contrary, that "the ugliest of men, or a criminal, or an invalid, or a cripple, is still always a living man. The affirmative, life, subsists despite his defects, and it is this affirmative factor which is our theme here."[7] Thus, while the president is a mere human being, and a particularly power-hungry one at that, the bully pulpit—that is, the president's unique ability and burden to represent America to itself—remains. Because of the exigencies of American politics and American political history, the president is constrained to take on the task of union building. He must take the moral imperative brought up from political associations, and make it a national imperative, that is, make it incumbent upon the whole of the American people, indeed make it constitutive of American identity.[8] Government is the medium by and through which the people's judgment is communicated back to them. It is thus an indispensable and irreplaceable means for constructing a moral society.

The president's rhetoric is central to the pedagogical function of the bill; King's reaction speaks to that fact. At the same time, other institutions of the federal government—most relevantly, the legislature and the bureaucracy—likewise reflect the Hegelian notion of the state as a moral teacher and unifier. While the democratic majority and Johnson's unparalleled legislative abilities meant that the outcome was never in much doubt, the congressional debate was lively and sustained. On both sides, debate regarding the bill reflected the inevitable amalgam of self-interest and universal moral appeals. Yet on both sides, the debate also focused on the principles that undergird the American public moral consensus. Thus, for every high-minded statement supporting the inalienable right to vote, there was an equally ardent appeal to the principle of self-determination, and the danger of an all-usurping government. Sam Ervin (senator from North Carolina) argued that the bill was both unconstitutional and unfair. "I do not believe," he said, "that the Constitution of the United States permits Congress to degrade one State or six or seven States to such an extent that they are not on an equality with the other States of the Union."[9] Strom Thurmond (even then senator from South Carolina) argued vehemently that if the act were passed, Americans would find "a totalitarian state in which there will be despotism and tyranny."[10] The institutions of national government thus moved the debate over segregation to a level of medium party politics: each partisan had a self-interested stake in the matter, but each was constrained to present his or her case in terms of the American public moral consensus.

Thurmond's statement may have been hyperbolic, but it was not fatuous: the Voting Rights Act gave extraordinary powers of oversight and enforcement to the executive branch. The act authorized the U.S. attorney general to appoint federal officers as registrars and voting examiners, whose job was to be present at registration and voting facilities, in order to ensure that blacks were afforded free and equal access. This power was, according to Davison, "used sparingly,"[11] yet it was clearly effective.

> While only 28 percent (16 of 57) black-majority counties without examiners achieved black-majority electorates, 60 percent (19 of 32) of black-majority counties with federal examiners did so during the times. In fact, in Alabama, Georgia, Louisiana, and Mississippi, every county in which a majority-black electorate was registered in 1967 or 1968 either had had a federal examiner or was geographically adjacent to one or more counties that did.[12]

For the most part, these visits ended a mere five years after the passage of the act. As a result, the effects of federal registrars dropped off over time. Nevertheless, even a decade later, counties that were visited by federal examiners had a higher rate of black registration than those that were not.[13]

Just as important and just as controversial was section 5 of the act, which froze all voting statutes within the seven states of the Deep South. After passage of the act, any proposed change in voting practices had to be submitted to the Department of Justice for examination and "preclearance." Thus, these states had to convince the federal government that their new state law—the product of ostensibly legal and democratic procedures—did not "have the purpose or effect of denying or abridging the right to vote on account of race" *before* the change could be implemented. The extraordinary power outlined in this section was lost on no one (least of all the representatives of the affected states), but the admittedly strong encroachment of these states' autonomy was considered necessary to counteract the many ingenious forms of discrimination and voting dilution practiced therein.

For several years, this section was not applied at all. But in 1969, the Supreme Court took up a case that directly addressed the question of its constitutionality. *Allen v. the State Board of Education* concerned laws passed in Virginia and Mississippi that, it was alleged, were designed to dilute the effect of black votes by instituting at-large (as opposed to district) elections. Davison recounts the facts regarding the Mississippi statute:

> The 1966 legislature, without public debate, passed a package of election laws. . . . Among them was a bill requiring at-large election of all county boards of supervisors and boards of education. A senator explained that the change from wards to countywide elections would protect "a white board and preserve our way of doing business."[14]

The Supreme Court ruled in favor of the federal government. Writing for the court, Chief Justice Warren wrote that

> the Voting Rights Act was aimed at the subtle, as well as the obvious, state regulations which have the effect of denying citizens their right to vote because of their race. . . . The right to vote can be affected by a dilution of voting power as well as by an absolute prohibition on casting a ballot.[15]

This ruling gave newfound standing to the section, and the Justice Department created a special section to cope with the increased workload associated with statutory challenges. The effect of this section was even more important in changing the political and cultural landscape in the South. Lisa Handley and Bernard Grofman conclude that "[f]ederal intervention . . . as well as voting rights suits brought by private litigants, was primarily responsible for the significant increase in southern black officeholding, at least at the state legislative and congressional levels."[16]

My purpose here is merely to recount the fact that the Voting Rights Act did more than simply outlaw a set of discriminatory practices; it established powerful provisions regarding its enforcement. The attorney general, along with other officials appointed by the Department of Justice, was given sweeping authority to bring the law to the affected areas—in essence, to bring the judgment of the nation to bear on the actions of states, communities, and even individuals. Hegel argues that the bureaucrat's role is decisive in mediating the state's inherent moral dimension to the people. Again, in his words, "[t]he conduct and culture of officials is the sphere where the laws and the government's decisions come into contact with individuals and are actually made good."[17] In the contemporary climate, such judgments are subject to ridicule, and often such criticism is well deserved. It need nevertheless be said that in its enforcement of the Voting Rights Act, federal bureaucrats performed in a way that Hegel would recognize and even laud. The actions of the federal observers, registrars, and lawyers represented, concretized, and even personalized the universal interests of the state. By their very physical and professional presence, they manifested the inescapable fact that the nation's moral consensus had changed, and that all state and local political institutions would have to conform to that judgment.[18]

Thus, while all three institutions differ markedly from the Hegelian equivalents, they nevertheless fulfill certain essential Hegelian roles. With the Voting Rights Act of 1965, these institutions combined to effectuate nothing less than a radical rethinking of American morality and American identity. Indeed, they performed in just the way that Hegel describes.

Governmental Pressure on Civil Society

I must be clear. I am appealing to the Voting Rights Act to demonstrate a conceptual point. First, the actions of the federal government inevitably have a moral dimension. Second, because the federal government is a national institution, it is uniquely able to influence the beliefs and values, and constrain the independent actions, of all Americans. Because I have argued that the cultivation of social capital through the institutions of family, church, and neighborhood is abetted by, if it is not wholly dependent upon, ethnic and cultural homogeneity, and is thus wholly insufficient to the problem of a fraying social fabric, it makes sense to point to an instance where the actions of the federal government were able to define the American public moral consensus in a way that was explicitly transracial. Of course, the Voting Rights Act was hardly the only instance of this sort of definition. From Truman's desegregation of the armed forces, to Eisenhower's intervention at Little Rock, to the Civil Rights Act of 1964, the federal government demonstrated a slowly developing sense of resolve regarding the matter of segregation.[19] At the same time, the Voting Rights Act is unique. Few legislative acts so overtly demonstrate the moral dimension of politics. For that matter, few authorized a more intrusive and more selective form of federal power. While both facts make the conceptual point easier to draw, I am not arguing that all laws are, can be, or ought to be equally instructive. Also, while I contend that the positive action of the federal government is indispensable to the objective of building a more moral, more civic society, I am not making specific normative claims about what the relative power of the federal government ought to be.

Finally, the law is now over thirty years old, and has, therefore, an extensive history—involving several extensions and additions and an ongoing litany of Supreme Court decisions. Many now claim that some of those decisions and extensions have developed into policies that amount to a kind of affirmative action through politics (e.g., extending protections to language minorities, adopting new standards for legislative redistricting, etc.). These individuals thus contend that these changes have been counterproductive to the very goals of the act itself. Using the terms that engage this work, the argument, then, is that the operative goal of building a more moral society has led to a new institutionalization of identity politics, thereby undermining the very cause of unity—indeed, undermining the very objectives that motivated the law in the first place. In Abigail Thernstrom's words,

> We need electoral arrangements that deliver the right messages. . . . And the right messages are: that we are all Ameri-

cans, that we're in this together, that the government thinks of us and treats us as individual citizens with individual (not group) rights, that whites can represent blacks and blacks can represent whites, that we have no need for legislative quotas since distinct racial and ethnic groups are not nations in our society.[20]

I am neither qualified nor able to debate every dimension of the law, nor of every court case, nor of every extension of the original act. Nevertheless, a few points are necessary.

It does seem clear that the most important provisions of the 1965 law (sections 4 and 5) were included as emergency measures in order to respond to a specific state of affairs: i.e., rampant disenfranchisement of blacks and local white populations bent on using every available means to subvert the effort to alter that state of affairs. It is equally apparent that the law has been dramatically effective in this regard. In the Deep South, blacks are registered at levels that approach whites, and hundreds of blacks have been elected to local and state offices. Finally, I trust all would agree that there is a tension inherent within the law: provided these successes were to continue, the point would eventually come where the law's innate tendency to abet identity group politics would undermine and even override its ability to ameliorate past racial injustices. To be sure, not all would agree that we have now reached that point, but on this specific issue, at least, I must confess my sympathies with the arguments of Abigail Thernstrom and others. I have argued that the goal of a more moral society is premised on the existence of a more unified society, and the latter, it seems to me, is undermined by policies that foster group political identity. The tensions within the act itself makes any decision a judgment call, but to say the least, I would argue that the inadequacies inherent within the institutions of civil society make it particularly important that the federal government mandate electoral arrangements that, in Thernstrom's words, "send the right message."

But the question of whether Thernstrom and company are right is independent of my contention that the law of 1965 did what I said it did. If they are right, it merely demonstrates the rather basic point that the institutionalization of law does not end the matter.[21] Indeed, it would illustrate that Hegel's conception does not adequately describe the fabric of American democratic life. The pedagogy associated with American government is not a one-way street but rather completes the dialogic circle between government and civil society. Finally, if Thernstrom is right, it would also speak in a negative way to the more fundamental point that governmental action *will* instruct the citizenry about how it ought to understand moral and civil behavior. The only question is whether it does so well or poorly.

Again, the cards are stacked against a felicitous outcome. Often, if not always, politicians are, in Jim Sleeper's apt phrase, "moral dilettantes." The point then is not that citizens should rely on the state to tell them what the moral thing to do is. Politicians can surely provide needed leadership, but they must ordinarily be led to believe that there is a strong connection between a moral imperative and their own political interest. This discussion cannot, therefore, be taken to deny the primary status of political associations. The argument here has been that through these associations, politicians can be so led, and that when they are, their actions can play a critical role in constructing a more moral society. The Voting Rights Act of 1965 is representative of that role. Its passage and implementation helped to change the consensus in a way that made the society more moral, and it did so in a way that dramatically changed the expression of American civil society.

Initially, this change took the form of "massive resistance." Responding to the Supreme Court's 1954 decision in *Brown v. the Board of Education,* civic and political leaders in the South mobilized tremendous resources within and without civil society to preserve "the Southern way of life" against the latest round of interlopers, carpetbaggers, and scalawags. The virtual resurrection of the Ku Klux Klan in parts of the Deep South and the explosion of so-called citizen's councils, along with a flurry of new state legislation, all showed that the South was willing to employ every legal and extralegal mechanism available to preserve the edifice of segregation. The role of white churches was more mixed, but for every Christian community that joined the fight against Jim Crow, there were at least as many that emphatically defended segregation. Yet the majority of churches lined up in neither camp. Rather, most church leaders responded to the federal government's action by counseling a resolute disinterest in matters of this world, and, if anything, the parishioners' feelings on the matter were decidedly less ambiguous than those of the average church leader. In Numan V. Bartley's words, "[O]n the whole the church acted as a prosperous secular institution, unwilling to allow Christian principles to impede seriously its institutional success."[22] Labor unions in the South also reinforced established segregationist policies. In the face of calls for integration from George Meany and others in national leadership, many local members either ignored such entreaties, or quit the union and joined the KKK. Such responses do not constitute "massive resistance," but, to say the least, this policy of quietism coming from these two key institutions of civil society cleared the way for more virulent responses.

At the same time, this vindictive and widespread backlash is quite obviously not the end of the story. Few would deny that the formidable resources of the federal government lent credibility and force to black Southerners' pursuit of justice. It appears to me impossible to gauge the relative contribution of each factor, but it does seem fair to conclude that the reigning ethos of Jim Crow has been effectively destroyed, and that the actions of the federal government were crucial to effecting that change. James Button quotes a black Southern schoolteacher who offers this conclusion: "Integration here has been due to federal law; otherwise things would be the same way today. Things don't change easily in small, poor, Deep South towns."[23]

Civil society in the Deep South has changed, too. Citizens' councils are moribund if they exist at all, national labor unions are wholly integrated, and churches rarely explicitly express their support for policies of segregation. Indeed, Robert Wuthnow has noted that "[t]he effect of the civil rights legislation in the early 1960s . . . was to prompt religious organizations to form caucuses and coalitions oriented toward the promotion of racial equality."[24]

Of course, this is not to say that the issue of race, and the tension between race and the institutions of civil society, has gone away. The American dilemma remains just as relevant as it ever was. Neighborhoods and churches (not to mention local union halls, country clubs, and other private institutions) are only marginally less segregated now than they were in, say, 1955. One must not minimize these realities. But one must assess them in light of this fundamental fact: whatever the correlation between ethical thickness and ethnic or racial homogeneity, the acceptability of overt racism, either in an organization's ethos or its actions, is gone forever. Organizations that explicitly espouse racist beliefs, or implicitly affirm them in their practice, remain, of course. The state cannot do just anything: it can act only within the confines of a robust conception of individual and group rights. Nevertheless, the fact that such organizations in the South and elsewhere must operate either as social pariahs or in closeted silence cannot but be regarded as a rather dramatic and positive development. Indeed, much of the progress our society has made toward real and sustained integration must be attributable to this very fact.

Our society has changed. More specifically, it has changed morally. And that change has manifested itself within American civil society even though this change is not and could not be the result of civil society institutions alone. The Voting Rights Act of 1965 is one especially pertinent example of the American people using the mechanism of the federal government to express their considered judgment about the content and import of the American public moral consensus. And that judgment conditioned and changed the expression of American civil society.

This Hegelian analysis thus leads to an utterly Hegelian conclusion: "Particular interests should in fact not be set aside or completely suppressed; instead, they should be put in correspondence with the universal, and thereby both they and the universal are upheld."[25] The particularity of civil society makes it ill suited as a means for expressing universal moral judgments. That is the job of the state, and civil society is constrained, albeit not compelled, to operate within that expression.

Determining when constraint becomes compulsion, or, more strongly, when constraint becomes tyranny, is no easy matter, of course. Indeed, adjudicating the hard questions and the competing rights claims is the never-ending burden of the very institutions outlined in this chapter. Nancy Rosenblum's recent book *Membership and Morals* offers a strong case that the only way for a liberal society to preserve the benefits associated with civil society is to accept the fact that people will sometimes form noxious and almost wholly infelicitous groups.[26] While my position might differ at the margins, I share that belief. However, I also believe more must be said. For I would argue that a robust understanding of the freedom of association is all the more reason for politics to take up the task of articulating and concretizing just what it is that the larger society *does* believe. In his book, *Liberal Purposes,* William Galston offers the following analogy:

> Think of a society based on liberal public principles as a rapidly flowing river. A few vessels may be strong enough to head upstream. Most, however, will be carried along by the current. But they can still choose where in the river to sail, and where along the shore to moor. The mistake is to think of the liberal polity either as a placid lake or as a an irresistible undertow.[27]

Within very broad limits, it is the responsibility of government to make sure that groups can find eddies and pools within which they can do what they want with whom they want. But I would insist that for that very reason, society ought also to concern itself with the direction and speed of the current that will inevitably result from governmental action or inaction.

There is one other political point I want to make. For I suspect that some may be inclined to admit to the change in American society regarding the issue of race, but to dismiss it as either trivial or superficial. Americans' long-standing conversation about race (or shouting match, as you prefer) has recently produced a flurry of books. Many representatives of this cottage industry argue that even in this post–civil rights era, there is a political, conceptual, even metaphysical divide between black and white Americans. The title of Andrew Hacker's recent book epitomizes this position—two nations: black and white, separate, hostile, unequal.[28] As I have said before, it is indisputable that significant differences exist between black and white Americans on their evaluation of recent and historical events, and, most relevantly, on their attitudes about policy questions concerning race. The question is: How should one assess these differences. Are they, or are they not, cause for despair?

In *One Nation After All*, Alan Wolfe acknowledges "the huge racial rift" separating black and white Americans on questions of policy, but he insists on the importance of an underlying agreement:

> Principles . . . are least appreciated when most ubiquitous. It does not take a historian to remember a time when significant portions of the United States did not accept the principle that everyone was a moral equal regardless of race. The fact that nearly all Americans now do is what makes it possible to disagree about a policy such as affirmative action, for a substantial portion of that disagreement takes place within reasonable interpretations of what the common moral principle means.[29]

Thus, the question of this ongoing racial divide must be assessed within a proper and adequate frame of reference. Disagreement about policy is meaningful—indeed, is possible—only if an agreement on principles is already in place. Politics regarding questions of race run deep and are often hostile, even vituperative; but because of the sea change in principles, politics about these questions is, for the first time, truly possible. For it is now the case that discussions about affirmative action, racial gerrymandering, or what have you take place within a deep and established agreement that race is morally irrelevant, and that our society ought to develop so as to bring itself ever closer to that reality. This, too, is a dramatic and significant change, and it, too, is the result not of civil society, and surely not of civil society alone, but rather, it results from the actions of the state. It is due, most specifically, to the passage of civil rights legislation like the Voting Rights Act.

The Role of the State in the Contemporary Era

Again, my purpose has been conceptual. I have tried to show that the institutions of civil society are necessary but insufficient means for reinvigorating a more moral, more civic-minded society. Nevertheless, the very concerns that drive the civil society movement beg the question: What does this mean for our contemporary set of circumstances? What actions can government take that might help to advance the moral and civic condition of the polity, and which of these might have a felicitous regulative effect on American civil society?

A sufficient response would require another book, but I do want at least to point to a few relevant examples. My argument has been that the national government is the only common moral authority, and that, therefore, it is uniquely able to cultivate and promote a distinctively American ethos, one that transcends race, ethnicity, religion, ideology, and class. I therefore want to focus on issues and institutions that present just this sort of challenge: namely, the military, public education, and campaign finance reform.

The Military and Universal National Service

For much of our nation's history, military service was incumbent upon all (or almost all) able-bodied males. The American military was thus premised on the ideal of the citizen-soldier. Few would dispute the claim that this ideal has had important and felicitous effects in the broader society. The ideal of the citizen-soldier brought together individuals from various classes, ethnicities, and religions (and, after Truman's order, races) who would otherwise rarely have had a chance to interact. By living, training, and fighting alongside each other, American men (and a few American women) came to value and respect members of other diverse groups. The military's requisite level of commitment, sacrifice, and solidarity instilled a deep and abiding sense of regard for one's comrade. More than this, it also cultivated a broader but nevertheless meaningful sense of civic obligation. Thus, until the

Vietnam era, at least, American military service achieved many of the very objectives outlined by Adam Ferguson over two hundred years ago.[30] Their profound and common experience often left veterans uniquely filled with "the love of the public" about which Ferguson spoke and upon which, to some degree, any society depends.[31] In contrast to Ferguson, of course, military service in America was not limited to the aristocracy. Rather, universal conscription was a state institution by which a national identity was communicated, mediated, to the citizen who was also a soldier, and thus, ultimately, to society at large.[32]

To its almost universally acknowledged credit, the move to an all-volunteer military has not changed its commitment to, or its ability to achieve, this transethnic, transracial ethos.[33] To be sure, troubling questions about the status of women and homosexuals have, in the eyes of many, jeopardized the military's ability to maintain this role while remaining an effective fighting force. Still, most would agree with Thomas Ricks that "the Army may be the only institution in America where we can see what Lyndon Johnson's Great Society could have been."[34]

But the military's contemporary achievements and its felicitous social effects are naturally limited to those who volunteer, and one significant result of the transition to an all-volunteer military has been that the army now recruits disproportionately from lower (although, significantly, not the lowest) economic classes and from racial minorities. One must question whether the grave risks associated with national defense should be left primarily to those of limited means. If those risks were shared more equitably throughout society, one must also wonder how it would effect decisions about whether and when to employ military force. But more to the immediate point, the move to an all-volunteer military has affected its ability to foster these indirect social goods. Even as the goals of cultivating both civic-mindedness and a national ethos have become more exigent than ever, the fruitful intermingling between religions, ethnic groups, and especially classes has declined dramatically in the all-volunteer military. Just so, the sense of commitment and duty to the social order that is a collateral result of military service is now focused on a far smaller segment of the population. It is therefore worth attending once again to the question of compulsory and universal service.

Military downsizing in a post–Cold War world renders any questions about the desirability of universal *military* service wholly beside the point. The military simply no longer needs that many recruits. But while the military alone may not be able to function as a path of universal service, universal service need not be limited to the military. Many nations include nonmilitary options (including work in hospitals, social service, and the like) in which young citizens can fulfill these kinds of obligations. According to Charles Moskos, "Today, in Germany, which still has conscription, about 100,000-plus young men each year—approximately 30 to 40 percent of all eligible draftees—perform alternative civilian service."[35] These options ought not to be seen as equivalent—rarely does someone try to kill you in a hospital; military service must always be valorized and rewarded over and above any such civilian alternative. But assuming these options can be adjudicated in legislation,[36] the reintroduction of a truly universal service could enable our society once again to advance these civic goals even while respecting and accommodating the unique features of military life. And because so many draftees would serve in and with the broader community, that service would have an even greater potential for mediating and thus reinvigorating a spirit of solidarity and common purpose.

There is no denying that the political will for such a proposal is minimal, if not wholly absent. The libertarian streak runs strong in American history. But the legacy of the citizen-soldier is at least as strong, and we would do well to try to recapture the social benefits associated with that legacy. To my mind, the burden is on those who consider the moral condition of the American polity to be unsatisfactory to say why such a refashioning of this public institution is unacceptable or unworkable. At the least, it seems to me that civil society advocates should find here grounds for supporting the Clinton administration's Americore program. This weaker alternative is hardly likely to induce the level of change that might likely be associated with a truly universal program. But it seems to me to offer one noncoercive and relatively cheap mechanism by which some of these same civic objectives might be more fully extended to those from higher economic strata.

Moral Education and the Public School

Like the military, public schools have traditionally functioned to bring people together across lines of particularity. Middle-class movement to the suburbs has diminished the likelihood of integration across class and race lines, but even in the most elite suburb, public schools continue to expose children to different religious, ethnic, and ideological perspectives. But the importance of public schools does not end here. The public school is where the state is most directly engaged in the art of moral pedagogy. For it is the central and irreplaceable mechanism by which the state communicates the moral and civic dimensions of American citizenship.

In his classic book, *The Lively Experiment: The Shaping of Christianity in America,* historian Sidney Mead affirms the position of J. Paul Williams, who argues, in effect, that the public school system in the United States is the functional equivalent of the European established church. Whereas European nations have traditionally depended on "the Church" to take on the inculcation of a common set of morals, values, and social expectations, the endemic condition of American pluralism moved the task inexorably, if by default, into the hands of the state. The public school, in turn, became the natural locus within government for such a task. While any school—private or public, religious or secular—can communicate a moral ethos, public schools are, by definition, the only form of primary and secondary education that fully transcends particularity, and articulates a moral vision that is open to and incumbent upon all. Because of the American tradition of religious pluralism and religious freedom, that moral vision should not be identified with any one religious tradition. The state therefore must choose a minimalist and secular one: the religion of democracy. In terms that echo my discussion of the American public moral consensus, Mead and Williams want to promote a distinctively American set of beliefs and values that transcend the public expression of any specific religious tradition.[37]

While the basic outlines of this democratic religion, then and now, receive near universal assent, the specifics have always been inherently controversial. How should those propositions be taught? How do these values compare with each other? And how should they be given content? As I mentioned, the heavy-handed Protestantism associated with public education at the turn of the century led to the Roman Catholic parochial school system. Then, as now, the public school curriculum was fought over so vigorously precisely because the stakes were so high. For each participant implicitly acknowledged both that there *is* a universal set of beliefs and that that belief system, if left abstract and vague, is not enough.

But the contemporary climate *is* different. Earlier this century, Roman Catholics opted out of the system. Today, opponents demand that their objections be heard and their ideals affirmed. Every year, state legislatures take up proposals that stipulate yet another set of new and politically charged curriculum requirements; school board elections and the approval of new and revised textbooks are similarly subject to inevitable and often quite rancorous confrontations. The recent reaction to the voluntary standards developed by the National Center for History in the Schools is singularly evocative of the perceived stakes associated with public education in this country.[38] Much of this change manifests many of the same issues outlined throughout this book: the breakdown of public authority, the diminution of the idea of a common truth, and the rise of identity politics. In any event, the implications for democratic religion and the public school are severe. Our inability to agree on the terms under which we Americans will teach our children history appears to preclude the possibility that we could teach them anything about morality.

Certainly, there are a number of contentious moral issues that weigh heavily on the American civic fabric. We are unlikely to come to resolution soon on the moral questions associated with abortion, for example. To be sure, the argument against the epistemological viability of universal moral claims does not alter the necessity of such a foundation. Any society must be able to reaffirm and transmit certain fundamental values and virtues to its children if it is going to survive. But more to the point, it is a mistake to argue that the move from platitude to substance is so inherently controversial that moral education is inevitably parochial and sectarian. The continued resiliency of the American public moral consensus shows plainly that universal claims are yet possible. The task is to make the inculcation of those claims viable for our contemporary circumstances.

A few years ago, my family and I were going through old scrapbooks. We came across my mother's second-grade report card from McKinley Elementary School, North Platte, Nebraska, for the school year 1942–43. Here is what it says:

> Education for good citizenship must be the chief aim and end of schools which derive their support from public funds raised through taxes. The training of boys and girls to be good citizens is not so much a matter of teaching them facts as it is a matter of bringing forth in them the right spirit. The teachers desire to cooperate with the parent in fostering the right attitude.

The report card then goes on to report progress according to the following citizenship traits:

1. Self-control:
   a. respects rights of others
   b. is attentive
   c. respects authority
2. Thrift
   a. respects property, his own and others
   b. careful of books, furniture and other materials
3. Responsibility
   a. works diligently
   b. is dependable
   c. plays fair
4. Personal neatness
   a. posture
   b. cleanliness, hands, nails, face, teeth, etc.
5. Consideration of others
   a. responds courteously
   b. is kind and thoughtful

Some may want to add or subtract from the margins of this list. Some may be suspicious of any effort to put such a list into practice. But is there anyone—and more pertinently, any parent—who would object to it outright? Anyone who would view these objectives as culturally bound and therefore oppressive or, alternatively, contentless and therefore useless? And if so, what would they propose as an alternative?

I cannot conjure one. Indeed, margins aside, I take this to be a responsible and judicious assessment of the possibility and limits of moral education in public schools. First, the author argues that there are a series of virtues that are understood to be essential for preserving a well-ordered democratic society. Second, this task is argued to be a central goal of a publicly funded education. That is, *precisely* because a school is supported by all taxpayers and open to all children, it must attend first and foremost to the task of moral and civic education. Perhaps most importantly, appeals to the parent implicitly avow the very dialogic and cooperative relationship between civil society and the state that this book seeks to present. I judge that our republic would do well to reintroduce just this sort of perspective.

To be sure, the question of what role the *federal* government ought to play in reinvigorating moral education in the public schools is not answered by this account. And that question is likely to be utmost in the minds of civil society advocates. Tocqueville himself notes that American schools are a felicitous example of private associations. That is why they work. It would be dangerous, he believes, to have schools controlled by a single authority. The debate associated with national testing standards bears a similar refrain.[39] The incompetence and ham-handedness of the federal government make it inherently ill equipped to deal with the questions of how a local school district decides to educate its students.

This is a powerful rejoinder. Public schools are unique institutions, combining parental, local, state, and federal control. To my mind, there surely are issues where the involvement of the federal government ought *not* to overstep other loci of control and input. But circumspection is not silence. At the very least, I would argue that the federal government should offer guidelines and rhetorical support for developing a nationwide curriculum on the moral requirements of American citizenship. Indeed, I think this arena ably lends itself to the rhetorical devices of the presidency outlined in the previous chapter.

But the question of degree is secondary. The more fundamental point is that we Americans remain without an established church, and while the prospects for revitalization of a civil religion recede ever further, we continue to require an institution that takes on the same pedagogical role. There are (and for that matter, must be) some values and virtues that transcend our differences, and the inculcation of those values in the lives of future citizens remains primarily the burden of the state. Just so, the need for moral and civic renewal hinges on a more developed sense of moral unity and national moral identity, and that enterprise requires the involvement of the national government.

The effects of such a national initiative are, of course, difficult to predict. The notion that childrens' attitudes and behavior would not be positively affected by such a policy seems to me nearly impossible to sustain. That alone ought to be enough reason to develop such a proposal. But the pedagogical effects of public education have never been limited to the children alone. For many immigrant parents, the education of their children constituted their most important exposure to the American public moral consensus. For native-born citizens, too, helping their children with homework and attending school presentations and parent-teacher conferences have offered important reminders of the very lessons they themselves once learned. The same effects surely continue to this day. The inculcation of a thin but authoritative moral ethos would therefore likely affect the way grown-ups conduct themselves, as well—in political associations, civil associations, and even in their everyday exchanges. The pointing down of the state through public education could have a dramatic effect on the moral fabric on American society and on the moral standards achieved within American civil society. I can see no reason not to try.[40]

Campaign Finance Reform

Earlier, I recounted the efforts of Common Cause on the matter of campaign finance reform, but in this context, it is worth returning to the issue. For I am inclined to agree with that organization that the present state of affairs, and, for that matter, any effort to deal with it, raises fundamental questions about the values that constitute our American identity.

There can be little debate that whatever the office, campaigns are growing ever more expensive, and thus candidates are ever more dependent on campaign money. This money comes primarily from well-heeled individuals and organizations with clear economic or political agendas, and, as a result, the perception among the electorate is that these contributions come with an implicit quid pro quo. According to Hunter and Bowman, 81 percent of Americans agree that government "is pretty much run by a few big interests looking out for themselves."[41] Campaign or party contributions are increasingly seen as the condition for meaningful representation, and thus, the poor and middle class feel ever more irrelevant to the political process. Hunter and Bowman also report that among the poor, working, and lower middle classes, as well as the poorly educated, there is widespread affirmation of the idea that "people like me don't have any say about what the government does."[42]

According to Verba, Schlozman, and Brady, these perceptions constitute the most important challenge to the current campaign finance system.[43] Indeed, these perceptions go to the heart of our democratic order. For if any one principle can be taken as part of the American public moral consensus, it is the ideal of political equality, of one man, one vote, of liberty and justice for all. If equal protection of interests is non-existent, or even if a large portion of the population merely believes it to be nonexistent, the civic implications are profound.

To be sure, the matter is extraordinarily complex, and the constitutional issues loom large for any proactive program. The Supreme Court's ruling in *Buckley v. Valeo* is unequivocal: money is a form of political speech, and therefore the conditions under which the government can regulate its use are severely limited. While the court acknowledged the government's right to restrict contributions in the hope of limiting corruption, the desire to preserve or foster political equality is not a constitutionally valid objective. "[T]he concept that government may restrict the speech of some elements of our society in order to enhance the relative voice of others is wholly foreign to the First Amendment."[44] This ruling has been a matter of much controversy, of course.[45] Nevertheless, *Buckley* outlines the extremely narrow terms under which policy reforms must proceed. A whole host of ingenious state policy initiatives regarding restrictions on campaign expenditures or campaign contributions have foundered on the rocks of *Buckley v. Valeo.* And it seems likely that a number of recent proposals at the federal level would suffer a similar fate.[46]

At the same time, the credibility problems associated with the status quo are grave; a meaningful, guileless response is vital. What then to do? I submit that perhaps the focus should change. In short, if Congress is unable to lower the ceiling, then it seems to me prudent to find ways of raising the floor. Free or reduced TV and radio time and mail service are hopeful strategies for increasing the exposure of less well-known and well-funded candidates. I am also convinced that programs that exchange such airtime for voluntary spending limits could pass constitutional muster. Though far more indirect than placing restrictions on campaign expenditures or contributions, these proposals would lower the importance of contributions and thereby reduce the importance of financial contributors. Properly legislated, they might even raise the level of political discourse. Mickey Kaus offers the following scenario:

> What if, for the two weeks before an election, the evening drive time on radio plus a half hour following the evening news on television were reserved for candidates? Ratings would decline, in all probability. But elections would be public rituals far more absorbing than they are now—in no small part because it would be easier to mount a challenge to incumbents.[47]

Were such a proposal to be adopted, it would at the least signify a new articulation of basic American values. I would expect that the condition

of our political campaigns, and the civic condition of the polity generally, would improve from such an articulation.

Here, too, the political issues are daunting. Many wealthy constituents are quite content with the way things are now, and their feelings
about proposals like Kaus's are quite well known to members of the
House and Senate. Nevertheless, I think the political and constitutional
chances are much better here. Indeed, I suspect that something along
these lines may have been the direction the *Buckley* court was advocating in the first place. As Burt Neuborne has noted, "As originally written, the Buckley per curiam was probably intended to steer the nation
to public financing of elections as the only constitutional way to control
expenditures and enhance equality."[48] In any event, here again, my
more fundamental point is civic. The cynicism and distrust that per-
vade the contemporary political climate undermine the civic order; if
political equality is believed to be a false or obsolete ideal, democracy
itself is imperiled. The federal government is uniquely positioned, and
uniquely responsible, to articulate our shared commitment to values
like political equality and thereby to revitalize that commitment in the
hearts of Americans.

Conclusion

These examples are illustrative only. My objective is not to call for some
slate of legislation, let alone to offer an exhaustive account, but merely
to raise renewed attention to a very Hegelian point of view: namely,
that the federal government has an indispensable role in fostering the
moral identity of the American body politic. This moral dimension cannot be avoided; it can only be directed. I am calling for a politics that
acknowledges that fact.

Again, I readily acknowledge that politicians are, more often than
not, "moral dilettantes." In this regard, the civil society movement has
got it right: political leaders rarely start anything, and when they do
pick up a cause, it is rarely for reasons that do not involve their own
self-interest. But while a moral dialogue rarely begins in government,
its processes and institutions can, in a unique and indispensable way,
move that discussion to a national level. Government is the means by
which we citizens express our considered judgment about our identity,
our values, and our purposes back to ourselves. Again, while political
associations point up, laws, governmental rhetoric, and governmental
institutions point down. And it is only when both partners are engaged

that a dialogue is created and the moral condition of the society is properly advanced.

There is more that must be said. It is clear enough that I believe that the civil society movement is too inclined to disparage the role of the state. However, it is not enough merely to argue for a corrective. What is required is a civil society movement that tries to envisage a normative understanding of what the state is, what it does, and what relationship it ought to have with the institutions of American civil society. What is required is a movement that sees the institutions it is concerned with as operating within a moral universe that is largely expressed through the political process. Politics and government articulate a minimal set of moral parameters that preserves, directs, and legitimates the pluralistic, particularistic expressions of civil society. This, too, is a very Hegelian point:

> In contrast with the spheres of private rights and private welfare (the family and civil society), the state is from one point of view an external necessity and their higher authority; its nature is such that their laws and interests are subordinate to it and dependent on it. On the other hand, however, it is the end immanent within them, and its strength lies in the unity of its own universal end and aim with the particular interest of the individuals, in the fact that individuals have duties to the state in proportion as they have rights against it.[49]

Of course, to give the government and the political process such an important role in the construction of a moral society is fraught with danger. Hegel was so concerned that he constructed the merest veneer of democratic processes. He would have society take its chances with the bureaucratic class. But the essential distinction here is that in contrast to Hegel's state, the American body politic is democratic.

Tocqueville, too, was very aware that the state and its institutions can easily degenerate into paternalism at best, oppression at worst. But whether he was reluctant or not, Tocqueville *was* a democrat, and in contrast to Hegel, he recognized that the dangers exist on both sides: without strong state institutions to manifest and affirm an overriding set of mores, civil society can readily degenerate into demagoguery, extreme partisanship, and the tyranny of the majority. We live out our social lives on the slippery slope. As I have tried to show, Tocqueville maintained that the solutions to the problems of democracy can be found only within democracy. Thus, while he argued that civil society is an essential constraint on the natural excesses of the state, he also believed that the dangers associated with an unchecked civil society is mollified by an overarching (and at least partially institutionalized) moral consensus. The one serves as a check on the other: two permanent but dynamic, combative but not wholly antagonistic, interlocutors, through which a distinctively democratic and distinctively moral conversation is sustained.

The civil rights movement is paradigmatic of such a conversation. The movement began in churches, and it cannot be understood without acknowledging the deep religious convictions that sustained the vast majority of its participants. In terms that civil society advocates rightly celebrate, the social capital institutions of family, neighborhood, and church provided a thick moral fabric that gave them the fortitude to stand up against an unjust and un-American social structure. Just so, the Montgomery bus boycott was the first significant instance in which this thick set of moral demands moved to embrace an explicitly political agenda. That political organization, and similar ones, practiced medium party politics as well as well as any in our nation's history. For it argued its moral case in terms of the American public moral consensus, demanding that American society live up to its purported ideals. The movement is thus one of American civil society's crowning achievements, and rightly stands as representative of the inherent power of those institutions to create moral and civic renewal. But it is romantic and historically inaccurate to understand the achievements of the civil rights movement as the responsibility of these institutions alone. The actions of the government surrounding the Voting Rights Act of 1965 (like similar acts before it) brought the issue to the national stage, and then rendered a moral judgment on the matter. That judgment, too, was articulated in terms of the American creed and was therefore made morally incumbent upon all Americans and indeed upon all expressions of American civil society.

The achievements of the civil rights movement are thus the result of the concerted actions of civil society broadly construed—that is, a civil society that extends beyond social capital institutions to include local and national political associations—and governmental institutions. In the civil rights movement, all three institutions combined to give content and specificity to the American public moral consensus and thus to make our society more moral.

The problems that drive the civil society movement—problems of dissolving civility and growing anomie—are perhaps as profound as those that occupied the civil rights movement. What is more, like the American dilemma of race, those problems appear endemic to the modern American condition. There is no guarantee that we will do better at addressing them than all those who came before us. Indeed, in this late modern era, politics, government, and even the very notions of authority and universality have all been severely compromised. But for all this, the ideals and values that define the American identity continue to resonate in the hearts of Americans, and whatever their current status, the political institutions that for good or ill concretize those values and ideals remain, and remain under democratic control. Those concerned about the moral condition of American society are right to attend to the condition of American civil society, but they are wrong to denigrate or reject the government's inevitable and indispensable role as a moral pedagogue. The task is daunting, but that is all the more reason for us to marshal all the resources we have at our disposal.

Notes

Chapter One

1. He goes on to note that "[o]ne recent college graduate even observed sadly that her suburban Philadelphia neighbors 'don't even wave anymore.' " Bill Bradley, "Civil Society and the Rebirth of Our National Community," *Responsive Community* 5, no. 2 (spring 1995): 5.

2. Robert Putnam, "Bowling Alone, Revisited," *Responsive Community* 5, no. 2 (spring 1995): 28.

3. John Marks, "The American Uncivil Wars," *U.S. News and World Report,* April 22, 1996, 68.

4. Michael Sandel, *Democracy's Discontent: America in Search of a Public Philosophy* (Cambridge: Harvard University Press, Belknap Press, 1996), 353.

5. Robert Putnam, "Bowling Alone: America's Declining Social Capital," *Journal of Democracy* 6 (1995): 73.

6. William J. Bennett, in "The National Prospect: A Symposium," *Commentary,* November 1995, 29.

7. Nick Ravo, "Index of Social Well-Being Is at the Lowest in 25 Years," *New York Times,* October 14, 1996, A14.

8. Richard Morin, "Poll Finds Wide Pessimism about Direction of Nation," *Washington Post,* August 29, 1997, A28.

9. Robert Wuthnow, *Christianity and Civil Society: The Contemporary Debate* (Valley Forge, Pa.: Trinity Press International, 1996), 3.

10. Even at this level of generality, there is not universal agreement. While Americans commonly understand civil society to refer to a variety of independent, voluntary groups, associations, and institutions that are not under the direct control of the state, some British thinkers (e.g., Ernest Gellner and John Hall) use the term *civil society* to describe a society that is civil—that is, one that is free and democratic, and that both manifests and secures that freedom through the existence of voluntary associations. This subtle but surely significant difference further underscores the difficulties associated with this concept.

11. Ernest Gellner, *Conditions of Liberty: Civil Society and Its Rivals* (London: Penguin Books, 1994); Sandel, *Democracy's Discontent;* John Keane, ed., *Civil Society and the State: New European Perspectives* (London: Verso, 1988); Andrew Arato and Jean Cohen, *Civil Society and Democratic Theory* (Cambridge: MIT Press, 1994); and Robert Putnam, *Making Democracy Work: Civic Traditions in Modern Italy* (Princeton: Princeton University Press, 1993).

12. Putnam describes the importance of these organizations in *Making Democracy Work.*

13. I have in mind the usual suspects: Benjamin Barber, Jean Bethke Elshtain, Glenn Loury, Robert Putnam. Others who might qualify include Michael Walzer, Alan Wolfe, and Michael Sandel.

14. I argue that the Solidarity movement in Poland is one of the two main wellsprings from which much of the American movement draws its conceptual self-understanding. It is worth noting, therefore, that in 1989, Bronislaw Geremek, Solidarity's leader in the Polish parliament, noted that "defining" civil society was of no interest to him or his compatriots. "We don't need to define it, we see it and feel it." Quoted in Flora Lewis, "Foreign Affairs: Needs of Civil Society," *New York Times,* August 29, 1989, I19. In America and Poland, to define civil society is to limit it, and to limit it is inevitably to make it less capable of achieving the desired ends.

15. Alexis de Tocqueville, *Democracy in America,* trans. George Lawrence, ed. J. P. Mayer (Garden City, N.Y.: Anchor Books, 1969), 513.

16. The social and political impact of this feeling of crisis is, of course, hardly limited to the reemergence of civil society as a concept. It is also at the bottom of some fundamental political shifts in this country, including the rise of religious conservatism, the widespread cynicism expressed in and toward politics, and, similarly, the decline in party identification. Whatever else might account for these conditions, they surely can be understood as reactions to a deep and pervasive uneasiness about the condition of American society and American culture, and the apparent inability of politics to significantly alter this condition.

17. Nancy L. Rosenblum, *Membership and Morals: The Personal Uses of Pluralism in America* (Princeton: Princeton University Press, 1998), 26.

18. Dan Coats, "Re-funding Our 'Little-Platoons,' " in *Policy Review: A Journal of American Citizenship* 75 (January–February 1996): 25.

19. Bill Bradley, "America's Challenge: Revitalizing Our National Community," *National Civil Review* 84, no. 2 (spring 1995): 96.

20. See, e.g., James S. Coleman, "Social Capital in the Creation of Human Capital," *American Journal of Sociology* 94, supplement (1988): S95–S120.

21. Robert Putnam, "Tuning In, Tuning Out: The Strange Disappearance of Social Capital in America," *PS: Political Science and Politics* 28, no. 4 (December 1995): 665.

22. Ibid.

23. Putnam, "Bowling Alone," 76.

24. Not surprisingly, the fault line echoes the distinction I want to draw between the public and the theoretical debate. Elshtain, Wolfe, Putnam, and Sandel all mention the family as a significant social institution. For Gellner and Keane, the family is simply not a relevant category.

25. These points of distinction are not foreign to the civil society discussion. They are articulated by Hegel in his *Philosophy of Right.* In light of Hegel's pivotal role in the modern concept of civil society, this connection is very significant. I say more about that role in chapter 5.

26. Theoreticians Arato and Cohen stand as a powerful counterexample; they cite the family, and "the intimate sphere" generally, as an integral element of civil society. Indeed, they further maintain that a reinvigorated progressiv-

ism must center on politics within the family. See Arato and Cohen, *Civil Society and Democratic Theory.*

27. Mary Ann Glendon, "Forgotten Questions," in Mary Ann Glendon and David Blankenhorn, eds., *Seedbeds of Virtue: Sources of Competence, Character, and Citizenship in American Society* (New York: Madison Books, 1995), 2.

28. Putnam, "Bowling Alone," 73.

29. Bradley, "America's Challenge," 96.

30. David Popenoe, "The Roots of Declining Social Virtue: Family, Community, and the Need for a 'Natural Communities Policy,' " in Mary Ann Glendon and David Blankenhorn, eds., *Seedbeds of Virtue: Sources of Competence, Character, and Citizenship in American Society* (New York: Madison Books, 1995), 73.

31. Andrew Martin, "Neighborliness Tied to Lower Crime," *Chicago Tribune,* August 15, 1997, sec. 2, p. 3. While coauthor Robert Sampson speaks of the need for neighbors to trust each other and to be willing to intervene in the lives of neighborhood children, he cautions that a safer, more involved neighborhood neither equates with nor requires the kind of intimate, affective associations commonly associated with Putnam and other civil society advocates. "We're not calling for a return to a mythical urban village. . . . You can have neighborhoods that get things done and don't necessarily have close personal ties."

32. Jean Bethke Elshtain, "Marriage and Civil Society," *Family Affairs* 6, no. 1 (spring 1996): 4. In the interest of full disclosure, I should say that I edited this volume. Further on, I cite an essay by Don Eberly that also appeared there.

33. Popenoe, "The Roots of Declining Social Virtue," 97, 94, 98. It is interesting and significant that Popenoe's concern resonates forcefully with an observation of one of the patron saints of the civil society movement, Adam Ferguson. As part of the eighteenth-century Scottish Enlightenment, Ferguson argued that the virtues of community and union are ultimately inseparable from animosity and separation. "[O]ur attachment to one division, or to one sect, seems often to derive much of its force from an animosity conceived to an opposite one: and this animosity in its turn, as often arises from a zeal in behalf of the side we espouse." *An Essay on the History of Civil Society,* ed. Fania Oz-Salzberger (Cambridge: Cambridge University Press, 1995), 21. I will have more to say about Ferguson's analysis in the next chapter.

34. Alan Ehrenhalt, *The Lost City: The Forgotten Virtues of Community in the Chicago of the 1950s* (New York: Basic Books, 1995).

35. Sandel, *Democracy's Discontent,* 321.

36. The demand to conform often created lives of quiet desperation. One thinks of studies like David Riesman's *The Lonely Crowd* and William Whyte's *The Organization Man,* films like *The Man in the Gray Flannel Suit* and *Rebel without a Cause,* and Betty Friedan's lament, "Is this all there is?"

37. James Luther Adams rightly qualifies the claim that church membership is "voluntary." Within the Christian tradition, this notion includes significant theological presuppositions that are more commensurate with a Protestant understanding of church. See his "Mediating Structures and the Separation of Powers," in Michael Novak, ed., *Democracy and Mediating Structures: A Theological Inquiry* (Washington: American Enterprise Institute, 1980), 2–3.

38. Sidney Verba, Kay Lehman Schlozman, and Henry E. Brady offer significant empirical support for this claim in their voluminous study, *Voice and Equality: Civic Voluntarism in American Politics* (Cambridge: Harvard University Press, 1995). The authors found that churches are by far the most important means for sustaining political activity among the poor and uneducated. Just as significantly, churches and church organizations often exemplify the democratic ideal, by providing one of the few remaining opportunities in which people of different economic and education levels actually do intermingle as equals.

39. Adam Meyerson, "Letter to Our Readers," *Policy Review: The Journal of American Citizenship* 75 (January–February 1996): 5.

40. William Schambra, "By the People: The Old Values of the New Citizenship," *National Civic Review* 84, no. 2 (spring 1995): 109. It is important to note that Loury's comments reinforce the idea that institutions of civil society serve to support the moral and cultural inculcation that takes place within the family.

41. Quoted in Dan Coats and William Bennett, *Project for American Renewal* (Washington: Empower America, 1995), 23.

42. Ibid., 1.

43. As I noted, many on the left contend that such sentiments also betray a common inattention, if not outright hostility, toward the needs and demands of marginalized populations.

44. Schambra, "By the People," 103.

45. Quoted in Theda Skocpol, "Unraveling from Above," *American Prospect,* March–April 1996, 20.

46. Schambra, "By the People," 101 ff.

47. Robert Putnam, "Robert Putnam Responds," *American Prospect,* March–April 1996, 28.

48. This distinction recalls Berger and Neuhaus's minimalist and maximalist strategies, as outlined in their seminal work, *To Empower People: The Role of Mediating Structures in Public Policy* (Washington: American Enterprise Institute, 1977). In their latest writing, they effectively reject the maximalist strategy. I discuss this work and its influence on the contemporary movement in chapter 4.

49. Bradley, "America's Challenge," 99.

50. Francis Fukuyama goes farther than that, arguing that "[a]t most, the state can agree to do no further harm." In "The National Prospect: A Symposium," *Commentary,* November 1995, 56.

51. Glenn Loury, "Values and Judgments: Creating Social Incentives for Good Behavior," in T. William Boxx and Gary M. Quinlivan, eds., *Culture in Crisis and the Renewal of Civil Life* (Lanham, Md.: Rowman and Littlefield, 1996), 23.

52. Don Eberly's assessment is quite common:

The realm of civil society is often referred to as an intermediary sector because it stands as a buffer between the individual and the outer world of the state and the market. Civil society is not an economic sphere in which self-interested persons compete, nor is it oriented according to law and legal procedure; it is a sector where individuals are drawn together into horizontal relationships of trust and collaboration. ("Recovering Moral Cohesion," *Family Affairs* 6, no. 1 [spring 1996]: 8)

53. As I will argue below, one of the dominant threads that runs through the modern use of the term *civil society* relates to the desire to construct, as it were, capitalism with a human face.

54. Dale Russakoff and Steven Pearlstein, "Ma Bell's Changing Tone: In a Reordered Corporate World, It's Employees Who Pay the Toll," *Washington Post National Weekly Edition,* June 3–9, 1996, 6–9. Alan Ehrenhalt's description of the lives of workers on the southwest side of Chicago in the 1950s offers a similarly striking contrast to contemporary corporate life. See his *The Lost City,* esp. 101–4.

55. Francis Fukuyama's book *Trust: The Social Virtues and the Creation of Prosperity* (New York: Free Press, 1995), is a glaring exception. Fukuyama argues that these changes may ultimately undermine the free enterprise system itself. Capitalism depends on social norms of trust and reciprocity, and the inculcation of those norms can come only from outside the system itself. A decline in civil society may therefore ultimately leave Americans unable to compete in a global economy. Thus, just as the operation of the market affects the condition of social life, the condition of society is equally significant to achieving and maintaining an efficient, well-ordered market economy.

56. Sandel, *Democracy's Discontent,* 332.

57. See Robert Wuthnow, *Poor Richard's Principle: Recovering the American Dream through the Moral Dimension of Work, Business, and Money* (Princeton: Princeton University Press, 1997). See esp. chap. 1, "Having It All and Wanting More: The Social Symptoms of Cultural Distress." Alan Wolfe's study *One Nation After All* (New York: Viking Press, 1998) outlines similar conclusions. See 234–50.

58. Sue Schellenbarger, "Work and Family," *Wall Street Journal,* June 26, 1996, B1.

59. The Council on Families in America, *Marriage in America: A Report to the Nation* (New York: Institute for American Values, 1995), 14.

60. David Popenoe, "The Family Condition of America: Cultural Change and Public Policy," in H. Aaron, T. E. Mann, and T. O. Taylor, eds., *Values and Public Policy* (Washington: Brookings Institution, 1994), 92.

61. Jean Bethke Elshtain, *Democracy on Trial* (New York: BasicBooks, 1995), 14.

62. Benjamin Barber, "Searching for Civil Society," *National Civic Review* 84, no. 4 (spring 1995): 114. Here again, Berger and Neuhaus's analysis in *To Empower People* emerges as an essential precursor to this discussion. Their term *megastructures* closely recalls the point. It is also worth noting that their term explicitly includes both the market and the state.

63. The connection between the state and the market, then, is that both institutions have outgrown their traditionally imposed limits and threaten to swamp the more intimate forms of thinking and behaving that are associated with civil society. In what follows, I tie this notion to the thought of Tocqueville and, more recently, Berger and Neuhaus. But it is important to note that a

similar idea is found in the thought of Jürgen Habermas. Habermas claims that the systems of thought associated with the state and the market have "colonized" the "life-world" of the family, civil society, and the public square. For more on Habermas, see his *The Structural Transformation of the Public Square: An Inquiry into a Category of Bourgeois Society,* trans. Thomas Burger (Cambridge: MIT Press, 1989). See also Craig Calhoun, ed., *Habermas and the Public Sphere* (Cambridge: MIT Press, 1992).

64. Gregg Vanourek, Scott W. Hamilton, and Chester E. Finn, Jr. *Is There Life after Big Government?: The Potential of Civil Society* (Indianapolis: Hudson Institute, 1996).

65. Meyerson, "Letter to Our Readers," 5.

66. George Will, "The Politics of Soulcraft," *Newsweek,* May 13, 1996, 82.

67. To my knowledge, Pat Buchanan never invoked the term *civil society;* nevertheless, his economic populism expressed a similar belief that corporations act without considering the impact of their decisions on the local community. Buchanan's 1996 primary campaign was hardly removed from partisanship, but it is fair to say that his criticisms earned him the animosity of many mainstream Republicans.

68. Eberly, "Recovering Moral Cohesion," 9.

69. David Brooks, " 'Civil Society' and Its Discontents," *Weekly Standard,* February 5, 1996, 19.

70. Paul Starobin, "Rethinking Capitalism," *National Journal,* January 18, 1997, 106.

71. Alan Wolfe concludes *One Nation After All* by telling Republicans that "if . . . you want to be a party of morality, you will have to at some point condemn the capitalist mentality you otherwise so admire" (306–7). It appears that in very tentative ways, at least some conservatives are recognizing this basic tension.

72. E. J. Dionne, *Why Americans Hate Politics* (New York: Simon and Schuster, 1991). Alan Wolfe's study lends support to this conclusion as well. See *One Nation After All,* 307.

73. Putnam, "Bowling Alone," 68.

74. Bradley, "America's Challenge," 94–95.

75. Don Eberly, "The Quest for a Civil Society," *National Civic Review* 84, no. 4 (spring 1995), 124.

76. Elshtain, *Democracy on Trial,* 53.

77. Rogers Worthington, "On the Record: Todd Gitlin," *Chicago Tribune,* January 12, 1997, sec. 2, p. 3.

78. Arthur Schlesinger, Jr., *The Disuniting of America* (New York: Norton, 1992).

79. Bradley, "America's Challenge," 96.

80. To anticipate, the ability to distinguish between good and bad political association—i.e., between political associations on the one hand, and identity politics on the other—is itself a moral distinction. And I will argue that this moral distinction cannot be found or developed within the institutions of civil society themselves.

81. Alan Wolfe argues that "[c]ontemporary American conservatism can lit-

erally be defined as the defense of middle-class morality, an effort to protect the traditional neighborhoods, family ideals, religious beliefs, work ethic, schools, love of country, and security concerns of the lower-middle class, no matter how impolitically expressed, from the welfare state on the one hand, and the liberal defense of modernity on the other" (*One Nation After All*, 11).

82. As I go on to show, Putnam, for one, affirms a role for the state that appears to be similar to my own. But it is relevant to note that he, too, is compelled to argue against a conception of "civil society" that is strongly reminiscent of the conception I have outlined here. See chapter 8.

Chapter Two

1. John Keane, "Despotism and Democracy: The Origins and Development of the Distinction between Civil Society and the State, 1750–1850," in John Keane, ed., *Civil Society and the State: New European Perspectives* (London: Verso, 1988), 36; Krishan Kumar, "Civil Society: An Inquiry into the Usefulness of an Historical Term," *British Journal of Sociology* 44, no. 3 (September 1993): 375–95; and Andrew Arato and Jean Cohen, *Civil Society and Democratic Theory* (Cambridge: MIT Press, 1994) make virtually the identical argument.

2. Marvin Becker argues that it begins much earlier, in the sixteenth century, with Grotius and Pufendorf. He maintains that one can hear faint rumblings of the change as far back as Montaigne. See Becker, *The Emergence of Civil Society in the Eighteenth Century* (Bloomington: Indiana University Press, 1994).

3. For more on the constitutive features of modernity, see Talcott Parsons, "Evolutionary Universals in Society," in *Sociological Theory and Modern Society* (New York: Free Press, 1967), 490–520. Philip Selznick offers a splendid overview of the relevant issues in "Morality and Modernity," pt. 1 of his *The Moral Commonwealth: Social Theory and the Promise of Community* Berkeley: University of California Press, 1992.

4. Fania Oz-Salzberger, introduction to Adam Ferguson, *An Essay on the History of Civil Society* (Cambridge: Cambridge University Press, 1995), xv–xvi.

5. Adam Ferguson, *An Essay on the History of Civil Society*, ed. Fania Oz-Salzberger (Cambridge: Cambridge University Press, 1995), 238.

6. Ibid., 218.

7. Ibid., 256.

8. Keane, "Despotism and Democracy," 37.

9. David Brooks, " 'Civil Society' and Its Discontents," *Weekly Standard*, February 5, 1996, 20.

Chapter Three

1. Alexis de Tocqueville, *Democracy in America*, trans. George Lawrence, ed. J. P. Mayer (Garden City, N.Y.: Anchor Books, 1969), 12. (All further references to this work in this chapter will appear in parentheses in the text.)

2. This conception of history as the product of human freedom within the capacious confines of providence is very different from Hegel's. Tocqueville dismissed any notion of historical determinism as "cowardly." See Andre Jardin, *Tocqueville: A Biography*, trans. Lydia Davis and Robert Hemenway (New York: Farrar Straus Giroux, 1988), 269.

3. In contrast to many critics, I do not see a significant distinction between the first and second parts of *Democracy in America.* I am more inclined to view the work as a complete and coherent whole. Nevertheless, it is fair to say that the themes that emerge from this analysis are more closely connected to part 2.

4. Even more than 150 years after Tocqueville wrote, Americans still feel the shock of recognizing themselves in his analysis. At this point in the analysis, I forgo any dot connecting. Still, I cannot resist referencing the commonplace bumper sticker, "The one who dies with the most toys wins." The uneasy, self-condemnatory tone behind this sentiment readily recalls Tocqueville's analysis and belies the statement's ready humor. The decidedly Hobbesian character of Tocqueville's thinking is also worth noting.

5. Pierre Manent, *Tocqueville and the Nature of Democracy,* trans. John Waggoner, with a foreword by Harvey Mansfield (Lanham: Rowman and Littlefield, 1996), 59.

6. This problem hints at Tocqueville's famous discussion of the tyranny of the majority. Since the issue is not germane to my concerns, I leave off discussion of this central topic.

7. In chapter 5, I focus on Hegel and his followers, drawing out contrasts and similarities with the Tocquevillian tradition. To anticipate, however, I want to note that Tocqueville's fears in this regard are remarkably similar to Gramsci's discussion of hegemony: both describe a form of despotism that is comparatively benign, agreed to, and bought off with creature comforts. It also recalls the behavior of the Polish Communist government vis-à-vis its people. Cf. Jacques Rupnik, "Dissent in Poland, 1968–78: The End of Revisionism and the Birth of Civil Society," in Rudolf L. Tokes, ed., *Opposition in Eastern Europe* (Baltimore: John Hopkins University Press, 1979), 82: "relations between the authorities and the workers in Poland, as in the rest of the Soviet bloc, are based on a tacit social contract. . . . The regime provides job security and slow but regular increases in the standards of living. In exchange, workers forfeit their traditional union, political and civil rights." It is remarkable to note that in all three cases, an independent civil society was seen as the most effective means for combating this state of affairs.

8. In the phrase "liberal democracy," *liberal* is an adjective that, in Guido de Ruggiero's words, "has the force of a qualification." De Ruggiero, *The History of European Liberalism* (Oxford: Oxford University Press, 1927), 379. It describes a series of political and social mechanisms that curtail, direct, and control the rule of the people. In this basic sense, Tocqueville is the quintessential liberal. This is one central reason that his thought on civil society has come to dominate the liberal tradition, and especially the American liberal tradition.

9. See Tocqueville, *Democracy in America,* 305. Tocqueville's entire definition of mores is important.

> I mean it to apply not only to 'mores' in the strict sense, which might be called the habits of the heart, but also to the different notions, possessed by men, the various opinions current among them, and the sum of ideas that shape mental habits. So I use the word to cover the whole moral and intellectual state of a people.

Tocqueville considers mores "to be one of the great general causes responsible for the maintenance of a democratic republic in the United States" (287).

10. Tocqueville also distinguishes between civil and political society. Krishan Kumar notes this, but he says that Tocqueville defines civil society as "essentially the arena of private interests and economic activity." Kumar, "Civil Society: An Inquiry into the Usefulness of an Historical Term," *British Journal of Sociology* 44, no. 3 (September 1993): 381. In other words, civil society means something close to what Marx thought it meant. Political society, on the other hand, constitutes 'the art of association' within civilized society and includes both political and civil associations. There is certainly textual support for this claim (see, e.g., Tocqueville, *Democracy in America,* 586, and Jardin, *Tocqueville,* 204); nevertheless, I believe that Kumar's description is, at best, overstated. In the first place, Tocqueville notes on the first page that equality of conditions exercises dominion over "civil society as much as over the government" (9). Such a statement would appear to leave little room for political society as a separate social domain. Second, in one of his most famous discussions, Tocqueville explicitly includes "commercial and industrial associations" within his definition of civil associations (513; see also 521), thereby effectively precluding the claim that economic activity is something separate from civil society. I conclude that when Tocqueville uses the term "civil society," he means something very similar to the traditional liberal understanding: that part of society that is not the state and includes everything from the family to unions and political parties *and* large and small economic enterprises. When he does refer to political society, I take him to be referring to something like political culture—that is, the broader social effects of the principles and institutions of political organization.

11. Nancy Rosenblum rightly notes that this distinction, while legitimate, is not static. "[A]ssociations not formed for purposes of expression anticipate, foster, and mutate into political voices." *Membership and Morals: The Personal Uses of Pluralism in America* (Princeton: Princeton University Press, 1998), 206.

12. Compare the summary statement of Berger and Neuhaus (two of those who, I will argue, follow in Tocqueville's path) about associations as "schools of democracy": "However trivial, wrongheaded, or bizarre we may think the purpose of some associations to be, they nonetheless perform this vital function." Peter Berger and Richard Neuhaus, *To Empower People: The Role of Mediating Structures in Public Policy* (Washington : American Enterprise Institute, 1977, 34).

13. Tocqueville is thus translating even as he affirms the basic insight of Montesquieu. For the latter, the nobility (i.e., the aristocracy) is the most important "intermediate power." It keeps the monarch from becoming a despot.

14. Not only is local government more democratic, it is also, consistent with Tocqueville's analysis, more natural. Tocqueville notes that local government is an inevitable feature of human society; it is "well-rooted in nature" (62).

15. Tocqueville notes that any association, "be it political, industrial, commercial, or even literary or scientific, is an educated and powerful body of

citizens which cannot be twisted to any man's will or quietly trodden down, and by defending its private interests against the encroachments of power, it saves the common liberties." 697.

16. In their major study of American political activity, *Voice and Equality: Civic Voluntarism in American Politics,* Sidney Verba, Kay Lehman Schlozman, and Henry Brady offer an analysis wholly commensurate with Tocqueville's: "We show that both the motivation and the capacity to take part in politics have their roots in the fundamental non-political institutions with which individuals are associated during the course of their lives" (Cambridge: Harvard University Press, 1995), 3. It is also interesting and relevant that their study concluded that churches were among the most important of these nonpolitical institutions.

17. Manent, *Tocqueville,* 24–25. This analysis fits very easily within the confines of modern game theory. In famous configurations like the prisoner's dilemma, the objective is to find a way to develop a sense of trust, reciprocity, and cooperation. Tocqueville is saying that civic associations are essential means to this end. Putnam, *Making Democracy Work,* makes the same argument, with explicit references to game theory. See my discussion below, pp. 85–86.

18. Yet even in the more crass world of political organizations, over time, the effort to keep up the appearances affects one's outlook, until "what had been calculation becomes instinct" (512). There are interesting parallels here between Tocqueville's thinking and Pascal's wager (regarding a faithful life). In both cases, if you fake it long enough, eventually the actions and emotions can become genuine.

19. William E. Johnston, Jr., "Finding the Common Good amidst Democracy's Strange Melancholy: Tocqueville on Religion and the American's 'Disgust with Life.'" *Journal of Religion* 75, no. 1 (January 1995): 58.

20. In this context, the question of whether such claims are true is not directly relevant. The only question is whether they are socially useful. "At the moment," Tocqueville says, "I am only looking at religion from a purely human point of view" (445).

21. It is therefore not correct to see churches and other houses of worship as simply another manifestation of Tocqueville's civic associations. Churches are valuable because of what they add over and above the felicitous effects of association: namely, an authoritative and compelling set of moral beliefs. Indeed, Tocqueville thinks democracies would fare best under the cultural dominion of Roman Catholicism, precisely because of its more rigorous set of religious strictures and its hierarchical structure.

22. Ernest Gellner, *Postmodernism, Reason, and Religion* (London: Routledge, 1992), 5.

23. Throughout American history, a number of religious thinkers have expressed their extreme dissatisfaction with this bargain. In the contemporary arena, see, for example, the works of John Howard Yoder and Stanley Hauerwas.

24. William Mathie presents a compelling and disturbing analysis that claims that for Tocqueville, women choose the prevailing social norm because it is in their self-interest to do so. Everyone intuitively knows the importance of

mores and the importance of women in inculcating those mores, and therefore society makes life miserable for any women who would choose another path. Thus, a cloistered married life is the best and, in some sense, the only available option. It is this analysis, Mathie believes, that accounts for the sad but resolute condition of American women. Mathie's theory is controversial, but it is surely consistent with Tocqueville's operative principle: solutions to democratic problems are found through self-interest. See Mathie, "God, Women, and Morality: The Democratic Family in the New Political Science of Alexis de Tocqueville," *Review of Politics* 57, no. 1 (winter 1995): 7–30.

25. It is interesting to note the similarity between this description and Hegel's discussion. In the latter instance, the ethical immediacy of the family is destroyed when the young man finds he must go out on his own and earn a living in the heartless world of bourgeois society.

26. David Brooks, " 'Civil Society' and Its Discontents," *Weekly Standard*, February 5, 1996, 19. My frequent citations of Brooks's piece illustrate that I think it is an extremely perceptive analysis of the civil society movement. Nevertheless, on one central point I think he is dead wrong. Brooks offers the above litany without even a whisper of its uncanny similarity to Tocqueville's comparison between aristocratic and democratic life. That he then goes on to argue that Tocqueville "was not a believer in 'a limited life' " only compounds the error. Tocqueville's role as the theoretical lynchpin for this movement stems in large measure from his very willingness to affirm the moral superiority of a more egalitarian, but quieter and less heroic conception of society.

27. Another point of connection between Tocqueville and the contemporary movement bears mentioning. Tocqueville says that American exceptionalism is, in part, simply a matter of good fortune. America bypassed the feudal era of Europe and therefore equality and democracy were established without the severe social strife that Europe endured. But in contemporary America, the social institutions that served as our functional equivalents for the aristocracy—namely associations, religion, and family—are either waning or changing. We Americans are therefore left with a feeling of social crisis very much like eighteenth- and nineteenth-century Europe, only we are without even the vestiges of European solutions. Joshua Mitchell has noted this irony as well. "As Christian religion recedes in Europe and America, by an ironic twist of history the Europeans will be better able to cope with the political consequences because the *residual* aristocratic elements there counter the short-term tendencies of the democratic soul." Mitchell, *The Fragility of Freedom: Tocqueville on Religion, Democracy, and the American Future* (Chicago: University of Chicago Press, 1995), 254. In other words, those features of American society that were strengths may be turning into liabilities.

I can only speculate, but what Mitchell calls this "ironic twist of history" might explain the European character associated with much of the contemporary movement. Most significantly, perhaps, the fact that the movement can be characterized as populist traditionalism (i.e., the conservatism born of the desire to maintain the useful parts of the old social order) can be explained precisely because the old and uniquely American mechanisms are giving us cause for concern. Thus, though there is hardly a hint of aristocratic thinking in our history, America is, of necessity, turning to a political view that has clear ties to the European aristocracy.

Another example: Tocqueville says that in the aristocracy, fathers were the inculcators of mores. Fathers in democratic society, he says, effectively abandoned this role, as relations between father and sons became more egalitarian. Now I have noted the intense focus on the family within the civil society movement and the ties between it and the fatherhood movement. Is it possible that the rise of the fatherhood movement in America is an intuitive response to the obsolescence of the old democratic solution? That is, since women no longer occupy a separate, cloistered status relative to democratic society, they therefore can no longer be counted on to single-handedly inculcate American mores. That being the case, the old aristocratic system emerges, almost by default, as the only other salient option. If this is true, then the feminist argument that the fatherhood movement wishes to restore the old, sexist order could not be more wrong. Rather, the whole movement is premised on the recognition that that former order is indeed gone forever. The objective, rather, is to restore something of the older, aristocratic order, albeit in a radically different context.

Again, this is admittedly all rather speculative, but I include it to make the broader point: namely, that the Tocquevillian analysis not only shows us why we have come to this state of social decline, it also points to the fact that we are, for the first time, inclined to consider solutions that are more closely associated with the aristocratic social order.

28. Tocqueville also had important, and typically ambiguous, things to say about partisanship, but I leave that discussion until chapter 10.

Chapter Four

1. For more on Durkheim, see the collection edited by Robert Bellah, *Emil Durkheim on Morality and Society* (Chicago: University of Chicago Press, 1973). Bellah's introduction to this collection is also very helpful.

2. I do not wish to imply that Tocqueville's influence is in any sense limited to these figures. Throughout the twentieth century, American political science and sociology are littered with Tocquevillian themes and ideas. Group theory, pluralism, game theory, and various expressions of American exceptionalism all manifest Tocqueville's legacy. I have chosen these figures because they are cited most frequently by contemporary civil society advocates, and because they address most directly the moral problems associated with modernity.

3. Robert Nisbet, *A Quest for Community: A Study in the Ethics of Order and Freedom* (San Francisco: ICS Press, 1990; originally published in 1953). See also Nisbet, *Community and Power* (New York: Oxford University Press, 1962).

4. Nisbet echoes Tocqueville's uneasy (at best) relationship with the capitalist order. It is not that capitalism is immoral; rather, both see capitalism as dependent upon local associations to sustain the values that keep it going. Yet capitalism also has an innate tendency to grow and consolidate, tendencies that are extremely unhealthy to these very associations. This leaves human beings like "a sand heap of disconnected particles of humanity. If it is, or is allowed to become, the latter, there is nothing that can prevent the rise of centralized, omnicompetent political power." For Tocqueville and Nisbet, as for

the contemporary movement, the concern over capitalism is born of the belief that capitalism, like democratic society itself, must be controlled if freedom is to be preserved. Nisbet, *Quest for Community,* 215.

5. Ibid., xxx.

6. Ibid., 156.

7. Ibid., 235. Nisbet argues that the state's growth is of a piece with the ascendancy of a particular conception of liberalism—namely, of freedom as the preservation and extension of the individual's autonomous choice. Sandel, *Democracy's Discontent,* presents a contemporary argument that is strikingly similar to Nisbet's.

8. Nisbet, *Quest for Community,* 45.

9. Nisbet's attention to alienation, disintegration, and the innate drive for community reflects the influence of Durkheim.

10. Nisbet, *Quest for Community,* 239.

11. Ibid., 171.

12. Ibid., xxix–xxx.

13. Ibid., xxix.

14. Peter Berger and Richard Neuhaus, *To Empower People: The Role of Mediating Structures in Public Policy* (Washington: American Enterprise Institute, 1977), 15.

15. Ibid., 2.

16. Ibid., 3, 4. Part of the relevancy of these institutions stems from the fact that they "have demonstrated a great capacity for adapting and innovating under changing circumstances."

17. In this sense, the language and tenor of Durkheim come to fore. Durkheim is also explicitly cited in the text. See ibid., 4.

18. Peter L. Berger and Richard John Neuhaus, "Response," in *To Empower People: From State to Civil Society,* ed. Michael Novak (Washington: AEI Press, 1996), 153.

19. Berger and Neuhaus, *To Empower People,* 2.

20. Ibid., 7.

21. It is worth saying more here. Berger and Neuhaus's formulation certainly contains hints of the Catholic principle of subsidiarity (see chapters 7 and 9), and for that reason, many have seen this work as a seminal point in bringing Catholic social thought to bear on the American experiment. Perhaps. But I believe that the connection is more coincidental than referential. In a symposium on the book, Neuhaus himself notes the similarity, and states that "[w]e have no problem with that" (Richard John Neuhaus, "Response to Mechling and Price," *Soundings* 62, no. 4 [winter 1979]: 406). That is, it seems to me, a ringing statement of consistency, but nothing more. They do not mention him, but I believe one could make just as strong a case that it is John Stuart Mill who is being echoed, not Pius XI. Later in the same response, Neuhaus goes on to say this: "[T]o put it quite bluntly, their choice [the choice of individuals and groups] is none of our business so long as they do not infringe upon the liberty of others to make different choices" (ibid., 407). The ardent libertarianism behind this statement is not representative of Catholic social thought; it is, however, quite representative of Millian liberalism.

22. I believe that this is the source for the incessant, if often uncontextualized, reference in the contemporary debate.

23. Peter L. Berger, "Response to Mechling and Price," *Soundings* 62, no. 4 (winter 1979): 398.

24. Neuhaus, "Response to Mechling and Price," 405.

25. Jay Mechling, "Myth and Mediation: Peter Berger's and John Neuhaus's Theodicy for Modern America," *Soundings* 62, no. 4 (winter 1979): 348.

26. Berger and Neuhaus, *To Empower People,* 6.

27. Berger and Neuhaus, "Response," 150.

28. Berger and Neuhaus, *To Empower People,* 1.

29. In chapter 12, I make almost the same point to argue for the indispensable role of the state. The difference between us is that while I believe the state's pedagogical role is most clearly manifested in questions involving race, I do not believe it does or ought to end there.

30. Berger and Neuhaus, *To Empower People,* 19.

31. Berger and Neuhaus, "Response," 151.

32. Ibid., 150.

33. Michael Novak, introduction to *To Empower People: From State to Civil Society,* ed. Michael Novak (Washington: AEI Press, 1996), 2.

34. Berger and Neuhaus, "Response," 145.

35. Novak, introduction, 5.

36. The first sentence of Putnam's book formulates the question: "Why do some democratic governments succeed and others fail?" The basic formulation is essentially a recasting of Tocqueville's question: "Why does democracy work in America?" The cohesion between the two works starts at the very beginning. Robert Putnam, *Making Democracy Work: Civic Traditions in Modern Italy* (Princeton: Princeton University Press, 1993).

37. Ibid., 167–76. See my definition and discussion of social capital in chapter 2.

38. In stark contrast to Berger and Neuhaus, Putnam argues that the actions of the state (specifically, the reorganization of the institutions of local government) are critical agents in effecting this kind of change. For Putnam, clearly, the state is not an irrelevancy.

39. Putnam, *Making Democracy Work,* 88.

40. Robert Putnam, "Bowling Alone: America's Declining Social Capital," *Journal of Democracy* 6 (1995): 66.

41. Ibid., 77.

42. The following list is representative, but it is by no means exhaustive. See, for example, "The Solitary Bowler," *Economist,* February 18, 1995, 21–22; Richard Morin, "So Much for the 'Bowling Alone' Thesis," *Washington Post National Weekly* Edition, June 17–23, 1996, 37; John Clark, *Shifting Engagements: Lessons from the "Bowling Alone" Debate,"* Hudson Briefing Paper 196 (Indianapolis: Hudson Institute, 1996); Richard Stengel, "Bowling Together: Civic Engagement in America Isn't Disappearing but Reinventing Itself," *Time,* July 22, 1996, 35–36; Robert Samuelson, "Harvard Scholar Misses the Point of 'Real Life,' " *Chicago Tribune,* April 26, 1996, sec. 1, p. 29. See also a two-part series with a number of commentators entitled "Unsolved Mysteries: The Tocqueville

Files" in the *American Prospect*, March–April and May–June 1996. The March–April issue includes a response by Putnam.

43. Morin offers a blunt but fairly accurate summary of this position. "In short, reports of the disappearance of social capital in American life are premature—if not simply wrong."

44. There is a more substantive criticism, lodged by Jean Cohen and others, that claims that Putnam offers no explanation for how face-to-face interactions in choral groups and the like result in a sense of trust toward the social world as a whole. This is a criticism that I accept, and that anticipates my argument that the civil society agenda is necessary but incomplete. See chapter 9. See also Jean Cohen, *American Civil Society Talk*, working paper no. 6 (Washington: The National Commission on Civic Renewal, 1997), 8–21.

45. In response to a question about Putnam's work, Peter Berger presents a similar distinction. He notes that it is "true that people don't participate in organizations the way they used to—they participate in less organized ways and move from one to another." He concludes, "[I]t's the mode of participation that has changed, not the fact of participation." "Epistemological Modesty: An Interview with Peter Berger," *Christian Century*, October 29, 1997, 973.

46. Transcript, First Plenary Session, National Commission on Civic Renewal, Washington, January 25, 1997 (Washington: National Commission on Civic Renewal), 43. Alan Wolfe echoes this distinction: "[T]he literature dealing with civic decline has tracked something important, but not necessarily in the right way: it is not the overall decline in group membership that is crucial—for when added up properly, there may not be that much of a decline—but a change in the qualitative nature of those ties that matters." *One Nation After All* (New York: Viking Press, 1998), 261.

47. In their voluminous study of American political participation, Verba, Schlozman, and Brady conclude that "the evidence is mixed as to whether Americans are a nation of gregarious organizational activists or have retreated to the privacy and relative inactivity of checkbook participation." *Voice and Equality: Civic Voluntarism in American Politics* (Cambridge: Harvard University Press, 1997), 65.

48. The distinction is echoed in Putnam's own words. In "Tuning In, Tuning Out: The Strange Disappearance of Social Capital in America," *PS: Political Science and Politics* 28, no. 4 (December 1995), he notes that social capital is not identical to political participation. The latter, he says, focuses on our "relations with political institutions," the former "refers to our relations with others" (665).

49. The case against television was only hinted at in "Bowling Alone." It was developed in "Tuning In, Tuning Out."

50. Berger and Neuhaus, *To Empower People*, 19.

51. Putnam, "Bowling Alone," 671.

52. Berger and Neuhaus, *To Empower People*, 18.

53. One could say that in Tocquevillian terms, Berger and Neuhaus are more concerned with the primary function of political associations, while Putnam is more focused on civic associations.

54. Martin E. Marty, *The One and the Many* (Cambridge: Harvard University Press, 1997), 138.

55. Tocqueville was among the first to notice war's unique attractiveness to "men of democracies." Because democracy has left humanity's natural desire for power and comfort significantly less restrained, democratic citizens, both as individuals and as a collective, approach war much as they would a hopeful acquisition. As a result, "no kind of greatness is more pleasing to the imagination of a democratic people than military greatness which is brilliant and sudden, won without hard work, by risking nothing but one's life." *Democracy in America,* 657–58. Hegel makes a strikingly similar point: "War has the higher significance that by its agency . . . 'the ethical health of peoples is preserved in their indifference to the stabilization of finite institutions . . .' " (*Philosophy of Right,* P 324, p. 210). Both quotations speak prophetically to the disquiet that seems to characterize our post–Cold War society.

56. Nisbet, *Quest for Community,* 36.

57. Ibid., 34.

58. Ibid., 36.

59. Ibid., 231.

60. Sandel, *Democracy's Discontent,* 278.

61. One could similarly speculate that the end of the Cold War accounts for the comparatively muted reception to the works of Nisbet and Berger and Neuhaus. So long as that struggle continued to occupy American consciousness, their concerns fell on fallow ground.

62. Putnam, *Making Democracy Work,* 179.

Chapter Five

1. John Keane, "Despotism and Democracy: The Origins and Development of the Distinction between Civil Society and the State, 1750–1850," in John Keane, ed., *Civil Society and the State: New European Perspectives* (London: Verso, 1988), 44–50.

2. Andrew Arato and Jean Cohen, *Civil Society and Democratic Theory* (Cambridge: MIT Press, 1994), 90.

3. Quoted in Krishan Kumar, "Civil Society: An Inquiry into the Usefulness of an Historical Term," *British Journal of Sociology* 44, no. 3 (September 1993): 392 n. 8.

4. Arato and Cohen, *Civil Society and Democratic Theory,* 91.

5. W. F. Hegel, *Hegel's Philosophy of Right,* trans. with introduction and notes by T. H. Knox (New York: Oxford University Press, 1967), 12.

6. As often happens with Hegel, one suspects his analysis here is undermined by the restrictions of his dialectic. My purposes here, however, are more expository. For more on this interesting topic, see Merold Westphal, "Hegel's Radical Idealism: Family and State as Ethical Communities," in *The State and Civil Society: Studies in Hegel's Political Philosophy,* ed. Z. A. Pelczynski (Cambridge: Cambridge University Press, 1984), 77–92.

7. Z. A. Pelczynski notes that the political apparatus associated with the bourgeois state includes elements of what we might call "the welfare state," that is, institutions that preserve individual livelihood. The fact that such insti-

tutions are included within civil society and not the state is born of, on the one hand, the different foci Hegel attaches to the civil and political realms, and on the other, to his apparent justification for such institutions. I.e., welfare-type assistance is justified not as an expression of the common good but as an essential element of individual rights. See Z. A. Pelczynski, "Political Community and Individual Freedom," in *The State and Civil Society*, ed. Z. A. Pelczynski (Cambridge: Cambridge University Press, 1984), 70–71. I say more about Hegel's concept of the state in chapter 8.

8. Hegel's term *bürgerliche Gesellschaft* can be translated both ways.

9. Hegel, *Philosophy of Right*, addition 116, P 182, p. 266.

10. Ibid., P 183, p. 123. Recall that for Tocqueville, too, commonalty is born of shared self-interest. But it is worth pointing out that Tocqueville also saw economic institutions as important examples of social institutions that help build a morally unified society.

> Men chance to have a common interest in a certain matter. It may be a trading enterprise to direct or an industrial undertaking to bring to fruition; those concerned meet and combine; little by little in this way they get used to the idea of association. The more there are of these little business concerns in common, the more do men, without conscious effort, acquire a capacity to pursue great aims in common.

Alexis de Tocqueville, *Democracy in America*, trans. George Lawrence, ed. J. P. Mayer (Garden City, N.Y.: Anchor Books, 1969), 520.

11. T. H. Knox, notes to Hegel, *Philosophy of Right*, 353–54. Francis Fukuyama is the most important contemporary advocate of Hegel's conception of the social role of the marketplace. See Fukuyama, *Trust: The Social Virtues and the Creation of Prosperity* (New York: Free Press, 1995).

12. Hegel, *Philosophy of Right*, P 213, p. 137.

13. Knox, notes to Hegel, *Philosophy of Right*, 360.

14. Hegel, *Philosophy of Right*, P 252, p. 153; recall for a moment the frequency with which corporate employees refer to themselves as "more like a family."

15. Hegel's Corporations thus exemplify the contemporary notion that the institutions of civil society are "mediating" institutions. (See ibid., P 302.) Knox quotes from a discussion of Mussolini's Italy, in which "Corporations are to act as decentralized administrative bodies, in order to achieve an organization and a morale half-way between the public irresponsibility and the technical agility of private enterprise and the pubic responsibility and heavy routine of the ordinary departments of state." Knox concludes that this summary "might almost pass as an exegesis of Hegel's own meaning." Ibid., 361 n. 83.

16. Ibid., P 253, p. 153.

17. Ibid., P 265, p. 163.

18. Ibid., P 270, p. 168.

19. Arato and Cohen, *Civil Society and Democratic Theory*, 113.

20. Hegel, *Philosophy of Right*, P 295, p. 192.

21. Peter Berger, "The Socialist Myth," *Public Interest* 44 (summer 1976): 7.

22. Karl Marx, "On the Jewish Question," in *The Marx-Engels Reader*, ed. Robert Tucker (New York: Norton, 1978), 43.

23. Karl Marx, "Contribution to the Critique of Hegel's *Philosophy of Right,*" in *The Marx-Engels Reader,* 17.

24. Karl Marx, "The German Ideology," in *The Marx-Engels Reader,* 163.

25. Marx, "On the Jewish Question," 44.

26. Kumar, "Civil Society," 379.

27. Gellner, *Conditions of Liberty: Civil Society and Its Rivals* (London: Penguin Books, 1994), 1.

28. Antonio Gramsci, *Selections from the Prison Notebooks,* ed. and trans. Q. Hoare and G. Nowell Smith (New York: International Publishers, 1972), 12.

29. Ibid., 264–65.

30. Jeff Weintraub has called Gramsci "the Marxist de Tocqueville," and in many respects that is a fair assessment. But notice this fundamental distinction: for Tocqueville, one of the most basic functions of civil society is to protect society against the state's benign despotism, while for Gramsci, at least the operative function of civil society is exactly the opposite. Civil society serves to shore up and protect the state apparatus from any destabilizing social independence. Quoted in Kumar, "Civil Society," 381.

31. Noberto Bobbio, "Gramsci and the Concept of Civil Society," in *Civil Society and the State: New European Perspectives,* ed. John Keane (London: Verso, 1988), 88.

32. Antonio Gramsci, *Il Grido del popolo,* September 14, 1918, quoted in Joseph A. Buttigieg, "Gramsci on Civil Society," *boundary 2,* vol. 22, no. 3 (1995): 14.

33. Antonio Gramsci, quoted in Buttigieg, "Gramsci on Civil Society," 20.

34. This strategic shift—using civil society against the capitalist order—also helps to account for Gramsci's belief that economic relationships and organizations were analytically separate from the concept of civil society. In other words, if the capitalist order was the enemy, then any elements of that order were at best irrelevant to the task of fostering revolution. In private correspondence, Francis Fukuyama blames Gramsci for the fact that the contemporary discussion shows such little interest in economic organizations. He rightly points out that before Gramsci, not only were economic institutions not ignored, they were taken as *representative* of civil society.

Chapter Six

1. The official toll was 45 dead and 1,165 injured. See Jacques Rupnik, "Dissent in Poland, 1968–78: The End of Revisionism and the Birth of Civil Society," in Rudolf L. Tokes, ed., *Opposition in Eastern Europe* (Baltimore: John Hopkins University Press, 1979), 70, 106.

2. There were, of course, many others in Eastern Europe who were formulating similar responses. Vaclav Havel and the Charter 77 movement in Czechoslovakia and Marc Rokovski and George Konrád in Hungary were all part of this developing strategy. What is more, the thought of Havel in particular has been important to a number of American intellectuals, including Jean Bethke Elshtain, Michael Walzer, and others. Nevertheless, I judge that a more complete accounting is not necessary. It is fair to say that the movement to find an alternative strategy of resistance had its beginnings in Poland. More impor-

tantly, it is almost beyond dispute to say that the Solidarity movement was the event that proved most significant in reintroducing the concept of civil society to Western audiences.

3. Adam Michnik, "The New Evolutionism," in *Letters and Papers from Prison,* trans. Maya Latynski (Berkeley: University of California Press, 1985), 145.

4. In the 1950s and 1960s, Kołakowski came to reject and condemn Marxist dogmatism—especially the passivity born of a belief that the coming revolution had been scientifically established. Thus, "Kołakowski identified his ideas with Antonio Gramsci's epistemology." Norbert A. Zmijewski, *The Catholic-Marxist Ideological Dialogue in Poland, 1945–1980* (Hants, England: Dartmouth Publishing, 1991), 131. At the same time, it is fair to say that Kołakowski most often presents a conception of civil society that focuses heavily on economic institutions. To this degree, he is following a strain of Hegelian thought not associated with Gramsci. See Kołakowski, "The Myth of Human Self-Identity: Unity of Civil and Political Society in Socialist Thought," in *The Socialist Idea,* ed. Lesek Kołakowski and Stuart Hampshire (London: Weidenfeld and Nicolson, 1974), 18–35.

5. Lesek Kołakowski, "Hope and Hopelessness," *Survey* 17, no. 3 (summer 1971): 37–52.

6. Ibid., 46.

7. David Ost, *Solidarity and the Politics of Anti-politics* (Philadelphia: Temple University Press, 1990), 66.

8. Michnik, "The New Evolutionism," 142.

9. Ost, *Solidarity,* 68.

10. On the other hand, acknowledgment of the connection between Gramsci and Solidarity and its forebears can be found, sporadically at least, in the secondary literature. Z. A. Pelczynski notes, for example, that

> Gramsci's reformulation of the state–civil society relation . . . did not of course provide a viable action programme in Italy or elsewhere in the West. . . . [I]t has proved, from the standpoint of revolutionary praxis, a dead end. Amazingly, however, developments in Eastern Europe, especially Poland, have given the Gramscian approach—albeit in a radically modified form—a new lease on life. It is this so-to-speak revisionist, upside-down, neo-Gramscian version of Gramsci which has been found theoretically fruitful . . . by the theorists of the "democratic opposition" or "new evolutionism" of the East. . . . An analytical framework for considering developments in advanced, Western bourgeois society has been transformed into a framework for analyzing the situation in the contemporary socialist countries of East Europe.

Z. A. Pelczynski, "Solidarity and the 'The Rebirth of Civil Society' in Poland," in John Keane, ed., *Civil Society and the State: New European Perspectives* (London: Verso, 1988), 365–66.

11. Private correspondence, June 29, 1997.

12. Andrew Arato and Jean Cohen, *Civil Society and Democratic Theory* (Cambridge: MIT Press, 1994), 71.

13. Rupnik, "Dissent in Poland," 83.

14. In fact, the members subsequently changed the name of the organization to KSS-KOR (Social Self-Defense Committee–Workers' Defense Committee) in order to reflect more accurately this broader mission.

15. The phrase "act as if you are free" illustrates well the mutual-support system, and long-standing conversation, among the dissident writers of Eastern Europe. It appears in Havel's writings, and is also found in George Konrád's *Antipolitics,* trans. Richard E. Allen (Orlando, Fla.: Harcourt Brace Jovanovich, 1984), the Bible of the Hungarian underground. Konrád writes: "[T]he greatest action on behalf of freedom is to behave toward everyone as though we were free men—even toward those who we fear. If we act that way with them, they will think we are not really afraid of them" (82).

16. The commitment to nonviolence is one point on which these partisans break company with Gramsci. The commitment was both philosophical and strategic in nature. It was genuine and sorely tested, and, as I shall argue below, it served to cement further the alliance between the church and the secular intelligentsia.

17. The similarity between this list and the concrete proposals outlined in Gramsci's writings is, I trust, a point that I need not belabor. For more on the flying university and the independent presses, see Rupnik, "Dissent in Poland," 94–96.

18. Jan Jozef Lipski, *KOR: A History of the Workers' Defense Committee in Poland, 1976–1981,* trans. Olga Amsterdamska and Gene M. Moore (Berkeley: University of California Press, 1985), 76–77.

19. Ost, *Solidarity,* 70.

20. Ibid., 31.

21. Quoted in ibid., 77.

22. Timothy Garton Ash, *The Polish Revolution: Solidarity* (London: Granta Books, 1991), 84.

23. The idea that revolutionary strategy requires that civil society be both pluralistic and united is not unknown to Gramsci.

> The hegemonic forces therefore include not only the party but all the other institutions of civil society (in Gramsci's meaning of the term) which have some connection with the elaboration and diffusion of culture. As regards its function, hegemony *aims not only at the formation of a collective will capable of creating a new state apparatus and transforming society but also at elaborating and propagating a new conception of the world.*

Noberto Bobbio, "Gramsci and the Concept of Civil Society," in John Keane, ed., *Civil Society and the State: New European Perspectives* (London: Verso, 1988), 93; italics added.

24. Quoted in Pelczynski, "Solidarity," 370.

25. Garton Ash, *Polish Revolution,* 370.

26. Ost, *Solidarity,* 107.

27. See, e.g., Garton Ash, *Polish Revolution,* 224–27.

28. One must acknowledge the reality that this near identification of religion and culture both fostered and was furthered by the near extermination of a large Jewish minority during the Holocaust.

29. Osa, "Creating Solidarity: The Religious Foundations of the Polish Social Movement," *East European Politics and Societies* 11, no. 2 (spring 1997): 351.

30. George Weigel, *The Final Revolution: The Resistance Church and the Collapse of Communism* (Oxford: Oxford University Press, 1992), 72–74.

31. Michnik, "The New Evolutionism," 145. Michnik was among the first on the secular left to embrace the church as a partner in peaceful opposition to the state. His book *The Church and the Left,* trans. David Ost (Chicago: University of Chicago Press, 1993), calling for a rapprochement, was first published in France in 1977.

This work is relevant because of what I have said above. Like the very leftists Michnik was addressing, Gramsci believed that the Catholic Church in Italy and elsewhere was concerned solely with the maintenance of its own status and authority—it was thus little different from the state, content to add its support to shoring up the oppression of the working class. In order to advance the cause of revolution, Michnik had to dispel this notion.

32. Lipski, *KOR,* 75.

33. See Rupnik, "Dissent in Poland," 90. Osa maintains that the rise of Solidarity would not have been possible, and cannot be adequately understood, without attending to Wyszynski's words and actions throughout the postwar years.

34. Weigel notes that many churches became de facto sanctuaries from the state, possessing a kind of "moral extra-territoriality." Weigel, *The Final Revolution,* 151.

35. Michael H. Bernhard, *The Origins of Democratization in Poland: Workers, Intellectuals, and Oppositional Politics, 1976–1980* (New York: Columbia University Press, 1993), 136.

36. Weigel, *The Final Revolution,* 101. See also 125: church leaders again echoed the themes of the secular left, calling upon Christians "to live 'as if' they lived in a free country."

37. Ibid., 151.

38. One such moral principle is "subsidiarity," that is, the idea that the direction and control over any group of individuals ought to remain in the hands of the individuals involved. If that authority is to be removed, it is to be removed to no higher a level than is necessary to effect control. The idea was first articulated by Pope Pius XI in the encyclical *Quadragesimo Anno:*

> Just as it is gravely wrong to take from individuals what they can accomplish by their own initiative and industry and give it to the community, so also it is an injustice and at the same time a grave evil and disturbance of right order to assign to a greater and higher association what lesser and subordinate organizations can do.

This principle has received serious attention in recent Catholic social thought. For example, the idea is central to the American bishops' letter on the economy, published in 1985. Subsidiarity is also a common theme in the thought of John Paul II. Most importantly, his encyclical *Centesimus Annus,* written in 1991, just after the fall of Communism, repeatedly references the idea. The concept of subsidiarity bears significant associations with the contemporary interest in civil society, and quite often that connection is made explicit. I think it is fair to assume that the pope's leadership in condemning the reach of the Communist state is principally behind the contemporary interest in this idea.

39. Garton Ash, *Polish Revolution,* 239. Though I postpone discussion until chapter 7, note the similarity between this list and the triumvirate listed in chapter 1.

40. Ibid., 290.

41. Ost, *Solidarity,* 9.

42. Garton Ash, *Polish Revolution,* 294.

Chapter Seven

1. As I noted in chapter 6, the principle of subsidiarity maintains that, as a general rule, power should stay in the hands of the affected parties (groups, families, individuals). Accordingly, the power of the state is and ought to be limited.

2. Benjamin Barber, "Searching for Civil Society," *National Civic Review* 84, no. 2 (spring 1995): 114.

3. Adam Michnik, "The New Evolutionism," in *Letters and Papers from Prison,* trans. Maya Latynski (Berkeley: University of California Press, 1985), 144. Even in 1989, after Solidarity had become part of an overtly corporatist power relationship with the crumbling Communist Party, movement leaders continued to claim that their actions, as well as the answers to Poland's problems, were independent of political concerns.

4. Krishan Kumar, "Civil Society: An Inquiry into the Usefulness of an Historical Term," *British Journal of Sociology* 44, no. 3 (September 1993): 386.

5. Actually, the romanticism exhibited by these anti-Marxists is very reminiscent of the Marxian belief that the stateless society would grow spontaneously out of the authoritarian socialist state. In turn, the romanticism of the Solidarity movement is clearly echoed in the typically conservative belief that thousands of manifestations of civil society are lying fallow in American society, waiting only for the recession of the state to signal their emergence. It is extremely ironic that this right-wing belief is the mirror image of Marxian ideology.

6. Kumar, "Civil Society," 389.

7. George Konrád, *Antipolitics,* trans. Richard E. Allen (Orlando, Fla.: Harcourt Brace Jovanovich, 1984), 35.

8. David Ost, *Solidarity and the Politics of Anti-politics* (Philadelphia: Temple University Press, 1990), 15.

9. Here is another sign of the congruence with, and almost surely the influence of, Catholic social thought. It is at best unlikely that John Paul II's repeated condemnations of both capitalism and communism as materialistic, and thus inattentive to the spiritual worth of each individual, did not have an impact on the Polish dissident movement.

10. Ost, *Solidarity,* 77.

11. Wlodzimierz Weslowski, "The Nature of Social Ties and the Future of Postcommunist Society: Poland after Solidarity," in *Civil Society: Theory, History, Comparison,* John A. Hall, ed. (Cambridge: Blackwell Publishers, Polity Press, 1995), 114.

12. Konrad, *Antipolitics*, 92.

13. Quoted in Ost, *Solidarity*, 69.

14. Jacques Rupnik wrote an early and very influential article entitled "Dissent in Poland, 1968–78: The End of Revisionism and the Rebirth of the Civil Society" (in Rudolf L. Tokes, ed., *Opposition in Eastern Europe* [Baltimore: John Hopkins University Press, 1979]). In 1981 and 1982, Andrew Arato wrote two articles that furthered the connection: "Civil Society against the State: Poland 1980–81," *Telos* 47 (spring 1981): 23–47; and "Empire vs. Civil Society: Poland 1981–82," *Telos* 50 (winter 1981–82): 19–48.

15. Michnik, "A Year Has Passed," *Letters and Papers from Prison*, 124.

16. Ost, *Solidarity*, 19.

17. Quoted in Flora Lewis, "Foreign Affairs: Needs of Civil Society," *New York Times*, August 29, 1989, I19.

18. Michael Walzer, "The Idea of Civil Society," *Dissent* 38, no. 2 (spring 1991): 293.

19. At this stage, it is true that interest in civil society was located primarily within the academy. Nevertheless, the term did begin to emerge in more popular circles. The connection between Solidarity and civil society was reinforced perhaps most importantly by the writings of Flora Lewis, then senior foreign correspondent for the *New York Times*. During the revolutions of 1989, she wrote an ongoing series of articles regarding Poland and the rebirth of Solidarity. (Incidentally, Lewis also wrote an article in 1989 that connected the actions of Solidarity to the thought of Antonio Gramsci. She used Gramsci's analysis to declare that "the Communist ideal is destroying itself as the century ends because it could not create the 'fortresses and earthworks' of civil society, nor accommodate them.") Lewis, "Foreign Affairs: The Rise of Civil Society," *New York Times*, June 25, 1989, sec. 4, p. 27.

20. Alan Wolfe, *Whose Keeper: Social Science and Moral Obligation* (Berkeley: University of California Press, 1989), 2, 13. Wolfe thus reiterates my claim that the civil society movement seeks to address social discontents that are endemic within modernity.

21. I have not considered Jürgen Habermas's work in this book. I judge that while his work is of remarkable significance within the academy, it has not greatly influenced the *public* debate about civil society in America. On the other hand, Wolfe's book draws heavily from the Habermas's work. Therefore, if one were to make the alternative case that Habermas and the idea of the public square have had some impact on the public debate, it would rest primarily on Wolfe's book and other secondary sources. For more on Habermas, see chapter 1, note 64.

22. Robert Putnam, "Bowling Alone: America's Declining Social Capital," *Journal of Democracy* 6 (1995): 77.

23. So far as I can determine, the term "civil society" also does not appear in *Making Democracy Work* or any other relevant work of Putnam's published prior to 1996.

24. Robert Putnam, "Robert Putnam Responds" (part of a series entitled "Unsolved Mysteries: The Tocqueville Files"), *American Prospect*, March-April 1996, 28.

25. I might reiterate here that the term also does not appear at all in the original version of *To Empower People*. The alternative term in that work is "mediating institutions." The twentieth-anniversary edition of the work, published in 1996 (by the AEI Press), added the subtitle *From State to Civil Society*.

26. One notable exception is David Dyssegaard Kallick, "Why Civil Society?" *Social Policy* 26, no. 4 (summer 1996): 2–8.

Chapter Eight

1. W. F. Hegel, *Hegel's Philosophy of Right*, trans. with introduction and notes by T. H. Knox (New York: Oxford University Press, 1967), P 300, p. 292 n. 178.

2. Z. A. Pelczynski, "Political Community and Individual Freedom," in *The State and Civil Society: Studies in Hegel's Political Philosophy*, ed. Z. A. Pelczynski (Cambridge: Cambridge University Press, 1984), 56.

3. Hegel, *Philosophy of Right*, P 253, p. 153.

4. Ibid., P 271, p. 174.

5. Ibid., P 279, p. 183

6. What's more, Hegel wants it to be a hereditary monarchy, so that the person of the king might also represent the continuity and development of the life of the nation.

7. Hegel, *Lectures on the Philosophy of History*, trans. J. Sibree (New York: Dover, 1956), part 4, sec. 3, chap. 3, p. 456.

8. Hegel, *Philosophy of Right*, addition 171, P 280, p. 289.

9. Ibid., P 301, p. 196.

10. Ibid., P 294, p. 191. Hegel's regard for Plato's *Republic* is reflected, superficially at least, in the clear similarities between Hegel's bureaucrats and Plato's guardian class.

11. Hegel also regards public opinion and the freedom of the press as essential means by which the public is involved in the ongoing debate about the form and content of the common good. Nevertheless, Hegel believes that public opinion is invariably subject to caprice, shortsightedness, and prejudice. The freedom of the press is, therefore, similarly constrained.

12. Hegel, *Philosophy of Right*, P 273, p. 176.

13. Ibid., P 258, p. 156; italics added.

14. Stephen Smith, "What Is 'Right' in Hegel's *Philosophy of Right*?" *American Political Science Review* 83, no. 1 (March 1989): 14.

15. Hegel, *Philosophy of Right*, P 260, p. 160; italics added.

16. Ibid., P 261, p. 161.

17. Ibid., P 261, pp. 161–62.

18. Before moving on, I should also return briefly to Gramsci's thought in this regard. Recall that for Gramsci, the modern capitalist state was such a formidable power precisely because it had achieved control over both the state and civil society. Domination and hegemony, power and persuasion, were thus united, controlled by the same oppressive forces. The institutions of civil society offered the only way in which revolutionaries could attempt to break this hammerlock. Gramsci thus believed that in the modern (that is, the capitalist) epoch, neither civil society nor the state was adequate to the purposes of social control. After the revolution, however, things become quite murky indeed in

Gramsci's thought. On the one hand, Gramsci appears true to the Marxian idea that after the revolution, the state will ultimately wither away. In a classless society, Gramsci believed, the state would be "reabsorbed" into civil society. At the same time, it is not clear that Gramsci thought that the withering away of the state would take place concomitant with the revolution. Indeed, there are also elements within Gramsci's thought that evince his continued support for Lenin's Soviet Union, even going so far as to refer to a "progressive" form of totalitarianism. I am not equipped to resolve this question. More to the point, it is not germane to our purposes. While Gramsci's revolutionary strategy resonates in the contemporary concept, his postrevolutionary theory, whether utopian or draconian, is of little use to us here.

19. Alexis de Tocqueville, *Democracy in America,* trans. George Lawrence, ed. J. P. Mayer (Garden City, N.Y.: Anchor Books, 1969), 190.

20. Ibid., 194.

21. Ibid.

22. Ibid., 433–34.

23. Ibid., 287.

24. Ibid., 274.

25. Ibid., 275.

26. Ibid., 264.

27. Ibid.

28. Marvin Zetterbaum, "Tocqueville," in *The History of Political Philosophy,* ed. Leo Strauss and Joseph Cropsey (Chicago: University of Chicago Press, 1987), 774.

29. Tocqueville, *Democracy in America,* 267.

30. Ibid., 288.

31. Ibid. It goes without saying that Tocqueville was speaking about Roman Catholicism in the mid–nineteenth century. It is an interesting question whether and to what degree the reforms of Vatican II and demographic changes within the American Catholic Church would have changed Tocqueville's argument. For my immediate purposes, however, such questions are not germane.

32. Ibid., 289. It must be noted that Verba, Schlozman, and Brady present data that support the alternative, and historically more common, claim that the ecclesiological structure of Catholic churches leaves less opportunities for the development of civic skills. They conclude that there is "a dramatic difference between Catholic and Protestant respondents in terms of both opportunities to exercise politically relevant skills in church and time devoted to church-related educational, social, or charitable activity." Sidney Verba, Kay Lehman Schlozman, and Henry E. Brady, *Voice and Equality: Civic Voluntarism in American Politics* (Cambridge: Harvard University Press, 1995), 321–22.

33. Tocqueville, *Democracy in America,* 93. The idea that government is a powerful alien force and that citizens, in turn, have neither responsibility nor potency is captured in a favorite anecdote of Amitai Etzioni. During a television talk show regarding the savings and loan crisis, one exercised participant said: "Taxpayers shouldn't have to pay for that mess; government should pay for it."

34. Tocqueville, *Democracy in America*, 94–95.

35. Ibid., 87.

36. Ibid.

37. See also Andre Jardin's comment: "[P]ublic opinion had to be educated, [and] a civic spirit had to be created through the laws." *Tocqueville: A Biography*, trans. Lydia Davis and Robert Hemenway (New York: Farrar Straus Giroux, 1988), 176.

38. I am inclined to think that many contemporary scholars are too quick to associate these themes with Tocqueville's Catholic background. The historical case for this assertion is, to my mind, strained at best. While the idea circulates in Catholic thought from the time of Thomas Aquinas, Pope Pius XI did not coin the term itself until 1931 in his encyclical *Quadragesimo Anno*. On the other hand, the influence of John Stuart Mill's political thought on Tocqueville (and, for that matter, vice versa) is well established. Nevertheless, I admit that the case at hand is compelling circumstantial evidence for what one might call the Catholicity of Tocqueville's thought.

39. Pius XI, *Quadragesimo Anno*, P. 80, in *Church and State through the Centuries*, ed. Sidney Ehler and John Morrall (Westminster, Md.: Newman Press, 1954), 435.

40. Tocqueville, *Democracy in America*, 75.

41. Ibid., 94.

42. Ibid., 516; emphasis added.

Chapter Nine

1. Robert Putnam, "Bowling Alone: America's Declining Social Capital," *Journal of Democracy* 6 (1995): 77.

2. Alan Wolfe offers a similar assessment:

Being modern will always require some way of linking both intimate and distant obligations. Although in theory that balance could just as easily be found by engendering outward obligations inward, *the proper balance will more realistically be found by extending inward obligations outward*. . . . We need civil society—families, communities, friendship networks, solidaristic workplace ties, voluntarism, spontaneous groups and movements—not to reject, but to complete the project of modernity.

Wolfe, *Whose Keeper: Social Science and Moral Obligation* (Berkeley: University of California Press, 1989), 20. In contrast to Putnam, Wolfe argues that civil society is an independent and apparently self-sufficient source for creating and instilling moral obligations; it is the social realm where people "create their own moral rules" (ibid., 262).

3. Margaret Levi, "Social and Unsocial Capital: A Review Essay of Robert Putnam's *Making Democracy Work*," *Politics and Society* 24, no. 1 (March 1996): 47.

4. Jean Cohen, "American Civil Society Talk," *Working Paper #6, The National Commission on Civic Renewal*, 1997, 16. With a fair amount of derision, Nancy Rosenblum refers to this translation from a one arena to another as "the transition belt model." *Membership and Morals: The Personal Uses of Pluralism in America* (Princeton: Princeton University Press, 1998), 48.

5. Contemporary political science usually refers to this overarching moral consensus by the term "political culture." Within the discipline, the term's utility is by no means established, but the primary reason for rejecting it stems from the fact that this term obviously centers on orientations toward law, government, and political procedures; the idea common to Tocqueville and Hegel is broader than this. One might be tempted to call it simply "culture," but that would include a variety of common cultural experiences that have little or no moral content, and thus have little relevance. What is more, the issue at hand concerns those norms, values, and beliefs common to all or virtually all and that thus define a nation's identity. Perhaps "public" or "civic culture" would serve as the best alternative term.

6. Z. A. Pelczynski, "Political Community and Individual Freedom," in *The State and Civil Society: Studies in Hegel's Political Philosophy*, ed. Z. A. Pelczynski (Cambridge: Cambridge University Press, 1984), 56. Note that Pelczynski argues for a distinction within Hegel's understanding of ethical life or *Sittlichkeit*. He believes that at other points in Hegel's corpus, it is "a wider concept of national spirit. . . . It corresponds in many respects to our contemporary concept of culture. The state from this viewpoint is a political community because it is a cultural community."

7. Tocqueville and Hegel's agreement on this issue is perhaps the most significant sign of their shared debt to the work of Montesquieu.

8. The American public moral consensus and its metaphysical status are the subject of my book *Pluralism and Consensus: Conceptions of the Good in the American Polity* (Chicago: CSSR Press, 1998).

9. James Davison Hunter and Carl Bowman, *The State of Disunion: 1996 Survey of American Political Culture* (Ivy, Va.: In Media Res Educational Foundation, 1996), ix.

10. Ibid., 16

11. Ibid., 32.

12. This metaphor has always been used to express belief in an open, tolerant society that finds its strength through a mixture of commonality and difference. At the same time, the vast majority agree that this ideal is far from actualized. According to Hunter and Bowman, 83 percent believe children should also be taught that "our nation betrayed its principles by its cruel mistreatment of Blacks and Indians": ibid., 6.

13. Ibid., 5–6.

14. Ibid., 8–9. The survey acknowledges that affirmation is one thing, actual participation is something else. The actual percentage of Americans who voted in the 1996 election was 49 percent, the lowest turnout since 1924.

15. Ibid., 8.

16. Ibid., 4.

17. These findings find further support in Alan Wolfe's book *One Nation After All* (New York: Viking Press, 1998). Wolfe applies the term "middle-class morality"

> to characterize the values of those people in America who strive to earn enough money so that they feel that their economic fate is in their own hands, but who also try to live by principles such as individual

responsibility, the importance of family, obligations to others, and a belief in something outside oneself. (5)

Like Bowman and Hunter's, Wolfe's study found that this belief system was nearly ubiquitous within suburban, middle-class America.

18. Ibid., 76. This conclusion appears somewhat at odds with Hunter's better-known work, *Culture Wars* (New York: Basic Books, 1991). In that work, Hunter documents, to the contrary, that there is a pervasive and fundamental ideological division within American society. It is possible that Hunter could reconcile the two sets of data. For example, it may be that the agreement documented here is limited to mere platitudes, and once it becomes a question of implementation, ideological division emerges. Such an answer would seem to fit with his distinction between the ideal and the substance of political culture. But given the stark juxtaposition between these two works, this speculation is not sufficient; more of an answer is required.

19. Ibid., 10.

20. Ibid., 12.

21. Hunter and Bowman, *State of Disunion*, 21–22.

22. Ibid., 71.

23. Alexis de Tocqueville, *Democracy in America*, trans. George Lawrence, ed. J. P. Mayer (Garden City, N.Y.: Anchor Books, 1969), 162.

24. Incidentally, these data also lend support to those championing governmental devolution and "a new federalism." I say more about these issues in chapter 11.

25. Obviously, the moral teaching that goes on in churches is not solely, or even primarily, indirect. Again, the issue of religious teaching and American civil religion is an issue I take up below.

26. Gunnar Myrdal, *An American Dilemma: The Negro Problem and Modern Democracy*, 2 vols. (New York: Harper and Brothers, 1944).

27. Martin Luther King Jr., "Commencement Address at Lincoln University, June 6, 1961," in *A Testament of Hope: The Essential Writings of Martin Luther King, Jr.*, ed. James M. Washington (San Francisco: HarperCollins, 1986), 208.

28. Ellis Cose, *A Nation of Strangers: Prejudice, Politics, and the Population of America* (New York: Morrow, 1992).

29. Cohen, "American Civil Society Talk," 18.

30. Ibid.

31. Tocqueville, *Democracy in America*, 604.

32. Fox Buttlefield, "Study Links Violence Rate to Cohesion of Community," *New York Times*, August 17, 1997, A27.

33. While the very term *neighborhood* is amorphous, the relevant understanding here is determined by the objective of building social capital. Robert J. Chaskin has noted that "those who define the neighborhood in terms of social relationships are more likely to describe a smaller unit than those defining the neighborhood in terms of institutions." If this is so, the number of neighborhoods that could be considered truly integrated becomes even smaller. Chaskin, *Defining Neighborhoods: History, Theory, and Practice* (Chicago: Chapin

Hall Center of the University of Chicago, 1995), 10–11. Chaskin's report is extremely helpful as a conceptual foundation for considering the nature and social function of neighborhoods.

34. R. S. Sampson, S. W. Raudenbush, and F. Earls, "Neighborhoods and Violent Crime: A Multilevel Study of Collective Efficacy," *Science* 277, no. 5328 (August 15, 1997): 918–24.

35. Buttlefield, "Study."

36. Andrew Martin, "Neighborliness Tied to Lower Crime," *Chicago Tribune,* August 15, 1997, sec. 2, p. 3.

37. Glenn Loury, "The Conservative Line on Race," *Atlantic,* November 1997, 153.

38. Ibid.

39. Paul Numrich and William Peterman, "Rogers Park: Congregations in a Changing Community Area," in *Religious Organizations and Structural Change in Metropolitan Chicago: The Research Report of the Religion in Urban America Program,* ed. Lowell Livezey (Chicago: Office of Social Science Research, University of Illinois at Chicago, 1996), 22.

40. Nancy Tatom Ammerman, *Congregation and Community* (New Brunswick: Rutgers University Press, 1997), 4.

41. The question of homogeneity as it relates to families (the remaining social capital institution) is much more complicated. On the one hand, interdenominational, interreligious, interethnic, and interracial marriages are all on the rise. One could speculate therefore that such families are the vanguard of an emergent universal ethos. On the other hand, there is widespread evidence that such marriages lead to inevitable clashes—especially when it comes to the religious upbringing of the children. Such evidence would appear to reinforce the point that one must prune one's ethical commitments when one leaves ethnic, religious, or racial homogeneity. Both are likely true to some degree, but it goes without saying that a couple that shares a religious, cultural, or ethnic identity is more readily able to construct a thick moral environment for its children.

42. Political associations, on the other hand, depend on coalition building, and thus almost invariably cross racial and ethnic boundaries. I say more about this in chapter 10.

43. Paul Martin Du Bois, Jonathan J. Hutson, and Mary Ann Statham, *Interracial Dialogue Groups across America: A Directory* (Brattleboro, Vt.: Center for Living Democracy, 1997), 73.

44. Rosenblum, *Membership and Morals,* 22.

45. Putnam argues that this conclusion reveals the importance of using the state to institute democratic institutions. Over many years, perhaps generations, that intervention will change people's mores and thereby foster more democratic forms of civil society. With this latter claim, I have no disagreement. Indeed, I want to argue something very similar.

46. Of course, throughout American history, there have been wholly legitimate, even laudable examples of American civil society that argued against the dominant understanding of the American moral consensus. The abolitionists, for example, were surely a good form of civil society and the Ku Klux

Klan is surely bad even though both operate contrary to the prevailing moral conception. In chapter 10, I argue that the distinction centers on the form the argument takes and the manner in which it is presented.

47. Robert Ezra Parks, *Human Communities: The City and Human Ecology* (New York: Free Press, 1952), 47. Quoted in Chaskin, *Defining Neighborhoods*, 4.

48. For more on the question of civil society and race, See Jean Bethke Elshtain and Christopher Beem, "Civil Society and Race: A Democratic Conversation," in *Civil Rights and Social Wrongs*, ed. John Higham (College Station: Penn State University Press, 1997), 151–62.

49. The role of churches in the South during the 1960s renders this question far more complicated. To say the least, there were as many churches working against the civil rights movement as there were working for it. I say more about this issue in chapter 11.

50. There is another, equally important set of questions: Within the neighborhoods of the 1940s and 1950s, the price for homogeneity was racial, religious, and ethnic intolerance. And how does the civil society movement deal with that? Is not the civil society movement leaving itself open to charges that it abets (whether consciously or not) those who would perpetuate patterns of discrimination in our society? How might we Americans work toward racial and ethnic justice while at the same time working to remake neighborhoods into ethically formative institutions? The analysis of social capital institutions certainly does not resolve these questions, but it must at least raise the possibility that integration (particularly in matters of housing) may not always be the most appropriate means by which to address this two-sided objective. On the other hand, for those who are yet unwilling to abandon the dream of integration, it seems to me that there are only two alternatives. In the first place, we could rely on the Hyde Parks of this nation to fashion specific forms of ethical and cultural homogeneity that are in no way tied to ethnicity or race. To be sure, many are drawn to communities like this precisely because they seem to have more fully overcome tensions associated with race and ethnic differences. Yet for all their value, Hyde Park and other communities like it (Cambridge, Berkeley, etc.) are parochial in their own way, and are not liable to ameliorate significantly our nation's unraveling social fabric. The other alternative is that we Americans work to firm up, thicken, an ethical framework that is significantly less specific, that is, an ethic that is less thick, but nevertheless thick enough to integrate (in both senses) families of various ethnicities, religions, and races. In other words, the fact that neighborhoods appear to work best when they reflect a measure of ethical and cultural homogeneity further reveals the need for a stronger, more operative, and more concrete American public moral consensus.

51. This is E. E. Schattschneider's point in *The Semisovereign People: A Realist's View of Democracy in America* (New York: Holt, Rinehart, and Winston, 1960). I say more about this work in the next chapter.

52. In *Membership and Morals*, Nancy Rosenblum takes issue with President Clinton, who, following the Oklahoma City bombing, excoriated militias and other paramilitary groups, arguing that "there is nothing patriotic about hating

your government or pretending that you can hate government and love your country. How dare you suggest that we in the freest nation on earth live in tyranny." Rosenblum argues to the contrary that "[i]t *is* possible to love your country and hate its government." Rosenblum, 317. Perhaps the matter turns on what one means by the word "hate," but this discussion no doubt makes it clear that I am more inclined to support the president's understanding of the matter.

53. See Wuthnow's description of the latter in *The Restructuring of American Religion* (Princeton: Princeton University Press, 1988), 3.

54. Wolfe, *One Nation After All,* 55.

55. See Beem, *Pluralism and Consensus.*

56. Tocqueville, *Democracy in America,* 290.

57. Ibid., 291.

58. Tocqueville's position cannot be readily dismissed. In private correspondence, Francis Fukuyama relates his theory that "most of the problems discussed by Putnam are in fact very much related to the disruption in gender relations that took place some time beginning in the 1960s with the movement of women into the workplace, the rise of feminism, etc."

59. Hegel, *Philosophy of Right,* P 270, p. 168.

60. Ibid. Hegel did say that the state could not dictate which church its citizens attended. At least to this degree, he was more latitudinarian that his sometime mentor, Rousseau

61. See Michnik, "Troubles" (written in 1987), in Michnik, *The Church and the Left,* ed. and trans. David Ost (Chicago: University of Chicago Press, 1993), 245–72.

62. Incidentally, I would not want to make the same argument for the so-called "moment of silence."

63. Quoted in Joe Klein, "In God They Trust," *New Yorker,* June 16, 1997, 42.

64. The best days of the Promise Keepers appear to be behind them. As of the spring of 1998, attendance at rallies has fallen off and the organization was forced to revert to an unpaid leadership. See Christine Leigh Heyrman, "Reviving a Revival," *New York Times,* February 24, 1998, A21. If this is so, it would appear to lend further credence to the doubts expressed here. It would also tend to belie the ready hopes for racial reconciliation attached to this association.

65. Incidentally, the rather far-fetched fears of NOW and others regarding the Promise Keepers—i.e., that they are really a tool for constructing an American theocracy and for returning women to subordinate, even servile roles, finds some limited explanation in the Tocquevillian equation. As I have noted, Tocqueville believes that the viability of American civil religion hinges on the separate, even cloistered condition of American women. Perhaps, just perhaps, those on the left who appear to be so vehemently against such things as religious commitment, racial reconciliation, better marriages, and more responsible, loving fathers are motivated by an intuitive sense that Tocqueville is right: you cannot have a cultural revival without a return to a culture in which women are second-class. Hence, if you want the former, then, necessarily, you must want the latter. To my mind, the answer is simply to state that the objec-

tives of Promise Keepers do not extend beyond the men inside the rallies, and those who need to be there. That is to say, in other words, that the goals are not political. This is, incidentally, very similar to what the movement's leaders have said. It is also entirely consistent with a form of political quietism that (for all the exposure of groups like the Christian Coalition) remains the most common attitude within evangelical Christianity.

Chapter Ten

1. I leave off discussing the market on this point. I do not do so because I believe that the question of whether and how economic institutions foster a common moral consensus is uninteresting or unimportant. Indeed, for the issues outlined here, the question is particularly relevant. For it is surely the case that in contemporary American society, most interactions between individuals of different ethnic and racial groups take place within the working environment. I believe works like Francis Fukuyama's *Trust* (New York: Free Press, 1995) and Robert Wuthnow's *Poor Richard's Principle* (Princeton: Princeton University Press, 1996) reveal the importance of this question, but I am not qualified to address it further. I only say that whatever virtues emerge through the market, they do not gainsay the anticivic strains that economic rationality places on the polity. This fact, to my mind, only reinforces the necessity of politics.

2. Sidney Verba, Kay Lehman Schlozman, and Henry Brady, *Voice and Equality* (Cambridge: Harvard University Press, 1995), 42. This voluminous work is essential to understanding the independent political activity of contemporary Americans.

3. *Oxford English Dictionary*, 2d ed., s.v. "partisan."

4. Don Eberly, "Civil Society: The Paradox of American Progress," *Essays on Civil Society: An American Conversation on Civic Virtue* 1, no. 1 (September 1995): 4.

5. Putnam, "Bowling Alone: America's Declining Social Capital," *Journal of Democracy* 6 (1995): 71.

6. Another reason: I have shown that civil society advocates are prone to reject the state. Yet, by definition, these associations affirm what civil society advocates would deny: that the state is a moral pedagogue and that the moral content of its actions inevitably affects the citizenry. I will say more about the state in the next two chapters.

7. For an overview of the Texas IAF, see Dennis Shirley, *Laboratories of Democracy: Building Political Power in Urban Schools and Neighborhoods* (Austin: University of Texas Press, 1997).

8. In *Voice and Equality*, Verba, Schlozman, and Brady present the unsurprising conclusion that "those who engaged in political activities usually performed in a social context—campaigning, protesting, getting involved in an informal community effort, or serving on a local governing board—were much more likely to mention some kind of social gratification as very important" in accounting for their participation (115–17). The concept of social capital also figures centrally in Shirley's analysis.

9. The same can be said for local politics themselves. In city, county, or

school board politics, the interactions between legislators and their constituents are far more likely to operate in a face-to-face manner. Indeed, this very fact explains why although civil society advocates routinely speak disparagingly about the state, they are less concerned about, and often even laud, local government. For they rightly maintain that politics that is local shares (or at least *can* share) many of the positive features associated with social capital institutions.

10. Shirley, *Laboratories of Democracy,* 184–85.

11. E. E. Schattschneider, *The Semisovereign People: A Realist's View of Democracy in America* (New York: Holt, Rinehart, and Winston, 1960), 40.

12. Wilson Carey McWilliams has pointed out to me that this distinction calls to mind Roberto Michels's "iron law of oligarchy": Very briefly, Michels holds that the larger an organization becomes, the more it tends to develop an elite cadre of leaders who are cut off from and indifferent to the rank and file. For the rank and file, on the other hand, membership is often constituted by nothing more than a commitment of financial support, and accordingly, the only way members can "vote" is with their feet, i.e., by deciding to withhold future contributions. Clearly, most (though not all) national organizations reflect Michels's gloomy analysis. The fact that these associations are less able to produce social capital is simply a reflection of this condition.

Michels's analysis surely underscores the importance of local, face-to-face associations. But I would also note that the oligarchical nature of national political associations does not alter the basic function outlined below: namely, that such associations are uniquely able to foster a national conversation about shared ideals and values. Also, it seems to me that an organization that wholly alienates itself from its membership would (or at least should) compromise its public standing no less than an organization that practices a wholly uncivil form of politics. Indeed, I suspect that these two tendencies are often found together.

13. Alexis de Tocqueville, *Democracy in America,* trans. George Lawrence, ed. J. P. Mayer (Garden City, N.Y.: Anchor Books, 1969), 175.

14. My use of Tocqueville's distinction here draws upon the discussion by Jean Bethke Elshtain and me of the 1996 presidential campaign. See Jean Bethke Elshtain and Christopher Beem, "Economics, Culture, and Small Party Politics," in *The Elections of 1996,* ed. Michael Nelson (Washington: Congressional Quarterly Press, 1997), 106–20.

15. All three of these presidents are what Stephen Skowronek calls "great repudiators"; that is, they broke dramatically with the policies and politics of the previous administration. Yet Skowronek also argues that all three strove to justify these minirevolutions "in constitutional terms broadly construed as the protection, preservation, and defense of values emblematic of the body politic." Indeed, for Skowronek, balancing these contradictory impulses of revolution and conservation is constitutive of the office itself. See his important work, *The Politics Presidents Make: Leadership from John Adams to Bill Clinton* (Cambridge: Harvard University Press, Belknap Press, 1997), 32, 20.

16. Tocqueville discusses temperance societies in a section on political activity. Interestingly, however, he places that discussion in a footnote on the effect

of mass personal pledges on social mores, thereby effectively demonstrating the movement's desire to effect massive policy changes. Tocqueville, *Democracy in America*, 242.

17. Although not always. William Lloyd Garrison and others argued that slavery showed that the very terms of American moral consensus were incorrigible, not simply its contemporary articulation. Because of what he regarded as its two-faced capitulation to the slave-holding interests, William Lloyd Garrison burned a copy of the Constitution in public, and called that document "a covenant with death and an agreement with hell." The rank sinfulness that pervaded that document forced a decision upon the Christian that is the antithesis of the inclusive conception: "we must either cease to sanction it, or give up our profession of Christianity." William Lloyd Garrison, *Liberator*, September 13 and September 20, 1844. Quoted in John L. Thomas, *The Liberator: William Lloyd Garrison* (Boston: Little, Brown, 1963), 330–31. Clearly, Garrison's words are an example of great party politics. Similarly, one could well argue that the eradication of slavery, at least in the South, was literally revolutionary, for it amounted to a wholesale rejection of the established social order.

18. Wilson Carey McWilliams has offered a very similar commentary on Tocqueville's analysis. "Tocqueville's formulation," McWilliams writes, "points toward a desirable synthesis, a party both lion and fox that acknowledges self-interest but relates it to broader political principles." McWilliams, "Tocqueville and Responsible Parties: Individualism, Partisanship, and Citizenship in America," in *Challenges to Party Government*, ed. John Kenneth White and Jerome M. Mileur (Carbondale: Southern Illinois University Press, 1992), 192.

19. Schattschneider, *The Semisovereign People*, 7–8.

20. Ibid., 27.

21. This thin consensus cannot be inconsistent with, or contradict, the thick set of beliefs and norms that constitute an individual's or group's identity. King, for example, was masterful at showing that while his Christian motivation was primary, it was also fully consistent with the terms of the national consensus. For the sake of building political support, King made his appeals in language that was universal, i.e., that was American. Ernie Cortes, leader of the Texas IAF, often makes similar arguments. For more on King, see my "American Liberalism and the Christian Church: Stanley Hauerwas vs. Martin Luther King Jr.," *Journal of Religious Ethics* 15, no. 2 (spring 1995): 119–33. For more on Cortes, See Shirley, *Laboratories of Democracy*, 76–86.

22. Grant McConnell, *Private Power and American Democracy* (New York: Alfred A. Knopf, 1966), 366–67. As is the case with Schattschneider, the analysis outlined in this section parallels McConnell's argument on several key points.

23. The debate is also continued through voting, but, as the authors of *Voice and Equality* acknowledge, "the vote is singularly limited in its ability to communicate detailed information about needs and preferences" (Verba, Schlozman, and Brady, 530).

24. It bears emphasizing that the notion of universality operative here is utterly Hegelian; it is universality as *Sittlichkeit*. The shared moral consensus

is understood to be constitutive of *American* identity. For my purposes here, I want to beg questions about the future of the nation-state on the one hand and the existence and contents of a transnational—that is, a *human*—moral consensus on the other. But I want to note that, epistemologically speaking, these intranational moral claims have a transnational status. They are not understood to be true merely for Americans; they are used to judge the actions of other nations. Further, there are some political associations that take on a role in the international arena that is roughly equivalent to medium party political associations. Doctors without Borders and Amnesty International are examples of international organizations whose actions appear to presuppose, and give content to, this transnational moral consensus.

25. *The Concord Coalition: An Initial Statement*, September 1992, 30, 32.

26. See, for example, Stephen Glass, "The Holy Trinity," *New Republic*, January 27, 1997, 16–19; and John B. Judis, "The Great Savings Scare," in *New Republic*, January 27, 1997, 19–24.

27. William A. Galston, *Liberal Purposes* (Cambridge: Cambridge University Press, 1991), 224–25.

28. John Gardner, *In Common Cause* (New York: W. W. Norton, 1972), 16.

29. Ibid., 102–3.

30. Press release of Common Cause president Ann McBride, February 12, 1997. I say more about campaign finance reform in chapter 12.

31. Verba, Schlozman, and Brady, *Voice and Equality*, 79.

32. Rhys Williams, "Is America in a Culture War?: Yes—No—Sort Of," *Christian Century*, November 12, 1997, 1041.

33. James Davison Hunter quotes from a consultant on fund raising through the mail: "Find . . . a nasty enemy. Tell people they're threatened in some way. . . . It's a cheap trick, but it's the simplest." Hunter, *Culture Wars* (New York: Basic Books, 1991), 167.

34. For one example, note this account of the Concord Coalition:

> The Coalition's army . . . has made it a force in politics. The force comes not just from the quantity of its supporters, but the quality. The group's active members are passionate and committed well beyond the norm in politics . . . it is not really a matter of politics or economics; it is a matter of faith.

Glass, "The Holy Trinity," 16. (Although Glass was fired for fabricating reportage, the commentary quoted here seems correct and well stated.)

35. Verba, Schlozman, and Brady, *Voice and Equality*, 529.

36. Quoted in Nancy Rosenblum, *Membership and Morals: The Personal Uses of Pluralism in America* (Princeton: Princeton University Press, 1998), 337.

37. Many of these organizations call themselves nonpartisan (that is, they profess no official relationship with any political party), but in reality, most every American would consider such organizations (and many others) to be strongly associated with one party and strongly partisan in their approach to politics.

38. McWilliams points out that this celebration is rather uneasy. He notes that Tocqueville is careful to state that no such parties exist "[a]t the present time." The issue of slavery makes such a qualification necessary, and is an ever-

present subtext for Tocqueville's discussion. See McWilliams, "Tocqueville and Responsible Parties," 193.

39. Nancy Rosenblum makes a similar point about the public display of Christian symbols during Christmastime. "At least public debate surrounding these cases advances civic understanding, at a minimum insight into theological and ideological differences on the question of religion in public life." *Membership and Morals,* 107.

40. Verba, Schlozman, and Brady, *Voice and Equality,* 500–506.

41. Charles W. Colson, "Stop Smearing the Religious Right," *Washington Post,* May 9, 1995, A19. Quoted in Robert Wuthnow, *Christianity and Civil Society: The Contemporary Debate* (Valley Forge, Pa.: Trinity Press International, 1996), 57.

42. For more on the dialogic virtues that are constitutive of genuinely democratic politics, see Amy Guttman and Dennis Thompson, *Democracy and Disagreement* (Cambridge: Harvard University Press, Belknap Press, 1996). See also chapters 6 and 7 of Michael J. Perry, *Love and Power: The Role of Religion and Morality in American Politics* (Oxford: Oxford University Press, 1991).

Chapter Eleven

1. In fact, the goals of civil society advocates often conflict with their rhetoric about the state. For all the accusations they lodge against the Nanny State, these advocates are often intimately associated with the political process, and they frequently voice their support for certain specific policy changes. To be sure, this action often focuses on policies that would (ostensibly) help to restore social capital institutions, but to say that state action can achieve that goal is to acknowledge (at least) that the state is not irrelevant to the enterprise of building a moral society.

2. Here, too, it is worth pointing out that things are not so simple. In chapter 9, I noted that civil society is grounded on notions of the individual right to association. Therefore, it will not exist, or at least will not thrive, unless it exists within a system of political freedom. Civil society cannot function without independent judiciary, strong and competing political parties, freedom of association, freedom of religion, freedom of the press. Yet while these freedoms circumscribe the power of the state, the state is the mechanism by which those rights are secured against the majority. Thus, to celebrate the free activity of American civil society requires one to affirm the state at least to the degree that the latter is necessary to secure the existence of the former. A wholly incompetent state makes civil society itself, let alone a civil society solution, impossible to sustain.

3. For a salient argument to this effect, see John D. Donahue, "The Disunited States," *Atlantic Monthly,* May 1997, 18–22.

4. Rhys Williams, "Is America in a Culture War?: Yes—No—Sort Of," *Christian Century,* November 12, 1997, 1042.

5. William Galston argues that the decline in what he calls "traditional morality" began with the civil rights movement. For while the movement was essentially "conservative," i.e., argued in terms of America's founding principles, "[i]t was also an effort to legitimize social difference." This effort, and its

success, Galston argues, became "an inspirational metaphor for other aggrieved groups. In ensuing years, the subordination of women to men, of youth to age, of heterodox sexuality to traditional families, of nonbelief to religion—all of these hierarchies and more were challenged in the name of freedom, equality, and recognition of legitimate differences." Galston, *Liberal Purposes* (Cambridge: Cambridge University Press, 1991), 268–69. Galston implies, but does not say, that some of these later efforts were less interested in presenting a "conservative" justification for their claims, that is, a justification that centers on America's founding principles.

6. Warren E. Miller and Santa Traugott, *American National Election Studies Data Sourcebook: 1952–1986* (Cambridge: Harvard University Press, 1989), 256. This period also accounts for the steepest decline in people's beliefs about whether or not other people can be trusted. See ibid., 287.

7. John Courtney Murray, *We Hold These Truths: Catholic Reflections on the American Proposition* (Kansas City: Sheed and Ward, 1988), 17.

8. Given the fact that the presidency is the only office that can take on this role, the development of what Jeffrey Tulis calls "the rhetorical presidency" strikes me as inevitable. My use, below, of the work of Wayne Fields further conveys my sense that this rhetorical dimension has been part of the presidency since the dawn of the republic. This position is not what Tulis argues, however. Tulis, *The Rhetorical Presidency* (Princeton: Princeton University Press, 1987).

9. Wayne Fields, *Union of Words: A History of Presidential Eloquence* (New York: Free Press, 1996), 6.

10. Ibid., 19. The language of particular and general has an inescapable Hegelian connotation.

11. Ibid., 20.

12. Ibid., 21.

13. Ibid., 115.

14. The other almost universal feature of inaugural addresses is the affirmation of divine providence and invocation of divine guidance. The American legacy of civil religion is profound and, at this level, the effect seems to me almost wholly benign. The expression of such sentiments in legislation is, of course, another matter entirely. And, as I argued in chapter 8, the difficulty comes in the fact that the distinction between law and mere rhetoric is extremely difficult to maintain.

15. Fields, *Union of Words*, 228.

16. Ibid., 276.

17. Cf. Knox's n. 64 to P 300 of Hegel's *Philosophy of Right:* "The Estates are the classes of civil society given a political significance." In W. F. Hegel, *Hegel's Philosophy of Right,* trans. with introduction and notes by T. H. Knox (New York: Oxford University Press, 1967), 372.

18. David Easton, *The Political System: An Inquiry into the State of Political Science,* 2d ed. (Chicago: University of Chicago Press, 1971), 129.

19. The position that politics ought to be neutral, or at least strive to be neutral, about questions of morality remains strong within liberal political theory. I cannot adequately address this argument here. I would recommend the reader consult George Sher's splendid book, *Beyond Neutrality: Perfectionism and Poli-*

tics (Cambridge: Cambridge University Press, 1997). To my mind, Sher effectively dismantles the neutrality position.

20. The mores of which Tocqueville spoke possess both moral content and at least a form of authority. And again, Tocqueville believed these were cultivated primarily through the institutions of civil society. But I have also shown that Tocqueville did not regard these institutions as sufficient for creating and sustaining a moral society. As for the many other distinctive features of American culture—the English language, our celebration of pragmatism and independence, for instance, or, more mundanely, fast food, television programs, and professional sports—both the moral and authoritative dimension of these cultural characteristics are, comparatively speaking, minimal.

21. It is also true, as Robert Wuthnow argues, that capitalism runs on "legitimating accounts that tell us why it is good to be committed to our work." He is also correct to argue that because these accounts "invoke fundamental definitions of reality . . . suggest conceptions of the good . . . tell us how to behave—they are fundamentally *moral* rather than economic." Wuthnow, *Poor Richard's Principle: Recovering the American Dream through the Moral Dimensions of Work, Business, and Money* (Princeton: Princeton University Press, 1996), 137. Again, I do not dispute the claim that the economic dimension, for good or ill, helps to inculcate a fairly widespread set of moral norms. But I do dispute the claim (though I do not believe this is a claim Wuthnow makes) that this effect allows one to ignore or even denigrate the pedagogical role of government.

22. Philip B. Heymann, "How Government Expresses Public Ideas," in *The Power of Public Ideas,* ed. Robert B. Reich (Cambridge: Harvard University Press, 1990), 96.

23. Glenn Loury, "Values and Judgments: Creating Social Incentives for Good Behavior," in *Culture in Crisis and the Renewal of Civil Life,* ed. T. William Boxx and Gary M. Quinlivan (Lanham, Md.: Rowman and Littlefield, 1996), 26.

24. Joseph M. Bessette, *The Mild Voice of Reason: Deliberative Democracy and American National Government* (Chicago: University of Chicago Press, 1994), 28.

25. Bessette calls it a combination of "democracy and deliberation" (38). He also makes a very Tocquevillian point about "self-interest rightly understood." A legislator is nothing if not ambitious and self-serving. But a number of the legislators he profiles show that one good way to receive notice and respect is to be worthy of it. That is, they serve their self-interest by serving the public interest.

26. Arthur Maass likewise argues against the dominant models of interest group theory, rational choice theory, and the like. He contends that such modes of analysis constitute "a vast oversimplification" of the real world, for they fail to accommodate the House's operative (if not determinative) concern for the broader public good. See his *Congress and the Common Good* (New York: Basic Books, 1983).

27. Hegel, *Philosophy of Right,* P 295, p. 192.

28. Philip Selznick notes that according to the *American Heritage Dictionary,* "in American usage, *bureaucrat* is almost invariably derogatory unless the con-

text establishes otherwise." Quoted in Selznick, *The Moral Commonwealth: Social Theory and the Promise of Community* (Berkeley: University of California Press, 1992), 274.

29. See John J. DiIulio Jr., Gerald Garvey, and Donald F. Kettl, *Improving Government Performance: An Owners Manual* (Washington: Brookings Institution, 1993).

30. The classic defense is Charles T. Goodsell, *The Case for Bureaucracy: A Public Administration Polemic* (Chatham, N.J.: Chatham Publishers, 1983). See also Jerry Mashaw, *Greed, Chaos, and Governance: Using Public Choice to Improve Public Law* (New Haven: Yale University Press, 1997). Mashaw argues against the indiscriminate use of public choice theory, and for the very Hegelian proposition that the bureaucracy is often a better and more accountable institution for the drafting and execution of law than the legislature.

31. James Q. Wilson, "The Rise of the Bureaucratic State," in *The American Commonwealth: 1976,* ed. Nathan Glazer and Irving Kristol (New York: Basic Books, 1976), 77–78.

32. Of course, the federal bureaucracy is often deeply involved in *drafting* public policy as well. See Randall Ripley and Grace Franklin, *Congress, the Bureaucracy, and Public Policy*, 4th ed. (Chicago: Dorsey Press, 1987). See also Peter Woll, *American Bureaucracy,* 2d ed. (New York: W. W. Norton, 1977).

33. This is not to say that undoing any bureaucratic agency or policy is an easy task. Examples of rent seeking are well known.

34. Mark Dowie notes that government makes the law, but often government does not enforce the law. "[C]itizens and citizen groups must do so themselves through litigation." Dowie thus identifies another way that political associations help to concretize the American public moral consensus: they demand that government agencies enforce, i.e., mediate, the moral claims inherent in its legislation. See Mark Dowie, *Losing Ground: American Environmentalism at the Close of the Twentieth Century* (Cambridge: MIT Press, 1996), 37.

Chapter Twelve

1. Wayne Fields, *Union of Words: A History of Presidential Eloquence* (New York: Free Press, 1996), 165.

2. Ibid., 265.

3. Ibid.

4. David J. Garrow, *Bearing the Cross: Martin Luther King, Jr., and the Southern Christian Leadership Conference* (New York: William Morrow, 1986), 408–9.

5. Tulis argues convincingly that during the "War on Poverty" campaign, Johnson's desire to step out of Kennedy's shadow caused him to stress rhetoric over policy. The legislation passed, but its overall quality suffered as a result. See Tulis, *Rhetorical Presidency,* 161–72.

6. Chandler Davidson, "The Recent Evolution of Voting Rights Law Affecting Racial and Language Minorities," in *Quiet Revolution in the South: The Impact of the Voting Rights Act 1965–1990,* ed. Chandler Davidson and Bernard Grofman (Princeton: Princeton University Press, 1994), 30.

7. W. F. Hegel, *Hegel's Philosophy of Right,* trans. with introduction and notes

by T. H. Knox (New York: Oxford University Press, 1967), addition 152, P 258, p. 279.

8. It likely goes without saying that a person who is or who appears to be honorable is much better able to fulfill this role. Therefore, questions about a president's or candidate's character are wholly legitimate, even central.

9. U.S. Congress, Senate, Judiciary Committee, *Voting Rights: Hearings before the Committee on the Judiciary, U.S. Senate,* Eighty-ninth Congress, First Session, on S. 1564 (to enforce the Fifteenth Amendment to the Constitution of the United States), April 2, 1965 (Washington: U.S. Government Printing Office, 1965), 797.

10. Chandler Davidson, "The Voting Rights Act: A Brief History," in *Controversies in Minority Voting: The Voting Rights Act in Perspective,* ed. Bernard Grofman and Chandler Davidson (Washington: Brookings Institution, 1992), 18.

11. Ibid., 20.

12. James E. Alt, "The Impact of the Voting Rights Act on Black and White Voter Registration in the South," in *Quiet Revolution in the South,* ed. Chandler Davidson and Bernard Grofman (Princeton: Princeton University Press, 1994), 368.

13. Ibid., 369.

14. Chandler Davidson, "Recent Evolution of Voting Rights Law," 32.

15. 393 U.S. 544, 565, 569 (1969).

16. Lisa Handley and Bernard Grofman, "The Impact of the Voting Rights Act on Minority Representation: Black Officeholding in Southern State Legislatures and Congressional Delegations," in *Quiet Revolution in the South,* ed. Chandler Davidson and Bernard Grofman (Princeton: Princeton University Press, 1994), 336.

17. Hegel, *Philosophy of Right,* P 295, p. 192.

18. Any discussion of federal civil servants ought not to discount the importance of the Supreme Court. Of course, the justices do not, in Hegel's words, engage in "direct and personal . . contact" (*Philosophy of Right,* P 295, p. 192) with the many parties affected by the law. Nevertheless, if anyone can fit Hegel's ideal description of a bureaucrat, it is a Supreme Court justice. "In those who are busy with the important questions arising in a great state, these subjective interests automatically disappear, and the habit is generated of adopting universal interests, points of view, and activities" (ibid., P 296, p. 193). Through their many rulings on the various sections of the Voting Rights Act, these civil servants were uniquely effective in concretizing and effectuating the government's moral judgment.

19. It is also important to mention the Civil Rights Bill of 1957. While the bill was without any meaningful provisions for federal enforcement, and was thus effectively a dead letter, it was the first civil rights bill since Reconstruction. Incidentally, all acknowledge that without Johnson's ardent support (he was then Senate majority leader) even that bill would not have passed.

20. Abigail Thernstrom, quoted in Jim Sleeper, *Liberal Racism* (New York: Viking Press, 1997), 65. Sleeper himself says liberals "blundered on voting rights," moving from "noble beginnings" to "bad faith" on questions of race

and representation. It is instructive that his account, too, begins with Johnson's speech before Congress and King's reaction. Ibid., 43–46.

21. Just as neither the *Dred Scot* decision nor *Plessy v. Ferguson* ended the moral questions associated with the political standing of blacks in this nation.

22. Numan V. Bartley, *The Rise of Massive Resistance: Race and Politics in the South during the 1950's* (Baton Rouge: Louisiana State University Press, 1969), 304.

23. James Button, *Blacks and Social Change: Impact of the Civil Rights Movement on Southern Communities* (Princeton: Princeton University Press, 1989), 182.

24. Robert Wuthnow, *The Restructuring of American Religion: Society and Faith since World War II* (Princeton: Princeton University Press, 1988), 115.

25. Hegel, *Philosophy of Right,* P 261, p. 162.

26. Rosenblum, *Membership and Morals: The Personal Uses of Pluralism in America* (Princeton: Princeton University Press, 1998).

27. William Galston, *Liberal Purposes: Goods, Virtues, and Diversity in the Liberal State* (Cambridge: Cambridge University Press, 1991), 296.

28. Andrew Hacker, *Two Nations: Black and White, Separate, Hostile, Unequal* (New York: Ballantine Books, 1992).

29. Alan Wolfe, *One Nation After All* (New York: Viking Press, 1998), 222.

30. For more on Ferguson, see chapter 2. The interesting point is that this connection illustrates once again Ferguson's ongoing relevance. It also reiterates the point that our problems and the means at our disposal for responding to those problems are, like Ferguson's, distinctively modern.

31. The experience of Vietnam veterans is, of course, different. But so, too, was the draft in that era. The opportunity for those from higher socioeconomic strata to delay or avoid service is too well documented to require recounting here.

32. Mickey Kaus, *The End of Equality* (New York: Basic Books, 1995), lists the crew of John F. Kennedy's PT 109 and their diverse backgrounds. It is hard to imagine how one could read that list and not feel that something profound has been lost. I turned to Kaus's work after one early reader of this book noted the similarities between his and mine. Though he is concerned almost exclusively with institutions that transcend class, his proposals for restoring what he calls "civic liberalism" resonate strongly with those I outline here.

33. For one strong counterargument, see Gregory D. Foster, "Failed Expectations: The Crisis of Civil-Military Relations in America," *Brookings Review* 15, no. 4 (fall 1997): 46–48.

34. Thomas E. Ricks, "The Great Society in Camouflage," *Atlantic Monthly,* December 1996, 24.

35. Quoted in *National Service: Getting it Right,* Cantigny Conference Series (Chicago: Robert M. McCormick Foundation, 1997), 29. This booklet is singularly helpful in understanding the issues surrounding national service and the Americore program.

36. See Kaus, *End of Equality,* 82–85. Kaus wants to have a draft ("with no civilian alternative") and national service for all those not selected. I am not sure that Kaus would want to deny draftees the possibility of conscientious

objection, but I know I would not, and I am confident that the proper combination of incentives (preferences in hiring and admissions policies, for example) would sustain a system of self-selection.

37. Sidney Mead, *The Lively Experiment: The Shaping of Christianity in America* (New York: Harper and Row, 1976), 68–71.

38. See Gary B. Nash, Charlotte Crabtree, and Ross E. Dunn, *History on Trial: Culture Wars and the Teaching of the Past* (New York: A. A. Knopf, 1997).

39. See, e.g., William Safire, "Flunk That Test," *New York Times,* October 1, 1997, A27.

40. In broad strokes, this argument parallels the position of the Character Education Partnership. It is no doubt apparent that I am deeply sympathetic to their concerns and objectives.

41. James Davison Hunter and Carl Bowman, *The State of Disunion: 1996 Survey of American Political Culture* (Ivy, Va.: In Media Res Educational Foundation, 1996), 30.

42. Ibid., 30–31.

43. Verba, Schlozman and Brady, *Voice and Equality* (Cambridge: Harvard University Press, 1995), 532.

44. *Buckley v. Valeo,* 424 U.S. 1 (1976).

45. *Buckley* accepted the idea of limits on contributions, but not on expenditures. This combination, in Burt Neuborne's words, "placed federal candidates between a virtually unlimited demand for money and severe restrictions on supply. The predictable results are a frenzied effort to find loopholes in the federal law, and the increased power of participants who can supply large amounts of money without violating federal law." Neuborne argues that many of the most problematic and disturbing features of the contemporary political landscape—political neophytes with unlimited financial resources, PACs, fundraising professionals, and soft-money donors who funnel their largesse to candidates "under the guise of 'party building' "all of these follow naturally from the court's ruling. See his *A Survey of Existing Efforts to Reform the Campaign Finance System,* Campaign Finance Reform Series (New York: NYU School of Law, Brennan Center for Justice, 1997), 9.

46. For more on these initiatives, and on campaign finance reform generally, see Anthony Corrado, Thomas E. Mann, and Daniel R. Ortiz, eds., *Campaign Finance Reform: A Sourcebook* (Washington: Brookings Institution, 1997).

47. Kaus, *The End of Equality.* 89.

48. Burt Neuborne, *Campaign Finance Reform and the Constitution: A Critical Look at Buckley v. Valeo* (New York: NYU School of Law, Brennan Center for Justice, 1997), 21.

49. Hegel, *Philosophy of Right,* P 261, p. 161.

Index